Economic and Industrial Performance in Europe

Economic and Industrial Performance in Europe

A report prepared for the Centre for Industrial Policy and Performance, University of Leeds

---

Edited by
David Coates
Professor of Contemporary Political Economy
University of Leeds, UK

Edward Elgar
Aldershot, UK • Brookfield, US

Published by
Edward Elgar Publishing Limited
Gower House
Croft Road
Aldershot
Hants GU11 3HR
UK

Edward Elgar Publishing Company
Old Post Road
Brookfield
Vermont 05036
US

British Library Cataloguing in Publication Data
Economic and Industrial Performance in
Europe: Report Prepared for the Centre for
Industrial Policy and Performance,
University of Leeds
I. Coates, David
330.941

Library of Congress Cataloguing in Publication Data
Economic and industrial performance in Europe: a report prepared for the Centre for Industrial Policy and Performance, University of Leeds / edited by David Coates.
272pp. 23cm.
1. Europe—Economic conditions—1945– 2. Europe—Economic policy. 3. Industries—Europe. 4. Industrial policy—Europe. I. Coates, David. II. University of Leeds. Centre for Industrial Policy and Performance.
HC240.E25 1995
330.94—dc20 95–5518
CIP

ISBN 1 85278 709 0

Printed and bound in Great Britain by
Hartnolls Limited, Bodmin, Cornwall

Contents

Tables and Figures

Tables

Figures

Contributors

Daniele Archibugi	Institute for Studies on Scientific Research of the Italian Research Council, Rome
David Coates	Professor of Contemporary Political Economy, University of Leeds, UK; Director, Centre for Industrial Policy and Performance, University of Leeds, UK
Paul Dunne	Senior Lecturer in Economics, University of Leeds, UK
David Harvie	Lecturer in Economics, University of Leeds, UK
Paul McVeigh	Researcher for the Centre for Industrial Policy and Performance University of Leeds, UK
Jonathan Michie	Judge Institute of Management Studies, University of Cambridge; formerly Senior Research Fellow in the Centre for Industrial Policy and Performance, University of Leeds, UK
Peter Nolan	Montague Burton Professor of Industrial Relations, University of Leeds, UK; Deputy Director, Centre for Industrial Policy and Performance, University of Leeds, UK
Mark Rudd	Policy and Research Executive, Leeds and Bradford Chamber of Commerce and Industry
Malcolm Sawyer	Professor of Economics, University of Leeds, UK
Mette Wiggen	Research Officer, Centre for Industrial Policy and Performance, University of Leeds, UK

1. Introduction

Paul McVeigh

There are lies, damned lies and statistics. So runs the popular phrase; and thus a healthy scepticism toward quantitative information is articulated. The widespread resort within political debate to an array of baffling and apparently inconsistent statistics has devalued their currency in political usage and perhaps encouraged an in-built indifference and resistance to statistics within society. And yet the urge to 'measure' social phenomenon in a similar way to the way in which a mathematician calculates an angle remains as testimony to the strength of the human compulsion to collate, analyse and quantify. Hence, a balance must be struck between satisfying the need to compile and compare information about society – with all of the beneficial consequences this may have for academic inquiry and policy making – and the need to produce meaningful information which avoids the pitfalls and abuses that can besiege the use of quantitative data.

This book aims to meet the rigorous challenge of striking such a balance. Its remit is the economic performance of the industrialised world, and especially Europe, since 1973. No such exercise could be undertaken without recourse to statistics, with all of the attendant dangers this involves. However, each of the contributors has sought to draw the attention of the reader to the shortcomings of the methodologies used in collecting data. All of the contributors sound a cautionary note regarding the validity of data. Despite the caveats that must be entered into a project akin to this one, both the range of data and the number of countries covered is impressively wide.

The book seeks to compare the fortunes of different nations in the period of economic restructuring, uncertainty, and generally slower growth that followed in the wake of the oil crisis in the 1970s. It seeks to show how the post-war boom – in which economic performance and economic trends were highly favourable across the developed world – has unravelled since 1973. This process of unravelling – influenced by the globalisation of both capital and production in the guise of the MNC, fuelled by the rise of the newly industrialising nations and given fresh impetus by the end of the Cold War – has impacted differently upon different national economies.

Whilst economic forces have acted adversely upon the vast majority of national economies since 1973, some have been better placed than others to shoulder the burden of the more intense, global, competitive pressures that have been part and parcel of the post-1973 world economy. In chapter two,

Jonathan Michie establishes that across Europe, economic performance has deteriorated and diverged in the period from 1973 to date, in comparison with the post-war boom. Even relatively small divergences in rates of growth have great political resonance when converted to levels of employment and unemployment. In this regard, Michie shows that all European economies have suffered in terms of higher unemployment rates. Rates have stabilised at levels higher than those which accompanied the post-war boom. In some nations the upward shift has been more pronounced, giving credence to the view that relative international competitiveness has had a bearing on the intensity of economic suffering felt by any individual national economy.

Low rates of growth are not sufficient to burn off this level of unemployment; perhaps because rates of growth themselves are constrained both by national competitiveness and by the buoyancy (or lack of buoyancy) of export markets. At any rate, unemployment levels are generally higher than before, throwing up profound social problems. In the past, macroeconomic expansion, concerted across the industrialised world, might have alleviated the situation but the differing relative economic strengths of nations and the rise of fierce global competition has forestalled serious pursuit of this option.

Nation states have thus looked inward, at domestic competitiveness, for improved economic performance. In chapter three, Malcolm Sawyer surveys some of the efforts made at improving the competitiveness of domestic industry. Much of the thrust of this effort has been involved in enforcing greater competition where private or public sector monopoly or oligopoly has been deemed incapable of delivering competitiveness vis-à-vis foreign producers. Competition policy has sought to prevent restrictive practises, break up monopolies, and scrutinise merger. The intensity of such efforts has varied. At times rhetoric has outpaced action; neo-liberals have been caught in a dilemma with takeover and merger. Is greater market power a reward for competitiveness? Or does it immediately lead to sloth? European level initiatives have their own dilemma. How does one combine the need to deliver internal (European) competition and external competitiveness (European competitiveness against Japanese/American/Far Eastern competition)?

Meanwhile, public sector concerns have been the subject of privatisation and deregulation. Sawyer concentrates attention on the former and charts the extent of privatisation pursued by the European states. In many cases, sales of public sector firms were encouraged by the alleged fiscal, financial, and political advantages on offer. Yet the philosophy of privatisation lying behind the sales contained the assertion that private ownership produces greater competitiveness and better economic results than public ownership. It must be ventured at this point that for all this frantic activity to improve the competitiveness of major domestic industrial concerns, the impetus to total employment has clearly been in a negative direction. In the short term, privatisation has entailed direct and large scale job losses. In the longer term, this rationalisation has had no detectable beneficial effect on general employment levels across economies.

Peter Nolan and David Harvie pick up this theme in chapter four. They are concerned that the whole wave of neo-liberal and 'Eurosclerosis' thesis is fatally flawed. In short, the notions that economic dynamism require deregulated labour markets free of institutional rigidities, and hence that devices such as the social charter 'cost' jobs are based on a fundamental misunderstanding of the nature of economic growth.

Taking the example of Germany, they demonstrate that Germany's economic miracle went hand in hand with collective bargaining, strong trade unionism and a rolling forward of workers' rights. Widening the debate, we can regard segments of the Japanese labour market to be similarly highly regulated with lifetime employment and large scale welfare provision through the firm itself. Again the Nordic countries have prospered despite this same degree of regulation and corporatism.

These countries have excellent growth rates which leave the UK and the US well behind since the Second World War. Indeed, as Nolan and Harvie argue, the very success of these economies may be linked to the extent of worker rights and participation. By gaining high real wages from employers, labour has pressured capital into a virtuous cycle of training and product and process innovation which allows specialisation in high skill production. Output is sold because of its quality, reputation, design and an array of other non-price factors. The fact that prices and costs may be higher does not matter since the product is highly differentiated and superior to low cost competition. It is therefore not price elastic making it less sensitive to any changes in price and cost including those brought about by a strong exchange rate.

In chapter five, Michie and Archibugi turn their attention to Science and Technology (S&T), and Research and Development (R&D). If privatisation and competition policy have had little effects on economic success, what of R&D? It appears more closely linked with the notion of technological advance, and hence of new products and processes for which monopoly rents may accrue to the innovator; allowing the kind of non-price competitiveness and high wage/high skill economy outlined above.

Yet R&D is a slippery concept to manage as the contributors illustrate. Which of the various measures of R&D and S&T are the ones to watch? There are many possible contenders; all possess flaws as well as advantages. Does it matter how much innovation and R&D a nation directly invests in? Is the rate of diffusion more important? Is there a conflict between innovation and diffusion such that the faster technology will diffuse the lesser are the incentives of monopoly rents to the innovator? Shop floor innovation may be at least as important as patenting, citations or R&D resourcing. Again, R&D resourcing may be a function of success as much as a precursor of it. The measurement of one's selected variable also must, therefore, matter. Qualitative factors must thus intrude into the analysis.

The importance of qualitative factors is also pointed out by David Coates and Mette Wiggen in their comparative analysis of state expenditure and debt in chapter six. In the most simplistic neo-liberal universe, mistrust of government extends to the endorsement of the thesis that the greater the level of state expenditure and debt, the worse for the economy. The material presented by Coates and Wiggen demonstrates that there is great similarity between the nations on the sheer quantity of state activity. There is no straightforward correlation between the level of state activity and economic performance that would indicate the plausibility of the neo-liberal position.

Indeed, the less developed nations studied have the least developed public sectors; yet over time their public sectors have grown. Simultaneously, they have actually 'caught up' significantly with the more developed nations in terms of GDP per capita. 'Catch-up' has co-existed with inflation of the public sector. Economic success has co-existed with the expansion of the state. Proponents of Eurosclerosis will doubtless contend that Europe as a whole suffers from excessively intrusive government in comparison with the 'Asian tigers'. This must surely be an area demanding more research; but it is noteworthy that if the 'Asian tigers' do subscribe to neo-liberal theories on the efficacy of minimal state intervention, their political leaders seem themselves to be thoroughly unwilling to accept this proposition.

Continuing the theme of the importance of qualitative factors within the entirety of state expenditure, Paul Dunne's contribution offers an analysis of the military economy. The thesis is underlined once again here that excessive military expenditure and an inflated military economy is damaging to long term growth prospects. The corollary is that in the aftermath of the Cold War, a rational and co-ordinated policy of reconversion and where necessary, compensation could provide an orderly and prompt restructuring of the military economy allowing the full benefits of a peace dividend to accrue.

Finally, in chapter eight, Mark Rudd emphasises not only as he puts it 'the social consequences of industrialism', but also I would argue the social consequences of industrial restructuring. The economic dilemmas illustrated by Michie in chapter two have found no easy solution in the chapters which followed. Competition policy and privatisation as described by Sawyer have not been panaceas providing a fast-growing, high employment European economy. Deregulating labour markets and reducing union and labour rights does not promote the progressive and virtuous move to a high wage/high skill economy but rather destroys such possibilities as Nolan and Harvie argue. Following Coates and Wiggen, simply reducing the size of the state is not likely to have the necessary impact; nor will the sheer infusion of money into R&D and S&T, though this may be part of the wider answer. Following Dunne, expenditure on the military and the sustenance of the military-industrial complex – one of the few areas of state spending neo-liberals have traditionally advocated – is ironically one of the least functional areas of spending for economic success; whilst leaving the inevitable restructuring of the military economy to the market will threaten to waste the potential benefits of the peace dividend.

Hence, the low growth and high unemployment which have punctuated the post-1973 European economy are still very much with us. Their social legacy is charted by Rudd whose statistics on poverty, homelessness and unemployment make nothing but grim reading and serve as a check on the complacency which all too frequently blurs the urgency of the issues. Despite the increases in state expenditure charted by Coates and Wiggen, and despite the creation of the welfare state, economic failure stares us most starkly in the face when we see high rates of unemployment, homelessness, urban decay and crime. Economic issues interest us because they claim to hold the solutions to combat social ills. In this sense, the overall state of Europe depicted in this book - for all the methodological problems inherent in such an exercise – is not a satisfactory one, and neither is the range of initiatives nor the conventional wisdom being pursued. Quite clearly, the accepted approaches to welfare policies and to industrial and economic regeneration are open to serious question.

In the wake of the collapse of Communism in Eastern Europe, there has been a good deal of triumphalism regarding the alleged victory of neo-liberalism and markets over state intervention. This triumphalism is such that any hint of sclerosis in the European economy is presented as a result of the allegedly statist and socialist influences at work in western European states. Though dwarfed by the all-pervasive statism of Soviet Communism, these influences are still felt by the Right to be fetters on the liberating power of markets. Hence, it is argued, western Europe has outperformed the Soviet bloc because of its greater reliance on markets; whilst areas of weakness within the European economy as against its Asian and American counterparts are said to be a result of the relics of a more limited statism in the capitalist western states.

In this version of events, the large role of the state in the economic miracles across the globe is frequently forgotten. Such miracles in Japan and the Far East, in western Europe after the last war, in Spain in the sixties, even, dare one say it, in the industrialisation of the Soviet Union, have almost always and everywhere gone hand in hand with large scale efforts by the state to modernise its national economic space. The regeneration of Europe's economy – so sorely needed in view of the current declining social fabric – will surely need to employ subtle and credible policies of state intervention. New policies and ideas are needed urgently to secure a level of economic performance, and a slicing of the economic cake which will permit a sustained assault upon the high levels of social and environmental deprivation still prevailing in western Europe.

The entire project was initially designed, and the relevant statistical material gathered, by Jonathan Michie in his then role as Senior Research Officer at the Centre for Industrial Policy and Performance. On his departure to

Cambridge, editorial responsibility passed to David Coates. Individual chapters were prepared by Jonathan Michie (chapter two), Malcolm Sawyer (chapter three), Peter Nolan and David Harvie (chapter four), Jonathan Michie and Daniele Archibugi (chapter five), David Coates and Mette Wiggen (chapter six), Paul Dunne (chapter seven) and Mark Rudd (chapter eight). The whole text was edited by Paul McVeigh, and set by Janet Pickering. Preliminary preparation of the final copy was the responsibility of Anne-Marie Land and Lorraine Sherriff, and the final text was prepared for publication by Janet Pickering.

2. Europe in Figures: National Income and Employment

Jonathan Michie

This chapter reports annual data from 1973 to 1990 for 18 European countries, covering the main economic indices. Data availability varies across countries but in most cases includes all the following series:

Table 2.i: National Accounts Statistics in national currencies
Government final consumption expenditure at 1985 prices
Private final consumption expenditure at 1985 prices
Investment at 1985 prices
Exports at 1985 prices
Imports at 1985 prices
Gross Domestic Product (GDP) at market prices, at 1985 prices

Table 2.ii: Employment
Male civilian employment
Female civilian employment
Total civilian employment
Wage earners and salaried employees
Manufacturing employment

Table 2.iii: Unemployment and Participation
Unemployment rate
Male unemployment rate
Female unemployment rate
Participation rate

Table 2.iv: Production and Prices
Index of manufacturing output (1985=100)
Average weekly hours worked in manufacturing
Index of hourly earnings in manufacturing (1985=100)
Consumer price index (1985=100)

for each country, listed alphabetically as follows:
Austria (1), Belgium (2), Denmark (3), Finland (4), France (5), Germany (6), Greece (7), Iceland (8), Ireland (9), Italy (10), Luxembourg (11), Netherlands (12) Norway (13), Portugal (14), Spain (15), Sweden (16), Switzerland (17), UK (18).

Commentary on each country is kept to a minimum due to space constraints but also to enable specific points to be picked up in the comparative analysis of subsequent chapters. Detail on data sources and methods are given in the Appendix to this Chapter. In general the data have been taken from the standard OECD sources, although certain adjustments have been made as explained in the Appendix. It was the OECD (called at the time the Organisation for European Economic Cooperation, OEEC) which after the second world war took over from the defunct League of Nations the work of developing national accounts. The body established a national accounts research unit in Cambridge where Richard Stone had become Director of the Department of Applied Economics. The United Nations took an interest in 1953 producing the report describing the *System of National Accounts*, also largely written by Stone, and therefore not very different from the second report produced for the OEEC. The report was revised in 1968 and is being revised again now. The work of the OECD means that the national accounting aggregates have much the same meaning for every country which produces them; this is not the case for other data such as literacy or education statistics.

The year 1973 – taken as the starting year for the data reported in this book – is generally considered to be a turning point for the world economy, marking the end of the post-war period of growth. Of course, this growth was still marked by economic cycles, and some countries suffered relative economic decline. Nevertheless, taken as a whole it was a period of historically fast economic growth and low levels of unemployment. Indeed, this was the only era yet witnessed in which the capitalist economies have managed to maintain near-full employment over their business cycles. Hence the depiction of this 25-year spell as marking the 'golden age of capitalism' (Marglin and Schor (eds), 1990). This era ended in 1973 with the first 'oil shock' (sometimes referred to as 'OPEC 1') which ushered in a decade of 'stagflation' (slow economic growth accompanied by high inflation). While 1973 is thus a convenient turning point, the factors which lay behind this breakdown had been building before then; (for a detailed analysis of this process, see Glyn, Hughes, Lipietz and Singh, 1990). The 1980s witnessed low inflation along with economic growth even lower than that experienced in the 1970s, despite some recovery of the world economy in the second half of the decade. The first four years of the 1990s have generally proved to be the worst – in terms of economic growth or unemployment levels – since before the second world war.

This immediately begs the question of how such factors are measured between countries and over time. Comparisons of national levels of unemployment are complicated by definitional problems and the paucity of consistent data. There are further problems in comparing unemployment performance over time, for instance, as methods of data collection change. Thus, for example, calculating the unemployment totals on a consistent basis would show that contrary to accepted opinion the extent of unemployment in

Britain was greater in the 1980s than it was during the Great Depression of the 1930s (see Kitson and Michie, 1994). The following tables of data nevertheless suggest broad trends in economic growth and other indicators for the European economies over the past 20 years along the lines referred to above: 1973 marked the end of the post-war boom, with widespread recession following 'OPEC 1', with the recovery from that recession then leading up to 'OPEC 2' at the end of the decade. The recovery from the recession of the early 1980s led into a period of fairly rapid economic growth in the second half of that decade. The expansion was fuelled by the drop in oil prices of 1985–6 and a considerable loosening of monetary policy following the October 1987 stock market crash, which it was feared would otherwise trigger a world slump in the manner of the 1929 Wall Street Crash. The average real rate of increase of GDP for the EC12 for the five years 1986–90 was thus 3.2%, with the real rate of increase of domestic demand at 3.9%. Investment rose on average by 5.9% with investment in equipment growing still faster at an average of almost 7.5%. In 1990, world GDP growth decelerated sharply from the strong growth rates of 1988 and 1989 (at 4.5% and 5.2% respectively) to about 2%, and this is reflected in the 1990 growth figures for most of the European countries covered by the following tables. For most of them, the final year of 1990 already indicates the arrival of the subsequent recession, with all the components of domestic demand being weak, contrasting with an average figure for growth in private consumption in the EC12 of 3% between 1985 and 1990.

The rate of GDP growth at which employment begins to increase has tended to be around 2% for most of these European economies since 1973. Given trends in population growth, demographics and participation rates, this means that a growth rate of around 2.5% has generally been required to prevent unemployment from increasing. During the second half of the 1980s an average growth rate for the EC12 of 3.2% reduced unemployment from 10.8% to 8.3% in 1990. Despite these modest falls, the EC countries continued to experience high rates of unemployment when compared to Japan, the USA or even non-EC European countries. Unemployment has generally been higher at the end of the period than the beginning, and has since risen further. European economies have also suffered a greater degree of deindustrialisation than did America or Japan over much of this period (see de Sousa and Castro, 1992).

1. Austria: Tables 2.1(i)–2.2(iv)

Manufacturing output as a percentage of GDP actually rose by 1.1% between 1973 and 1989, although manufacturing employment as a percentage of total employment declined by 5.7% over those years (OECD, *Historical Statistics, 1960–1990*, Table 5.2). Despite this fall, however, it can be seen from Table 2.1(iii) that unemployment rates remained relatively low throughout this period. Indeed, the Austrian economy appears to have been generally less prone to stagflation than most of the other economies. As noted below, there are other economies which enjoyed similarly favourable performances and these are, generally, those which displayed so-called 'corporatist' characteristics, although in most cases these characteristics have been eroded in the years after 1990. The Austrian economy over the 1973–1990 period could be characterised as corporatist and as relatively successful, particularly in avoiding large scale unemployment. Both of these facets of Austria's performance parallel the experience of the Scandinavian countries. (For a detailed discussion of corporatism as an economic system, and of the experiences of each of the corporatist economies, see Pekkarinen, Pohjola and Rowthorn (eds), 1992). Before 1973 the Austrian economy had been growing at an average rate (of real GDP per capita) during 1960–68 of 3.6% as against an OECD average of 3.9%, an average of 3.6% for the European OECD countries and an average of 3.9% for the smaller European economies. This improved to an average rate of increase during 1968–73 of 5.4% as against 3.6% for the OECD, 4.0% for the European OECD economies and 4.2% for the smaller European countries (see OECD, 1989). By 1970 Austria's GDP per capita was still 5% lower than the European OECD average and 20% lower than that of Germany; by 1985 it was 10% above the European OECD average and only 12% behind Germany's (see Guger, 1992). This was the result of a particularly good relative performance over the years 1973-79 when real GDP per capita grew at an average of 3.0% as against the averages for the OECD of 1.8%, European OECD of 1.9% and smaller European economies of 1.4%. While the average for 1979–87 of 1.6% growth was less than the 1.8% OECD average, this still outperformed the European OECD average of 1.3% or the average of smaller European countries of 1.2%. This was reflected in the low unemployment rates shown in Table 2.1(iii) along with participation rates which, as Table 2.1(iii) also indicates, actually increased over much of the period. Table 2.1(ii) demonstrates that these low unemployment and increased participation rates were achieved despite a growing labour force, resulting in absolute increases in total employment. However, the full employment policies which lay behind this successful performance were gradually abandoned after the Socialist Party under Bruno Kreisky lost its absolute majority in 1983, so that unemployment, which had peaked in that year, remained relatively high despite the European expansion over the latter half of the 1980s.

2. Belgium: Tables 2.2(i)–2.2(iv)

Belgium has a population of just under 10 million (9,947,800 in 1990) which makes it the second most densely populated of the EU countries (with a density of 327 inhabitants per square kilometre in 1990, as against an average for the EC12 of 146, and 439 for the Netherlands). GDP per capita in 1990 (in Purchasing Power Standards) was 19,091 ECU as against the EC12 average of 17,857 ECU. The breakdown between industry, services and agriculture as a percentage of GDP was, in 1989 (with the EC average figures in parentheses): industry 32.4% (34.4%), services 65.4% (62.5%) and agriculture 2.2% (3.1%). The respective employment percentages were: industry 28.9% (33.2%), services 68.3% (59.8%) and agriculture 2.8% (7.1%) (Eurostat, 1992). Manufacturing output as a percentage of GDP fell by 2.7% between 1973 and 1989, with manufacturing employment as a percentage of total employment falling by 13.9% over those years (OECD, *Historical Statistics, 1960–1990*, Table 5.2). Table 2.2(iv) indicates a relatively low level of hours worked in manufacturing – in fact Belgium has the shortest average working week of the 12 EC members, at 38.1 hours in 1989 for all full-time employees as against the EC average of 40.6 hours.

3. Denmark: Tables 2.3(i)–2.3(iv)

Denmark has a population of just over 5 million (5,135,500 in 1990). GDP per capita in 1990 (in Purchasing Power Standards) was 19,814 ECU as against the EC12 average of 17,857 ECU. The breakdown between industry, services and agriculture as a percentage of GDP was, in 1989 (with the EC average figures in parentheses): industry 27.1% (34.4%), services 68.3% (62.5%) and agriculture 4.6% (3.1%). The respective employment percentages were: industry 26.8% (33.2%), services 67.3% (59.8%) and agriculture 6.0% (7.1%) (Eurostat, 1992). Manufacturing output as a percentage of GDP actually rose by 0.1% between 1973 and 1989, with manufacturing employment as a percentage of total employment falling by only 1.1% over those years (OECD, *Historical Statistics, 1960–1990*, Table 5.2). Prior to 1973, Danish real GDP per capita had been increasing at an average rate of 3.8% during 1960–68 as against an average for the OECD of 3.9%, for the European OECD countries of 3.6% and for the smaller European economies of 3.9%. The average increases during 1968–73 were, then, 3.3% for Denmark, 3.6% for the OECD, 4.0% for the European OECD economies and 4.2% for the smaller European economies. Since 1973 the Danish performance was about average for the remainder of the 1970s but improved relatively in the subsequent decade. Thus the average increase in real GDP per capita over 1973–79 was 1.6% for Denmark as against 1.8% for the OECD, 1.9% for the European OECD countries and 1.4% for the smaller European economies, while over the 1979–87 years the average annual increase for Denmark was 1.9% as against only 1.8% for the OECD, 1.3% for the European OECD countries and 1.2% for the smaller European economies (see OECD, 1989).

4. Finland: Tables 2.4(i)–2.4(iv)

Prior to 1973, real GDP per capita in Finland had been increasing at an average rate of 3.3% during 1960–68 as against an average for the OECD of 3.9%, for the European OECD countries of 3.6% and for the smaller European economies of 3.9%. The average increases during 1968–73 were 6.5% for Finland, 3.6% for the OECD, 4.0% for the European OECD economies and 4.2% for the smaller European economies. Since 1973 the

Finnish performance was comparatively good, although the situation has deteriorated drastically with the collapse of Finland's Soviet markets. Thus the average increase in real GDP per capita over 1973–79 was 2.0% for Finland as against 1.8% for the OECD, 1.9% for the European OECD countries and 1.4% for the smaller European economies. Over the 1979–87 years the average annual increase for Finland was 2.9% as against only 1.8% for the OECD, 1.3% for the European OECD countries and 1.2% for the smaller European economies (see OECD, 1989).

5. France: Tables 2.5(i)–2.5(iv)

France has a population of 56,304,000 (1990 figures). GDP per capita in 1990 (in Purchasing Power Standards) was 20,207 ECU as against the EC12 average of 17,857 ECU. The breakdown between industry, services and agriculture as a percentage of GDP was, in 1989 (with the EC average figures in parentheses): industry 30.2% (34.4%), services 66.2% (62.5%) and agriculture 3.6% (3.1%). The respective employment percentages were: industry 30.1% (33.2%), services 63.5% (59.8%) and agriculture 6.4% (7.1%) (Eurostat, 1992). Manufacturing output as a percentage of GDP fell by 5.3% between 1973 and 1989, with manufacturing employment as a percentage of total employment falling by 6.7% over those years (OECD, *Historical Statistics, 1960–1990,* Table 5.2). This decline in output share is relatively large, with only the UK doing worse, although the fall in employment is actually relatively modest.

6. Germany: Tables 2.6(i)–2.6(iv)

The data in the following tables for Germany refer to West Germany alone throughout. Caution therefore has to be exercised in comparing these with data which include the former German Democratic Republic. Indeed, the rapid growth in GDP recorded between 1989 and 1990 was due in large measure to the increased demand levels resulting from the 'reunification'. To allow comparisons with the summary data given for the other EC countries, however, the relevant data are as follows: population in 1990 was 79,346,500; GDP per capita in 1990 (in Purchasing Power Standards) was 21,131 ECU as against the EC12 average of 17,857 ECU. The breakdown between industry, services and agriculture as a percentage of GDP was, in 1989 (with the EC average figures in parentheses): industry 39.4% (34.4%), services 59.0% (62.5%) and agriculture 1.6% (3.1%). The respective employment percentages were: industry 39.8% (33.2%), services 56.5% (59.8%) and agriculture 3.7% (7.1%) (Eurostat, 1992). Manufacturing output as a percentage of GDP fell by 4.2% between 1973 and 1989, with manufacturing employment as a percentage of total employment falling by 4.5% over those years (OECD, *Historical Statistics, 1960–1990,* Table 5.2). Given the fall in output share, the decline in employment share was, like France, relatively low. Prior to 1973, German real GDP per capita had been increasing at an average rate of 3.2% during 1960–68 as against an average for the OECD of 3.9%, for the European OECD countries of 3.6%. The average increases during 1968-73 were then 4.0% for Germany, 3.6% for the OECD and 4.0% for the European OECD economies. The average increase in real GDP per capita over 1973–79 was 3.2% for Germany as against 1.8% for the OECD and 1.9% for the European OECD countries, while over the 1979–87 years the average annual increase for Germany was 4.0% as against only 1.8% for the OECD and 1.3% for the European OECD countries (see OECD, 1989).

7. Greece: Tables 2.7(i)–2.7(iv)

Greece has a population of just over 10 million (10,046,000 in 1990). GDP per capita in 1990 (in Purchasing Power Standards) was 9,850 ECU as against the EC12 average of 17,857 ECU. The breakdown between industry, services and agriculture as a percentage of GDP was, in 1989 (with the EC average figures in parentheses): industry 27.1% (34.4%), services 55.9% (62.5%) and agriculture 17.0% (3.1%). The respective employment percentages were: industry 27.2% (33.2%), services 46.2% (59.8%) and agriculture 26.6% (7.1%) (Eurostat, 1992).

8. Iceland: Tables 2.8(i)–2.8(iv)

Iceland is of course a relatively small economy, with a total population of only 2,548,000 in 1990, although its GDP per capita is around the average for the EFTA countries (of Austria, Finland, Iceland, Norway, Sweden, Switzerland and Liechtenstein). Its relatively small manufacturing workforce is partly explained by the importance of the agricultural sector. The shares of employment in 1989 were (with the EFTA averages in parentheses for comparison): agricultural 10.5% (6.4% for EFTA), industry 26.3% (31.8% for EFTA) and services 63.2% (61.7% for EFTA). As a percentage of GDP these figures are 12.8% (3.9%), 32.5% (35.9%) and 54.7% (60.2%) respectively.

9. Ireland: Tables 2.9(i)–2.9(iv)

The Republic of Ireland has a population of 3,506,500 (1990 figure). GDP per capita in 1990 (in Purchasing Power Standards) was 12,819 ECU as against the EC12 average of 17,857 ECU. The breakdown between industry, services and agriculture as a percentage of GDP was, in 1989 (with the EC average figures in parentheses): industry 36.6% (34.4%), services 53.3% (62.5%) and agriculture 10.0% (3.1%). The respective employment percentages were: industry 28.4% (33.2%), services 56.5% (59.8%) and agriculture 15.1% (7.1%) (Eurostat, 1992). Manufacturing output as a percentage of GDP actually rose by 7.2% between 1973 and 1989, with manufacturing employment as a percentage of total employment falling by only 1.1% over those years (OECD, *Historical Statistics, 1960–1990,* Table 5.2).

10. Italy: Tables 2.10(i)–2.10(iv)

Italy had a population of 57,576,400 in 1990. GDP per capita in 1990 (in Purchasing Power Standards) was 19,187 ECU as against the EC12 average of 17,857 ECU. The breakdown between industry, services and agriculture as a percentage of GDP was, in 1989 (with the EC average figures in parentheses): industry 34.2% (34.4%), services 62.2% (62.5%) and agriculture 3.6% (3.1%). The respective employment percentages were: industry 32.4% (33.2%), services 58.2% (59.8%) and agriculture 9.3% (7.1%) (Eurostat, 1992). Manufacturing output as a percentage of GDP fell by 3.5% between 1973 and 1989, with manufacturing employment as a percentage of total employment falling by 5.3% over those years (OECD, *Historical Statistics, 1960–1990,* Table 5.2).

11. Luxembourg: Tables 2.11(i)–2.11(iv)

Luxembourg is a tiny country which would not justify separate data were it not for the fact that it is one of the twelve members of the European Union. It is therefore only included here for sake of completeness and, on a more practical level, since so many commentaries do include it, for example when reporting aggregate EU (or, previously, EC) data. The only economic fact of great significance regarding the Luxembourg economy is, perhaps, that it was the only one of the twelve member states which met the fiscal convergence criteria of the Treaty on European Union (the Maastricht Treaty) in 1993, although even Luxembourg failed the inflation criterion. Its population in 1990 stood at 378,400. GDP per capita in 1990 (in Purchasing Power Standards) was 24,303 ECU as against the EC12 average of 17,857 ECU. The breakdown between industry, services and agriculture as a percentage of GDP was, in 1989 (with the EC average figures in parentheses): industry 35.8% (34.4%), services 62.0% (62.5%) and agriculture 2.0% (3.1%). The respective employment percentages were: industry 31.2% (33.2%), services 65.4% (59.8%) and agriculture 3.4% (7.1%) (Eurostat, 1992).

12. The Netherlands: Tables 2.12(i)–2.12(iv)

The Netherlands has a population of around 15 million (14,892,600 in 1990). GDP per capita in 1990 (in Purchasing Power Standards) was 19,091 ECU as against the EC12 average of 17,857 ECU. The breakdown between industry, services and agriculture as a percentage of GDP was, in 1989 (with the EC average figures in parentheses): industry 32.5% (34.4%), services 62.8% (62.5%) and agriculture 4.6% (3.1%). The respective employment percentages were: industry 26.5% (33.2%), services 68.8% (59.8%) and agriculture 4.7% (7.1%) (Eurostat, 1992). Manufacturing output as a percentage of GDP actually rose by 0.5% between 1973 and 1989, although manufacturing employment as a percentage of total employment fell by 6.8% over those years (OECD, *Historical Statistics, 1960–1990,* Table 5.2). Prior to 1973, real GDP per capita in the Netherlands had been increasing at an average rate of 3.5% during 1960–68 as against an average for the OECD of

3.9%, for the European OECD countries of 3.6% and for the smaller European economies of 3.9%. The average increases during 1968–73 were 3.7% for the Netherlands, 3.6% for the OECD, 4.0% for the European OECD economies and 4.2% for the smaller European economies. Since 1973 the Netherlands' performance was about average for the remainder of the 1970s but deteriorated relatively in the subsequent decade. Thus the average increase in real GDP per capita over 1973–79 was 1.9% for the Netherlands as against 1.8% for the OECD, 1.9% for the European OECD countries and 1.4% for the smaller European economies. Over the 1979–87 years the average annual increase for the Netherlands was only 0.6% as against 1.8% for the OECD, 1.3% for the European OECD countries and 1.2% for the smaller European economies (see OECD, 1989).

13. Norway: Tables 2.13(i)–2.13(iv)

Prior to 1973, real GDP per capita in Norway had been increasing at an average rate of 3.6% during 1960–68 as against an average for the OECD of 3.9%, for the European OECD countries of 3.6% and for the smaller European economies of 3.9%. The average increases during 1968–73 were then 3.3% for Norway, 3.6% for the OECD, 4.0% for the European OECD economies and 4.2% for the smaller European economies. Since 1973 the Norwegian economy has done relatively well; thus the average increase in real GDP per capita over 1973–79 was 4.4% for Norway as against 1.8% for the OECD, 1.9% for the European OECD countries and 1.4% for the smaller European economies. Over the 1979–87 years the average annual increase for Norway was 2.9% as against only 1.8% for the OECD, 1.3% for the European OECD countries and 1.2% for the smaller European economies (see OECD, 1989).

14. Portugal: Tables 2.14(i)–2.14(iv)

Portugal has a population of just over 10 million (10,336,900 in 1990). GDP per capita in 1990 (in Purchasing Power Standards) was 10,369 ECU as against the EC12 average of 17,857 ECU. The breakdown between industry, services and agriculture as a percentage of GDP was, in 1989 (with the EC average figures in parentheses): industry 37.7% (34.4%), services 55.9% (62.5%) and agriculture 6.3% (3.1%). The respective employment percentages were: industry 35.3% (33.2%), services 45.7% (59.8%) and agriculture 18.9% (7.1%) (Eurostat, 1992).

15. Spain: Tables 2.15(i)–2.15(iv)

Spain has a population of almost 40 million (38,924,500 in 1990). GDP per capita in 1990 (in Purchasing Power Standards) was 14,556 ECU as against the EC12 average of 17,857 ECU. The breakdown between industry, services and agriculture as a percentage of GDP was, in 1989 (with the EC average figures in parentheses): industry 35.3% (34.4%), services 59.8% (62.5%) and agriculture 4.9% (3.1%). The respective employment percentages were: industry 32.9% (33.2%), services 54.0% (59.8%) and agriculture 13.0% (7.1%) (Eurostat, 1992). Spain has had a peculiar economic history having emerged from the second world war with its fascist regime intact under Franco. Multinational investment was attracted into the country under this regime despite - or perhaps in part because of - the protectionist policies pursued; the precondition for access to the Spanish market was direct investment because of the protective policies (see Recio, 1992). Such investment was also attracted by the peculiarly fascist combination of low wages with the existence of an industrial culture in the country. The integration of Spain into the EC which began in 1986, though, involved a sharp reduction in tariffs, affecting not only trade between Spain and other EC countries but also more generally as Spain adjusted to EC tariffs. While there have, therefore, been huge changes in the Spanish economy from 1973 there has also been some continuity, both since 1973 and from before that date. Bankers have managed to preserve much of their traditional economic and political power. Government economic policy throughout much of this period has been marked by high interest rates and by continued attempts to hold back wage levels. Thus, for example, it can be seen from Table 2.15(i) that private consumption actually fell between 1983 and 1984, during which time the total share of wages in GNP fell from 53.3% to 50.4% (or from 53.7% to 51.4% correcting for labour force changes - see Recio, 1992, p. 72) and the unemployment rate rose from 20.6% to 23.2%. Indeed, a striking aspect of the Spanish data is the high levels of unemployment. It can also be seen from Table 2.15(i) that imports were outstripping exports towards the end of the period. This has been balanced by capital inflows, but the nature of these is quite different from that seen from the 1960s referred to above; there has been a fall in direct investment in new plants, a growth in the purchase of established firms and increased spending - much of it speculative - on real estate and stock exchange investments. It can be seen that manufacturing employment was declining from 1975 until checked by the expansion in the second half of the 1980s, although as a percentage of the total labour force manufacturing workers fell from 14.3% in 1977 to 12.8% in 1985 before declining further to 11.5% in 1989. The most dramatic labour market changes over the past few years, however, has been the increase in the proportion of temporary labour within the overall labour force. This proportion has risen from 15.5% in 1987 to 29.9% by 1990 (Recio, 1992, p. 83).

16. Sweden: Tables 2.16(i)–2.16(iv)

Manufacturing output as a percentage of GDP fell by 2.8% between 1973 and 1989, with manufacturing employment as a percentage of total employment falling by 5.6% over those years (OECD, *Historical 1960–1990,* Table 5.2). Prior to 1973, Swedish real GDP per capita had been increasing at an average rate of 3.6% during 1960–68 as against an average for the OECD of 3.9%, for the European OECD countries of 3.6% and for the smaller European economies of 3.9%. The average increases during 1968–73 were then 3.1% for Sweden, 3.6% for the OECD, 4.0% for the European OECD economies and 4.2% for the smaller European economies. Since 1973 the Swedish performance was about average in terms of growth of per capita GDP, although this translated into a much better than average jobs outcome. Thus the average increase in real GDP per capita over 1973–79 was 1.5% for Sweden as against 1.8% for the OECD, 1.9% for the European OECD countries and 1.4% for the smaller European economies. Over the 1979–87 years the average annual increase for Sweden was 1.6% as against 1.8% for the OECD, 1.3% for the European OECD countries and 1.2% for the smaller European economies (see OECD, 1989).

17. Switzerland: Tables 2.17(i)–2.17(iv)

Prior to 1973, real GDP per capita in Switzerland had been increasing at an average rate of 2.7% during 1960–68 as against an average for the OECD of 3.9%, for the European OECD countries of 3.6% and for the smaller European economies of 3.9%. The average increases during 1968–73 were then 3.4% for Switzerland, 3.6% for the OECD, 4.0% for the European OECD economies and 4.2% for the smaller European economies. Since 1973 the performance was poor initially although it improved relatively in the 1980s. Thus the average increase in real GDP per capita over 1973–79 was: 0.1% for Switzerland as against 1.8% for the OECD, 1.9% for the European OECD countries and 1.4% for the smaller European economies. Over the 1979–87 years the average annual increase for Switzerland was 1.5% as against 1.8% for the OECD, 1.3% for the European OECD countries and 1.2% for the smaller European economies (see OECD, 1989).

18. The UK: Tables 2.18(i)–2.18(iv)

The UK has a population of almost 60 million (57,409,000 in 1990). GDP per capita in 1990 (in Purchasing Power Standards) was 19,726 ECU as against the EC12 average of 17,857 ECU. The breakdown between industry, services and agriculture as a percentage of GDP was, in 1989 (with the EC average figures in parentheses): industry 34.1% (34.4%), services 64.7% (62.5%) and agriculture 1.1% (3.1%). The respective employment percentages were: industry 29.5% (33.2%), services 68.4% (59.8%) and agriculture 2.2% (7.1%) (Eurostat, 1992). As a percentage of GDP manufacturing industry declined more rapidly in the UK over the period 1973–1989 than in any of the other major industrialised countries. Manufacturing output as a percentage of GDP fell by 6.1% over those years, with manufacturing employment as a percentage of total employment fell by 11.9% (OECD, *Historical Statistics, 1960–1990,* Table 5.2). The UK has the longest average working week of the 12 EC members; while table 2.18(iv) shows average hours worked in manufacturing of 42.2 hours in 1989, for all full-time employees the figure was 43.6 hours as against the EC average of 40.6 hours. The UK data also illustrate more instability than is the case for most of the other economies, with a relatively severe recession from 1979 followed by a more extreme boom in the second half of the 1980s, and with the subsequent recession, which is indicated by the GDP figures falling between 1990 and 1991, having continued into 1992. The consumer-led character of the 'Lawson boom' of the late 1980s can also be seen by comparing the figures for private as against government consumption in table 2.18(i) which show private consumption having increased by more than 30% from 1984 to 1989 during which time government consumption rose by less than 5%.

Data Appendix: Sources and Methods

The data were taken wherever possible from OECD sources. For the period up to 1988 consistent series had been constructed by Fabio-Cesare Bagliano, Andrea Brandolini and Alberto Dalmazzo of the LSE's Centre for Economic Performance, discussed in Bagliano *et al.* (1991) which gives a detailed account of the OECD sources and the methods used in constructing their database. Some minor corrections were made for the data reported in this chapter, and the series were updated to 1990 as detailed below. Up to 1988, the main data sources were as follows (full publication details are given in the References below): the OECD's *Annual National Accounts, Volume 1: Main Aggregates, 1960–1988*; *Labour Force Statistics, 1968–1988*; *Main Economic Indicators, Historical Statistics, 1969–1988*; *Industrial Production Historical Statistics*; and *Indicators of Industrial Activity*; the ILO's *Yearbook of Labour Statistics* and the UN's *National Accounts Yearbook.*

These series were updated as follows: For the first ('National Accounts Statistics') tables for each country, from OECD (1993), *National Accounts 1960–1991*. For the 'Employment' and 'Unemployment and participation' tables, from OECD (1992), *Labour Force Statistics, 1970–1990*, with the male and female unemployment percentages calculated from the figures given for unemployment and total labour force, and with participation rates calculated from the figures given for total labour force and population between 15 and 64. However, OECD (1992) does not give manufacturing employment for the UK after 1987, and the series in the UN (1992), *Yearbook of Labour Statistics, 1992,* includes mining and quarrying, so these data were taken from the *Employment Gazette* (June 1991) and linked.

For the 'Production and Prices' tables, manufacturing output was taken from OECD (1992), *Indicators of Industrial Activity*, number four, except for Iceland which had to be taken from the UN (1992), *Industrial Statistics Yearbook, 1990.* (The OECD's *Indicators of Industrial Activity* for 1991, number one, was also used for the Danish 1988 data.)

For hours worked (reported in the 'Production and Prices' tables), data were taken from the ILO (1992) *Yearbook of Labour Statistics* (and for earlier years where those from Bagliano *et al.* appeared suspect). In the case of Austria, this only gives monthly data, so these were adjusted according to a weighting derived from those years reporting both monthly and weekly data. For prices and hourly earnings (also reported in the 'Production and Prices' table for each country), OECD *Main Economic Indicators* were used (January 1993 and others). This did not give separate figures for Luxembourg; these were therefore taken from *European Economy* (December 1990). Likewise, price data for Portugal were taken from the ILO *Yearbook of Labour Statistics 1992,* which was also used for the earnings data for 1987 and 1988. 1989 and 1990 earnings data for Portugal had to be estimated from *European Economy* (December 1990, 'nominal wages per head'). Data from the ILO *Yearbook of Labour Statistics 1992* were also used to estimate 1989 and 1990 earnings data for Switzerland (using change in male earnings as a proxy).

Note that wherever possible, the series up until 1988 were left as reported by Bagliano *et al.*, since this gives detailed sources and methods, but in some cases these series were not consistent with those added for 1989 and 1990, in which cases the earlier series were altered accordingly. Thus the participation data for Italy were not consistent with those from OECD (1992), yet the latter only provides data back to 1977, so the 1973–6 data were adjusted by the weighting of 1977 data from OECD (1992) and the original series. The same procedure was used to adjust the 1973 and 1974 participation data for the Netherlands.

Bibliography

Bagliano, F.C., Brandolini, A. and Dalmazzo, A. (1991), *The CEP–OECD Data Set*, Centre for Economic Performance Working paper No. 118, LSE, London.

Commission of the European Communities (1990), *European Economy,* December, CEC, Brussels.

Commission of the European Communities (1993), 'Annual Economic Report for 1993', *European Economy,* No. 54, CEC, Brussels.

Department of Employment (1991), *Employment Gazette,* June, HMSO London.

Eurostat (1992), *Europe in Figures,* Third Edition, CEC, Luxembourg.

Glyn, A., Hughes, A., Lipietz, A. and Singh, A. (1990), 'The Rise and Fall of the Golden Age', in S. A. Marglin and J. B. Schor (eds), *The Golden Age of Capitalism,* Oxford University Press, Oxford.

Guger, A. (1992), 'Corporatism: Success or Failure? Austrian Experiences', in Pekkarinen *et al.*, (1992), *Social Corporatism: A superior economic system?,* Oxford University Press, Oxford.

ILO (1992), *Yearbook of Labour Statistics, 1992,* ILO, Geneva.

Kitson, M. and Michie J. (1994), 'Depression and Recovery: Lessons from the Interwar Period', in J. Michie and Grieve Smith (eds), (1994),

Unemployment in Europe, Academic Press, London.

Marglin, S. A. and Schor J. B. (eds), (19??) *The Golden Age of Capitalism,* Oxford University Press, Oxford.

OECD (1989), *Historical Statistics 1960–87,* OECD, Paris.

OECD (1990), *Annual National Accounts, Volume 1: Main Aggregates, 1960-1988,* OECD, Paris.

OECD (1990), *Labour Force Statistics, 1968–1988,* OECD, Paris.

OECD (1990), *Main Economic Indicators, Historical Statistics, 1969–1988,* OECD, Paris.

OECD (1992), *Indicators of Industrial Activity,* number 4, OECD, Paris.

OECD (1992), *Labour Force Statistics, 1970–1990,* OECD, Paris.

OECD (1993), *National Accounts 1960–1991,* OECD, Paris.

OECD (various issues), *Indicators of Industrial Activity,* OECD, Paris.

OECD (various issues), *Industrial Production Historical Statistics,* OECD, Paris.

OECD (various issues), *Main Economic Indicators,* OECD, Paris.

Pekkarinen, J., Pohjola, M. and Rowthorn, B. (eds), (1992), *Social Corporatism: A Superior Economic System?,* Oxford University Press, Oxford.

Recio, A. (1992), 'Economic Internationalisation and the Labour Market in Spain', in A. Castro, Méhaut and Rubery (eds), *International Integration and Labour Market Organisation,* Academic Press, London.

de Sousa, F.F. and Castro, A. (1992), 'Towards Greater European Co-operation: A Necessary But Difficult Road', in A. Castro, Méhaut and Rubery (eds), *International Integration and Labour Market Organisation,* Academic Press, London.

United Nations (1992), *Industrial Statistics Yearbook, 1990,* UN, New York.

United Nations (various issues), *National Accounts Yearbook,* UN, New York.

Weale, M. (1992), *Fifty Years of National Income Accounting,* Cambridge Discussion Papers in Accounting and Finance number 3, October, Department of Applied Economics, Cambridge.

1. Austria

Table 2.1(i) National Accounts Statistics, at 1985 prices; Million Schilling

	Gov't Cons'n	Private Cons'n	Invest-ment	Exports	Imports	GDP
1973	180720	581020	285970	276270	306800	1034300
1974	191020	598400	297320	305860	327980	1075100
1975	198620	617830	282590	298520	312740	1071200
1976	207080	645910	293380	331540	367210	1120200
1977	213820	681110	308320	345580	389850	1171100
1978	220890	671050	295770	370910	390230	1171800
1979	227450	700620	306150	414150	435800	1227400
1980	233520	711200	315280	435690	462830	1263200
1981	238710	713470	310930	456930	459320	1259500
1982	244190	722080	285550	469260	443990	1273000
1983	249600	758050	283910	484230	468590	1298400
1984	250140	757470	289910	513710	514990	1316007
1985	255000	775530	304410	549130	546810	1348400
1986	259240	787720	314830	534240	540420	1363800
1987	260270	811630	323810	547040	565660	1390400
1988	262030	835590	342580	595330	622230	1448300
1989	263185	872562	366279	657545	671428	1498375
1990	266316	905614	387344	710622	723947	1566957
1991	273332	927160	406477	769204	788105	1613305

Note: In this section the term "government consumption" is abbreviated to gov't cons'n and "private consumption" to private cons'n

Austria

Table 2.1(ii) Employment (1000s)

	Male Civilian	Female Civilian	Total Civilian	Wage & Salaried	Manufac-turing
1973	1916	1094	3010	2271	890
1974	1847	1163	3010	2409	910
1975	1814	1128	2942	2368	887
1976	1821	1126	2947	2380	873
1977	1846	1143	2989	2420	891
1978	1852	1163	3015	2470	895
1979	1876	1139	3015	2524	900
1980	1892	1178	3070	2545	907
1981	1901	1189	3090	2575	918
1982	1966	1220	3186	2677	946
1983	1948	1211	3159	2654	895
1984	1949	1286	3235	2740	921
1985	1957	1277	3234	2751	911
1986	1981	1301	3282	2795	925
1987	1980	1320	3300	2809	932
1988	1975	1336	3311	2822	915
1989	1987	1355	3342	2866	910
1990	2019	1393	3412	2929	922

Austria

Table 2.1(iii) Unemployment and Participation

	Unemployment			Participation Rate
	Total Rate %	Male Rate %	Female Rate %	%
1973	1.1	1.4	1.0	65.1
1974	1.3	1.0	1.9	65.0
1975	1.8	1.4	2.3	63.8
1976	1.8	1.4	2.4	63.8
1977	1.6	1.2	2.3	64.1
1978	2.1	1.6	2.8	64.5
1979	2.1	1.5	3.1	64.2
1980	1.9	1.3	2.8	64.6
1981	2.4	1.9	3.6	64.5
1982	3.5	2.8	4.8	66.4
1983	4.1	3.5	5.1	65.6
1984	3.8	3.9	3.6	66.3
1985	3.6	3.6	3.5	65.8
1986	3.1	3.2	3.1	66.3
1987	3.8	3.6	4.1	67.0
1988	3.6	3.2	4.0	66.9
1989	3.1	2.8	3.6	67.1
1990	3.2	3.0	3.5	67.7

Austria

Table 2.1(iv) Production and Prices

	Manufacturing Output (1985=100) (1985=100)	Hours worked in manufacturing	Hourly earnings (manufacturing)	Consumer Price Index
1973	76.4	36.0	37.7	51.4
1974	80.3	36.0	43.7	56.3
1975	73.6	33.9	52.6	61.0
1976	79.2	34.4	56.7	65.4
1977	81.8	33.9	62.3	69.0
1978	83.6	33.5	66.7	71.5
1979	90.2	33.6	70.4	74.2
1980	92.5	33.7	75.6	78.9
1981	90.2	33.4	81.0	84.3
1982	89.1	33.6	85.4	88.8
1983	90.3	33.3	90.1	91.8
1984	95.9	33.5	69.7	96.9
1985	100.0	33.4	100.0	100.0
1986	101.3	32.8	105.0	101.7
1987	99.8	32.3	110.0	103.1
1988	106.7	32.5	114.0	105.2
1989	115.0	32.2	120.0	107.8
1990	125.0	32.2	127.0	111.3
1991	127.0	31.9	135.0	115.0

2. Belgium

Table 2.2(i) National Accounts Statistics, at 1985 prices; Million Belgian Francs

	Gov't Cons'n	Private Cons'n	Invest-ment	Exports	Imports	GDP
1973	629960	2519200	803820	2608200	2781700	3829300
1974	651440	2584700	859600	2706100	2905000	3985900
1975	680780	2601200	843540	2483700	2642900	3926600
1976	705860	2726800	877230	2803200	2966600	4145500
1977	721910	2792000	877600	2865600	3108600	4165200
1978	765510	2856100	901860	2930700	3190700	4279100
1979	784510	2994000	877310	3137200	3477200	4370400
1980	796390	3053300	917660	3215800	3462400	4558900
1981	798460	3018000	769000	3288400	3351900	4511400
1982	787450	3059700	755580	3328600	3354400	4580700
1983	786990	3009600	722500	3419600	3311400	4598300
1984	788480	3045400	735130	3600300	3495900	4697000
1985	808930	3106200	739760	3641200	3522200	4737400
1986	818370	3183500	771140	3855400	3797100	4814300
1987	828270	3272000	811270	4101900	4122800	4904300
1988	816620	3349600	941050	4404000	4425700	5114600
1989	818593	3494177	1072545	4782800	4849200	5348169
1990	827801	3592618	1162222	4980100	5050600	5531092
1991	835449	3684956	1165433	5133000	5188100	5635491

Belgium

Table 2.2(ii) Employment (1000s)

	Male Civilian	Female Civilian	Total Civilian	Wage & Salaried	Manufac-turing
1973	2422	1234	3656	3028	1149
1974	2450	1265	3715	3094	1159
1975	2410	1253	3663	3048	1090
1976	2388	1253	3641	3034	1047
1977	2372	1250	3622	3023	1007
1978	2358	1270	3628	3021	967
1979	2367	1293	3660	3050	941
1980	2352	1305	3657	3051	921
1981	2283	1302	3585	2976	874
1982	2236	1301	3537	2924	842
1983	2198	1304	3502	2879	824
1984	2179	1318	3497	2867	815
1985	2177	1340	3517	2883	803
1986	2173	1368	3541	2901	790
1987	2161	1397	3558	2911	771
1988	2167	1443	3610	2955	766
1989	2196	1474	3670	3005	779
1990	2212	1514	3726	3051	782

Belgium

Table 2.2(iii) Unemployment and Participation

	Unemployment			Participation Rate
	Total Rate %	Male Rate %	Female Rate %	%
1973	2.4	1.9	3.4	62.2
1974	2.6	1.9	3.9	62.8
1975	4.6	3.4	6.8	62.6
1976	6.0	4.0	9.6	62.7
1977	6.8	4.3	11.3	62.5
1978	7.4	4.6	12.2	62.4
1979	7.7	4.6	12.9	62.8
1980	8.1	4.8	13.5	63.0
1981	10.4	7.2	15.5	63.3
1982	12.2	9.0	17.1	63.0
1983	13.5	10.3	18.3	62.8
1984	13.5	10.3	18.3	62.3
1985	12.6	9.1	17.7	62.0
1986	11.9	8.4	17.0	61.8
1987	11.6	8.1	16.4	61.8
1988	10.5	7.3	15.0	61.8
1989	9.3	6.1	13.7	62.1
1990	8.7	5.9	12.8	62.6

Belgium

Table 2.2(iv) Production and Prices

	Manufacturing Output (1985=100) (1985=100)	Hours worked in manufacturing	Hourly earnings (manufacturing)	Consumer Price Index
1973	89.2	37.6	33.9	41.3
1974	93.0	36.6	40.9	46.6
1975	83.5	34.8	48.6	52.5
1976	89.9	35.8	44.2	57.4
1977	90.6	35.1	59.5	61.4
1978	92.9	35.2	63.0	64.2
1979	97.5	35.4	67.7	67.1
1980	95.6	33.4	74.0	71.5
1981	93.3	33.8	82.1	77.0
1982	93.3	33.6	87.9	83.3
1983	95.3	33.5	92.6	89.7
1984	98.3	33.7	97.2	95.3
1985	100.0	33.1	100.0	100.0
1986	101.1	33.0	102.1	101.3
1987	103.5	33.0	104.1	102.9
1988	110.0	33.4	106.4	104.2
1989	115.0	33.6	111.0	107.3
1990	122.0	33.4	116.0	111.0
1991	117.0	–	122.0	114.6

3. Denmark

Table 2.3(i) National Accounts Statistics, at 1985 prices; Million Kroner

	Gov't Cons'n	Private Cons'n	Invest-ment	Exports	Imports	GDP
1973	108750	282970	128180	140620	182030	484550
1974	112570	274870	116830	145540	175110	480030
1975	114840	284970	102360	142950	166680	476860
1976	119960	307400	119890	148790	192660	507730
1977	122840	310730	116960	154910	192710	515970
1978	130450	313060	118260	156750	192940	523590
1979	138100	317360	117740	169850	202530	542150
1980	144010	305670	102900	178600	188820	539750
1981	147800	298610	83121	193250	185650	534940
1982	152340	302940	89007	198080	192660	551100
1983	152280	310760	90655	207700	196050	564980
1984	151650	321270	102340	214910	206740	589780
1985	155480	337220	115190	225570	223480	615070
1986	157780	350970	133900	224830	237800	633910
1987	160880	346760	123960	235480	233150	629400
1988	160270	342830	115930	248050	234620	626850
1989	161040	346237	120487	268438	247666	652119
1990	159470	347753	119935	289992	252798	663521
1991	157606	355816	116000	307526	262779	671762

Denmark

Table 2.3(ii) Employment (1000s)

	Male Civilian	Female Civilian	Total Civilian	Wage & Salaried	Manufac-turing
1973	1404	981	2385	1944	589
1974	1378	977	2355	1926	556
1975	1362	970	2332	1899	529
1976	1364	943	2307	1919	551
1977	1370	951	2321	1957	546
1978	1363	967	2330	1957	532
1979	1389	1050	2439	2059	568
1980	1385	1085	2470	2060	570
1981	1308	1061	2369	2023	505
1982	1299	1075	2374	2023	673
1983	1301	1088	2389	2037	503
1984	1338	1119	2457	2138	482
1985	1383	1139	2522	2209	516
1986	1438	1192	2630	2324	533
1987	1429	1217	2646	2337	521
1988	1445	1215	2660	2365	519
1989	1417	1193	2610	2317	506
1990	1422	1216	2638	2330	532

Denmark

Table 2.3(iii) Unemployment and Participation

	Unemployment			Participation Rate
	Total Rate %	Male Rate %	Female Rate %	%
1973	0.9	0.7	1.1	74.6
1974	3.6	3.6	3.6	75.6
1975	4.9	4.8	5.1	75.7
1976	6.4	6.0	7.0	76.0
1977	7.4	6.1	9.3	77.0
1978	8.4	7.0	10.4	77.7
1979	6.0	4.3	8.3	78.8
1980	6.9	6.7	7.2	80.0
1981	10.4	10.2	10.7	79.2
1982	11.1	11.0	11.2	79.5
1983	11.5	10.9	12.3	80.0
1984	8.6	7.7	9.6	79.3
1985	7.3	6.0	8.9	80.1
1986	5.5	4.1	7.2	81.6
1987	7.0	6.0	8.2	83.0
1988	7.3	6.4	8.2	83.4
1989	8.1	7.5	8.9	83.4
1990	8.3	7.7	8.9	84.1

Denmark

Table 2.3(iv) Production and Prices

	Manufacturing Output (1985=100) (1985=100)	Hours worked in manufacturing	Hourly earnings (manufacturing)	Consumer Price Index
1973	71.3	33.5	28.8	33.0
1974	72.6	34.2	35.0	38.0
1975	68.9	33.1	41.7	41.7
1976	77.1	33.2	47.1	45.4
1977	77.8	32.7	51.9	50.5
1978	79.2	32.6	57.3	55.5
1979	82.6	32.5	63.8	60.9
1980	82.6	32.6	70.9	68.3
1981	82.6	32.2	77.6	76.3
1982	85.1	32.5	85.4	84.1
1983	87.6	33.0	91.0	89.8
1984	96.7	33.0	95.4	95.5
1985	100.0	32.1	100.0	100.0
1986	104.1	32.8	104.8	103.6
1987	101.6	32.1	114.6	107.7
1988	105.0	31.8	122.0	112.7
1989	107.0	31.8	128.0	118.1
1990	108.0	31.5	134.0	121.2
1991	110.0	31.5	140.0	124.1

4. Finland

Table 2.4(i) National Accounts Statistics, at 1985 prices; Million Markkaa

	Gov't Cons'n	Private Cons'n	Invest-ment	Exports	Imports	GDP
1973	40645	136620	70063	60388	68398	240390
1974	42475	139050	72509	60005	72976	247670
1975	45404	143430	76819	51624	73386	250520
1976	47993	144740	70040	58207	71941	251190
1977	50017	143010	67596	67355	70857	251480
1978	52085	146550	62912	73373	68225	256960
1979	54055	154600	64811	79799	80752	275640
1980	56344	157700	71568	86509	87451	290320
1981	58767	159620	73118	90781	83372	294900
1982	60849	167050	76362	89792	85415	305460
1983	63113	171330	79468	92001	87959	314540
1984	64872	176040	77786	96993	88857	324190
1985	68218	181660	80052	98173	94893	334990
1986	70325	189110	80066	99498	97795	342020
1987	73458	199980	84415	102130	106570	355660
1988	75453	210070	91899	106120	118770	374080
1989	77117	218775	106412	107552	128834	395078
1990	80525	219293	101149	109236	127735	396460
1991	83032	210939	81900	102372	112731	370664

Finland

Table 2.4(ii) Employment (1000s)

	Male Civilian	Female Civilian	Total Civilian	Wage & Salaried	Manufac-turing
1973	1161	993	2154	1739	267
1974	1189	1030	2219	1816	280
1975	1177	1034	2211	1836	279
1976	1209	1059	2268	1939	252
1977	1171	1050	2221	1813	248
1978	1155	1035	2190	1802	237
1979	1188	1058	2246	1855	241
1980	1230	1088	2318	1920	249
1981	1234	1109	2343	1953	233
1982	1238	1129	2367	1980	226
1983	1239	1141	2380	1994	571
1984	1252	1151	2403	2025	563
1985	1255	1172	2427	2066	557
1986	1253	1168	2421	2061	550
1987	1250	1163	2413	2041	534
1988	1254	1166	2420	2052	519
1989	1282	1178	2460	2094	528
1990	1279	1179	2457	2098	524

Finland

Table 2.4(iii) Unemployment and Participation

	Unemployment			Participation Rate
	Total Rate %	Male Rate %	Female Rate %	%
1973	2.3	2.4	2.2	71.7
1974	1.7	1.6	1.9	72.8
1975	2.3	2.4	2.1	72.5
1976	3.9	4.7	2.9	75.5
1977	5.9	7.0	4.7	75.3
1978	7.3	8.4	6.0	75.0
1979	6.0	6.5	5.5	75.5
1980	4.7	4.7	4.6	76.4
1981	4.9	5.1	4.6	76.9
1982	5.4	5.6	5.2	77.5
1983	5.9	5.8	5.9	77.4
1984	5.2	5.4	5.0	77.4
1985	5.0	5.5	4.6	77.7
1986	5.4	6.1	4.6	77.7
1987	5.1	5.9	4.3	77.2
1988	4.6	5.1	4.0	76.9
1989	3.4	3.5	3.4	77.2
1990	3.4	4.0	2.8	76.8

Finland

Table 2.4(iv) Production and Prices

	Manufacturing Output (1985=100) (1985=100)	Hours worked in manufacturing	Hourly earnings (manufacturing)	Consumer Price Index
1973	68	33.4	24.2	28.9
1974	72	33.8	29.7	33.8
1975	69	33.8	36.2	39.8
1976	69	33.6	41.8	45.5
1977	68	32.8	45.5	51.3
1978	72	33.2	48.9	55.3
1979	80	33.4	54.5	59.4
1980	87	33.2	61.5	66.3
1981	89	32.8	69.3	74.3
1982	90	32.5	76.6	81.4
1983	93	32.4	83.9	88.2
1984	97	32.3	92.6	94.4
1985	100	32.3	100.0	100.0
1986	101	33.4	105.9	102.9
1987	105	32.1	113.6	107.1
1988	111	32.0	123.8	112.6
1989	115	31.8	134.0	120.0
1990	114	31.3	148.0	127.3
1991	102	–	158.0	132.6

5. France

Table 2.5(i) National Accounts Statistics, at 1985 prices; Million French Francs

	Gov't Cons'n	Private Cons'n	Invest-ment	Exports	Imports	GDP
1973	643250	2147500	929380	671410	827750	3633200
1974	651100	2173500	941310	730820	843660	3746200
1975	679630	2235400	880600	718490	761930	3735700
1976	707880	2344300	909340	777230	894750	3894300
1977	724730	2408500	892830	834480	895760	4019600
1978	762160	2497400	911520	883750	922450	4154200
1979	785170	2572800	940130	949680	1015800	4288900
1980	805050	2603600	964780	975330	1041000	4358600
1981	830300	2657000	946560	1011200	1019400	4409800
1982	861600	2748800	933580	994130	1045800	4522100
1983	879650	2774100	900290	1030800	1017800	4553500
1984	890010	2803800	876890	1102900	1045100	4613400
1985	910320	2871100	905290	1123900	1092600	4700100
1986	926120	2976200	935540	1111800	1168900	4808400
1987	953700	3056600	969840	1144700	1258700	4901700
1988	974470	3142400	1042200	1229900	1353900	5074500
1989	985665	3247133	1163479	1361732	1470475	5320876
1990	1003733	3334755	1199945	1434965	1564591	5440386
1991	1044881	3384284	1184676	1493572	1609237	5501546

France

Table 2.5(ii) Employment (1000s)

	Male Civilian	Female Civilian	Total Civilian	Wage & Salaried	Manufac-turing
1973	13141	7722	20863	16879	5882
1974	13225	7833	21058	17166	5953
1975	13015	7848	20863	17060	5798
1976	13019	7997	21016	17289	5745
1977	13028	8160	21188	17497	5721
1978	12972	8290	21262	17610	5640
1979	12935	8370	21305	17686	5556
1980	12913	8420	21333	17752	5495
1981	12771	8432	21203	17663	5321
1982	12708	8532	21240	17752	5249
1983	12567	8601	21168	17737	5136
1984	12356	8625	20981	17605	4997
1985	12238	8677	20915	17578	4853
1986	12206	8749	20955	17649	4749
1987	12203	8815	21018	17733	4637
1988	12277	8902	21179	17915	4572
1989	12389	9066	21455	18239	4584
1990	12514	9218	21732	18562	4623

France

Table 2.5(iii) Unemployment and Participation

	Unemployment			Participation Rate
	Total Rate %	Male Rate %	Female Rate %	%
1973	2.8	1.7	4.6	67.8
1974	2.9	1.8	4.8	68.0
1975	4.1	2.9	6.1	67.8
1976	4.5	3.1	6.8	68.1
1977	5.1	3.5	7.5	68.5
1978	5.3	3.9	7.6	68.4
1979	6.0	4.3	8.5	68.4
1980	6.4	4.4	9.4	68.1
1981	7.6	5.5	10.6	67.6
1982	8.3	6.2	11.2	67.3
1983	8.5	6.6	11.2	66.4
1984	10.0	8.1	12.6	66.1
1985	10.5	8.6	12.9	65.8
1986	10.6	8.7	13.1	65.8
1987	10.8	8.6	13.6	65.8
1988	10.2	8.0	13.1	65.6
1989	9.5	7.0	12.6	65.6
1990	9.0	6.7	12.0	65.9

France

Table 2.5(iv) Production and Prices

	Manufacturing Output (1985=100) (1985=100)	Hours worked in manufacturing	Hourly earnings (manufacturing)	Consumer Price Index
1973	94.8	43.6	22.7	30.3
1974	97.0	42.9	27.6	34.4
1975	87.5	41.7	31.8	38.5
1976	96.4	41.6	36.7	42.2
1977	98.0	41.3	41.4	46.1
1978	99.8	41.0	46.3	50.3
1979	103.9	40.8	51.8	55.8
1980	103.2	40.5	60.2	63.3
1981	101.0	40.3	69.2	71.8
1982	100.9	39.3	78.8	80.3
1983	100.2	38.9	88.9	88.0
1984	99.9	38.7	94.5	94.5
1985	100.0	38.6	100.0	100.0
1986	100.6	38.6	104.1	102.7
1987	102.4	38.7	108.5	105.9
1988	107.5	38.7	108.7	108.7
1989	113.0	38.7	115.0	112.7
1990	115.0	38.7	120.0	116.5
1991	113.0	38.7	125.0	120.2

6. Germany

Table 2.6(i) National Accounts Statistics, at 1985 prices; Million Deutsche Mark

	Gov't Cons'n	Private Cons'n	Invest-ment	Exports	Imports	GDP
1973	282560	825620	362780	344550	351150	1486000
1974	293850	831040	327990	386950	356140	1490000
1975	304780	857950	310630	360690	357370	1466300
1976	309380	889760	321760	395670	396900	1545700
1977	313610	927590	333280	411030	408600	1591300
1978	325650	963190	348900	424320	434300	1637000
1979	336680	998000	374130	442490	476850	1704900
1980	345340	1010500	384530	465030	495000	1728200
1981	351720	1005200	366080	501020	480650	1731100
1982	348760	991770	346830	517860	473660	1719900
1983	349580	1009000	357780	513520	482280	1745700
1984	358130	1024300	360590	554680	509610	1794900
1985	365660	1038300	360800	593490	527100	1830500
1986	375040	1073700	372620	590420	543540	1873400
1987	380500	1111500	380630	592910	565840	1907800
1988	388910	1141600	403250	626080	599160	1978300
1989	382670	1167370	419080	687020	645760	2027330
1990	391750	1230680	455460	758590	711740	2130500
1991	393600	1274630	485010	855860	794920	2209640

Germany

Table 2.6(ii) Employment (1000s)

	Male Civilian	Female Civilian	Total Civilian	Wage & Salaried	Manufac-turing
1973	16501	9910	26411	22395	9697
1974	16186	9852	26038	22113	9479
1975	15677	9608	25285	21489	9010
1976	15531	9528	25059	21407	8807
1977	15538	9476	25014	21496	8770
1978	15643	9526	25169	21734	8751
1979	15855	9661	25516	22132	8793
1980	15968	9829	25797	22478	8842
1981	15792	9818	25610	22335	8598
1982	15454	9723	25177	21904	8321
1983	15198	9595	24793	21519	8006
1984	15181	9658	24839	21573	7933
1985	15259	9751	25010	21744	8012
1986	15356	9911	25267	21996	8124
1987	16045	10581	26626	23610	8508
1988	16085	10750	26835	23834	8481
1989	16246	10963	27209	24229	8592
1990	16532	11414	27946	24983	8813

Germany

Table 2.6(iii) Unemployment and Participation

	Unemployment			Participation Rate
	Total Rate %	Male Rate %	Female Rate %	%
1973	1.0	0.9	1.2	69.4
1974	2.2	2.0	2.6	69.1
1975	4.1	3.8	4.5	68.6
1976	4.1	3.5	4.9	68.3
1977	4.0	3.2	5.1	68.1
1978	3.8	3.0	5.0	68.1
1979	3.3	2.6	4.5	68.3
1980	3.3	2.6	4.5	68.5
1981	4.7	4.0	5.9	68.3
1982	6.8	6.2	7.7	68.0
1983	8.3	7.7	9.3	67.5
1984	8.4	7.8	9.3	67.2
1985	8.4	7.8	9.4	67.6
1986	8.1	7.2	9.4	68.2
1987	7.7	7.0	8.8	68.6
1988	7.7	6.9	9.0	68.9
1989	6.8	6.0	8.1	68.8
1990	6.2	5.4	7.4	–

Germany

Table 2.6(iv) Production and Prices

	Manufacturing Output (1985=100) (1985=100)	Hours worked in manufacturing	Hourly earnings (manufacturing)	Consumer Price Index
1973	93.3	42.8	50.9	59.6
1974	91.2	41.9	56.3	63.8
1975	85.1	40.4	60.9	67.6
1976	91.0	41.4	64.8	70.7
1977	93.6	41.7	69.7	73.3
1978	92.6	41.6	73.2	75.2
1979	97.2	41.8	77.2	78.3
1980	97.2	41.6	82.0	82.6
1981	95.2	41.1	86.3	87.8
1982	92.1	40.7	90.6	92.5
1983	92.7	40.5	93.5	95.6
1984	95.6	41.0	95.8	97.8
1985	100.0	40.7	100.0	100.0
1986	102.4	40.4	103.6	99.9
1987	102.6	40.1	108.0	100.1
1988	106.8	40.0	112.7	101.4
1989	113.0	39.9	117.0	104.2
1990	119.0	39.5	123.0	107.0
1991	122.0	39.2	130.0	110.7

7. Greece

Table 2.7(i) National Accounts Statistics, at 1985 prices; Million Drachmae

	Gov't Cons'n	Private Cons'n	Invest-ment	Exports	Imports	GDP
1973	511640	2120400	1069900	502730	1051000	3414700
1974	573430	2134600	796350	503340	879750	3290500
1975	641870	2251200	798060	556860	935170	3489600
1976	674810	2370900	852470	648090	992670	3711500
1977	718840	2479400	918750	659580	1071800	3838800
1978	744030	2620300	973790	767720	1148500	4095900
1979	787520	2689300	1059500	818770	1230800	4247000
1980	789120	2693700	990950	875600	1132600	4321400
1981	842920	2748600	916610	823690	1173900	4323800
1982	862270	2855400	898970	764460	1256400	4340900
1983	885960	2863100	887210	825430	1338900	4358300
1984	912980	2911800	836970	965230	1341700	4478300
1985	942050	3025500	880370	977620	1513500	4617700
1986	936280	3034300	825420	1114900	1571100	4653300
1987	953130	3062300	760690	1293100	1831400	4650800
1988	1006500	3174500	829240	1390900	1950200	4834600
1989	1028677	3321410	938937	1427935	2191907	5019566
1990	1027155	3388926	992180	1440689	2454099	5017002
1991	1019623	3430141	972415	1477468	2542594	5107471

Greece

Table 2.7(ii) Employment (1000s)

	Male Civilian	Female Civilian	Total Civilian	Wage & Salaried	Manufacturing
1977	2279	983	3262	1553	633
1978	2290	986	3276	1574	647
1979	2327	984	3311	1608	661
1980	2362	994	3356	1668	675
1981	2423	1108	3531	1699	681
1982	2427	1075	3502	1720	674
1983	2384	1156	3540	1713	679
1984	2376	1177	3553	1744	679
1985	2371	1217	3588	1770	679
1986	2378	1223	3601	1774	718
1987	2362	1236	3598	1794	716
1988	2380	1277	3657	1845	707
1989	2386	1285	3671	1888	715

Note: Data not available pre-1977, nor for 1990. Manufacturing employment was 5600, 5660, 5700 and 6010 in 1973–1976.

Greece

Table 2.7(iii) Unemployment and Participation

	Unemployment			Participation Rate
	Total Rate %	Male Rate %	Female Rate %	%
1977	1.7	1.2	2.8	55.9
1978	1.8	1.3	3.0	55.5
1979	1.9	1.3	3.2	55.4
1980	2.8	2.2	4.1	55.9
1981	4.0	3.3	5.7	58.7
1982	5.8	4.7	8.0	58.7
1983	7.9	5.8	11.8	59.9
1984	8.1	6.0	12.2	59.8
1985	7.8	5.7	11.7	59.6
1986	7.4	5.1	11.6	59.1
1987	7.4	5.1	11.3	58.7
1988	7.7	4.8	12.5	59.5
1989	7.5	4.6	12.3	–

Greece

Table 2.7(iv) Production and Prices

	Manufacturing Output (1985=100) (1985=100)	Hours worked in manufacturing	Hourly earnings (manufacturing)	Consumer Price Index
1973	74.8	43.7	7.0	12.8
1974	73.3	43.8	8.9	16.2
1975	76.6	42.7	11.0	18.4
1976	84.7	41.8	14.2	20.8
1977	85.9	41.1	17.2	23.4
1978	92.5	41.3	21.2	26.3
1979	98.1	41.2	25.6	31.3
1980	99.0	40.7	32.6	39.1
1981	99.7	39.5	41.5	48.7
1982	97.6	38.6	55.4	58.9
1983	96.2	38.5	66.1	70.8
1984	97.4	38.2	83.5	83.8
1985	100.0	39.3	100.0	100.0
1986	99.3	39.2	112.7	123.0
1987	97.2	39.3	123.5	143.2
1988	102.2	41.1	146.2	162.5
1989	105.0	41.1	176.0	184.8
1990	102.0	41.1	210.0	222.6
1991	101.0	–	246.0	265.9

8. Iceland

Table 2.8(i) National Accounts Statistics, at 1985 prices; Million Kronur

	Gov't Cons'n	Private Cons'n	Invest-ment	Exports	Imports	GDP
1973	10799	47621	20669	27429	32587	73664
1974	11714	52505	22736	27203	36767	78315
1975	12807	47461	20721	27916	32232	79028
1976	13450	50034	20084	31154	31111	83831
1977	13742	56500	22504	34350	37387	91289
1978	14719	61560	21786	39556	38749	97646
1979	15522	63298	21831	42036	39704	102980
1980	15852	65436	24921	43170	40892	108850
1981	17017	70052	25163	43718	43614	113320
1982	18069	73766	25036	39519	43346	115540
1983	18922	69268	21964	43591	40899	111050
1984	18959	71458	23912	44898	44700	115170
1985	20136	74705	24255	49819	49051	118890
1986	21512	80660	23874	52914	49174	127630
1987	22820	93879	28380	55056	60418	138710
1988	23847	90121	27815	52734	58528	137270
1989	24360	85702	26224	54824	51999	138128
1990	25369	85219	26954	54616	52348	138680
1991	26690	90004	27754	51482	55707	140629

Iceland

Table 2.8(ii) Employment (1000s)

	Male Civilian	Wage & salaried	Manufacturing
1973	90.2	76.0	20.4
1974	93.3	78.4	20.6
1975	94.9	80.1	21.4
1976	98.3	83.4	22.1
1977	98.6	83.9	23.2
1978	101.5	86.7	23.6
1979	102.5	88.9	24.8
1980	105.9	92.1	25.9
1981	111.0	97.1	26.4
1982	113.9	99.6	26.3
1983	114.9	100.5	26.6
1984	116.6	101.8	27.2
1985	120.8	105.7	27.3
1986	124.5	107.7	27.6
1987	131.7	111.6	28.4
1988	128.8	108.5	25.6
1989	128.0	–	24.4

Iceland

Table 2.8(iii) Unemployment and Participation

	Unemployment	Participation Rate
1973	0.4	71.3
1974	0.4	72.2
1975	0.5	72.0
1976	0.5	73.3
1977	0.3	72.4
1978	0.4	73.6
1979	0.4	73.1
1980	0.3	74.3
1981	0.4	76.7
1982	0.7	77.6
1983	1.0	77.3
1984	1.3	77.6
1985	0.9	79.3
1986	0.6	80.8
1987	0.5	84.0
1988	0.6	80.1
1989	1.6	78.6

Iceland

Table 2.8(iv) Production and Prices

	Manufacturing Output (1985=100) (1985=100)	Hours worked in manufacturing	Hourly earnings (manufacturing)	Consumer Price Index
1973	67.1	–	1.4	1.1
1974	67.4	52.6	2.2	1.6
1975	67.0	50.5	2.8	2.4
1976	74.3	51.6	3.7	3.2
1977	84.4	49.5	5.1	4.2
1978	85.8	49.9	7.7	6.1
1979	91.8	49.6	10.9	8.7
1980	99.3	49.3	17.0	13.7
1981	102.6	49.9	25.9	20.8
1982	98.8	49.4	39.5	31.1
1983	92.6	48.7	61.5	57.9
1984	99.2	48.9	78.5	75.8
1985	100.0	48.6	100.0	100.0
1986	104.7	48.5	132.0	122.2
1987	112.6	49.2	184.6	144.6
1988	–	47.4	235.7	181.7

9. Ireland

Table 2.9(i) National Accounts Statistics, at 1985 prices; Million £

	Gov't Cons'n	Private Cons'n	Invest-ment	Exports	Imports	GDP
1973	2137	8092	3028	4282	6199	11396
1974	2299	8225	2676	4312	6057	11882
1975	2499	8293	2580	4637	5439	12554
1976	2564	8528	2929	5014	6236	12729
1977	2617	9105	3048	5717	7064	13774
1978	2824	9935	3623	6422	8173	14764
1979	2954	10375	4117	6837	9306	15218
1980	3163	10420	3922	7271	8888	15686
1981	3174	10597	4296	7414	9040	16208
1982	3277	9849	4149	7824	8758	16578
1983	3265	9932	3764	8642	9167	16537
1984	3242	10040	3716	10076	10070	17261
1985	3295	10415	3410	10738	10397	17664
1986	3373	10676	3308	11048	10982	17608
1987	3246	10948	3285	12527	11530	18467
1988	3106	11293	3296	13615	11980	19143
1989	3054	12141	3724	14990	13284	20780
1990	3213	12507	4105	16306	14084	22501
1991	3256	12546	3808	17113	14185	23072

Ireland

Table 2.9(ii) Employment (1000s)

	Male Civilian	Female Civilian	Total Civilian	Wage & Salaried	Manufac-turing
1973	769	288	1057	747	223
1974	775	296	1071	766	232
1975	764	297	1061	757	224
1976	754	296	1050	753	218
1977	769	299	1068	774	226
1978	785	310	1095	801	231
1979	808	321	1129	836	239
1980	808	333	1141	859	243
1981	794	337	1131	862	237
1982	788	345	1133	857	233
1983	764	346	1110	835	218
1984	752	338	1090	818	208
1985	727	332	1059	802	203
1986	729	339	1068	818	209
1987	722	352	1074	815	204
1988	728	350	1078	810	207
1989	724	352	1076	811	213
1990	744	371	1115	838	220

Ireland

Table 2.9(iii) Unemployment and Participation

	Unemployment			Participation Rate
	Total Rate %	Male Rate %	Female Rate %	%
1973	5.7	6.4	3.7	63.5
1974	5.4	6.2	3.3	63.0
1975	7.3	8.0	5.7	62.6
1977	9.1	10.0	6.6	62.1
1976	9.1	9.7	6.9	62.1
1978	8.3	9.1	6.1	62.3
1979	7.2	7.6	6.4	62.4
1980	7.4	7.6	7.0	62.3
1981	10.0	10.5	8.9	62.6
1982	11.6	12.3	9.7	63.0
1983	14.2	15.5	11.1	62.7
1984	15.8	17.3	12.2	62.0
1985	17.6	19.2	13.8	61.3
1986	17.6	19.3	13.7	61.4
1987	17.8	19.7	13.5	61.6
1988	16.9	18.9	12.3	61.0
1989	15.6	17.5	11.3	60.3
1990	13.7	15.5	10.0	60.8

Ireland

Table 2.9(iv) Production and Prices

	Manufacturing Output (1985=100) (1985=100)	Hours worked in manufacturing	Hourly earnings (manufacturing)	Consumer Price Index
1973	57.9	42.4	15.8	20.5
1974	58.7	41.5	19.0	24.0
1975	54.8	41.2	24.4	29.0
1976	61.9	41.3	28.5	34.3
1977	66.5	42.3	33.8	38.9
1978	71.8	42.5	38.8	41.9
1979	77.2	42.3	44.7	47.4
1980	76.5	41.3	54.2	56.1
1981	81.0	41.3	63.0	67.5
1982	80.1	40.5	76.4	79.1
1983	86.4	40.8	85.3	87.4
1984	95.8	41.1	92.3	94.9
1985	100.0	41.1	100.0	100.0
1986	102.9	41.4	106.8	103.8
1987	114.5	41.1	113.0	107.1
1988	129.0	41.9	118.2	109.4
1989	143.0	41.7	124.0	113.8
1990	149.0	41.5	131.0	117.6
1991	154.0	41.0	138.0	121.4

10. Italy

Table 2.10(i) National Accounts Statistics, at 1985 prices; Billion Lire

	Gov't Cons'n	Private Cons'n	Invest-ment	Exports	Imports	GDP
1973	96212	347150	156680	106590	139270	579480
1974	98494	360010	159880	112860	141220	610940
1975	100860	360690	148160	114920	123550	594740
1976	102990	378830	148230	126610	140110	633860
1977	106110	391290	150960	141330	142770	655260
1978	109870	403500	151910	154590	149820	679380
1979	113150	432210	160590	168100	167090	720060
1980	115540	458860	174560	153730	172320	750570
1981	118690	466170	169060	163230	165550	757760
1982	122080	470950	160280	163170	164420	760230
1983	125620	473070	158790	167480	161550	768780
1984	128750	483930	165870	178470	179880	791950
1985	133270	499590	168230	185020	188310	812750
1986	137130	522280	170860	189550	197720	833420
1987	142080	544510	182480	195650	218710	858270
1988	146360	567440	191450	206030	235690	891990
1989	146629	588427	200664	221144	245252	921714
1990	148471	607627	207190	242100	270963	942271
1991	151029	623253	209118	238685	275289	955817

Italy

Table 2.10(ii) Employment (1000s)

	Male Civilian	Female Civilian	Total Civilian	Wage & Salaried	Manufac-turing
1973	13555	5451	19006	13191	5240
1974	13734	5658	19392	13555	5422
1975	13773	5718	19491	13735	5443
1976	13745	5867	19612	13888	5370
1977	13646	6145	19791	14125	5441
1978	13680	6183	19863	14107	5386
1979	13703	6354	20057	14338	5371
1980	13774	6539	20313	14499	5438
1981	13775	6586	20361	14495	5333
1982	13688	6609	20297	14472	5233
1983	13671	6679	20350	14360	5080
1984	13670	6748	20418	14253	4881
1985	13677	6831	20508	14418	4766
1986	13638	6976	20614	14460	4719
1987	13519	7065	20584	14457	4639
1988	13665	7153	20818	14696	4699
1989	13605	7227	20832	14765	4729
1990	13696	7427	21123	15041	4757

Italy

Table 2.10(iii) Unemployment and Participation

	Unemployment			Participation Rate
	Total Rate %	Male Rate %	Female Rate %	%
1973	6.4	4.3	11.4	58.6
1974	5.4	3.7	9.4	58.4
1975	5.9	3.9	10.5	58.6
1976	6.8	4.3	12.0	59.2
1977	7.2	4.7	12.4	60.0
1978	7.3	4.8	12.4	59.7
1979	7.8	5.0	13.1	60.2
1980	7.7	4.9	13.0	60.8
1981	8.0	5.1	13.4	60.8
1982	8.7	5.9	13.9	60.2
1983	9.5	6.4	15.3	60.1
1984	10.1	6.7	16.3	59.8
1985	10.4	7.0	16.6	59.8
1986	11.2	7.6	17.6	60.5
1987	12.1	8.3	18.5	61.0
1988	12.1	8.3	18.6	60.9
1989	11.8	7.9	18.6	61.2
1990	10.8	7.2	17.0	61.1

Italy

Table 2.10(iv) Production and Prices

	Manufacturing Output (1985=100) (1985=100)	Hours worked in manufacturing	Hourly earnings (manufacturing)	Consumer Price Index
1973	84.1	41.3	9.5	17.7
1974	88.0	41.3	12.0	21.1
1975	79.2	41.4	17.8	24.6
1976	89.3	41.3	21.1	28.8
1977	90.3	41.5	26.6	33.7
1978	91.8	41.6	32.3	37.7
1979	98.2	41.2	38.3	43.3
1980	104.1	41.7	46.8	52.5
1981	102.4	41.8	57.3	61.9
1982	99.0	41.5	66.2	72.1
1983	95.6	41.5	72.4	82.6
1984	99.0	41.9	84.4	91.6
1985	100.0	–	100.0	100.0
1986	102.8	–	119.0	105.9
1987	106.8	–	141.6	110.9
1988	112.3	–	168.5	116.4
1989	118.0	–	126.0	124.2
1990	117.0	–	135.0	131.7
1991	114.0	–	148.0	140.2

11. Luxembourg

Table 2.11(i) National Accounts Statistics, at 1985 prices; Million Luxembourg Francs

	Gov't Cons'n	Private Cons'n	Invest-ment	Exports	Imports	GDP
1973	24310	88932	50543	157960	155440	166480
1974	25222	93305	47018	174450	164430	173500
1975	26056	98192	43524	146920	148950	162090
1976	26785	101260	41686	148360	150280	166200
1977	27567	103890	41653	154630	152530	168810
1978	28062	106920	42095	159500	161670	175690
1979	28688	110710	43682	174540	172530	179810
1980	29573	113730	49230	170940	178840	181320
1981	29987	115540	45580	163420	173240	180320
1982	30431	116010	45365	163150	172920	182360
1983	31008	116330	40136	171950	174780	187810
1984	31682	117610	40347	203180	198780	199440
1985	32306	120520	37883	222570	212920	205260
1986	33356	123460	48754	231890	221910	214310
1987	34235	128530	51935	243850	238370	220390
1988	35301	130830	53605	265640	256430	229900
1989	36183	141115	67802	280900	278518	249620
1990	37323	146748	69490	288105	290406	257561
1991	38754	156309	76304	298112	314455	265455

Luxembourg

Table 2.11(ii) Employment (1000s)

	Male Civilian	Female Civilian	Total Civilian	Wage & Salaried	Manufac-turing
1973	109.1	41.6	150.7	124.4	49.4
1974	111.1	43.8	154.9	129.3	51.0
1975	111.3	45.5	156.8	132.1	50.2
1976	109.7	46.9	156.6	132.5	48.5
1977	109.2	47.3	156.5	133.0	47.5
1978	107.7	48.9	156.6	132.6	44.6
1979	108.1	48.3	156.4	134.4	43.2
1980	108.8	48.7	157.5	136.3	42.1
1981	106.6	51.4	158.0	138.0	41.5
1982	106.7	50.9	157.6	138.0	40.6
1983	105.2	51.9	157.1	137.7	39.2
1984	105.1	52.9	158.0	138.8	38.8
1985	106.1	53.9	160.0	141.1	38.7
1986	108.5	55.9	164.4	145.9	39.4
1987	110.9	58.0	168.9	150.7	38.8
1988	114.1	60.1	174.2	156.2	37.4
1989	118.3	62.9	181.2	163.4	37.4
1990	123.7	65.2	188.9	171.2	37.4

Luxembourg

Table 2.11(iii) Unemployment and Participation

	Unemployment			Participation Rate
	Total Rate %	Male Rate %	Female Rate %	%
1974	0.1	0.1	–	65.2
1975	0.2	0.2	0.2	65.2
1976	0.3	0.3	0.4	64.8
1977	0.5	0.5	0.6	64.5
1978	0.8	0.6	1.0	64.0
1979	0.7	0.6	1.0	64.4
1980	0.7	0.5	1.2	64.4
1981	1.0	0.8	1.3	64.2
1982	1.3	1.0	1.7	63.9
1983	1.6	1.3	2.1	63.3
1984	1.7	1.3	2.4	63.4
1985	1.6	1.3	2.2	63.9
1986	1.4	1.1	1.9	64.9
1987	1.6	1.3	2.0	66.4
1988	1.4	1.3	1.6	68.1
1989	1.2	1.1	1.6	–
1990	1.1	0.9	1.7	–

Luxembourg

Table 2.11(iv) Production and Prices

	Manufacturing Output (1985=100) (1985=100)	Hours worked in manufacturing	Hourly earnings (manufacturing)	Consumer Price Index
1973	90.7	42.3	41.0	43.5
1974	94.5	42.4	47.5	47.6
1975	73.6	40.8	51.4	52.7
1976	76.7	40.6	59.4	57.9
1977	78.1	38.9	64.1	61.8
1978	81.1	39.8	68.0	63.7
1979	84.3	40.5	71.2	66.6
1980	81.8	40.0	76.5	70.8
1981	76.1	41.2	80.4	76.5
1982	77.5	41.2	86.8	83.7
1983	82.0	41.0	94.2	91.0
1984	93.6	39.7	97.1	96.1
1985	100.0	40.2	100.0	100.0
1986	101.8	40.5	103.8	100.3
1987	100.7	40.8	106.0	100.2
1988	109.3	41.2	112.6	101.6
1989	118.0	40.3	117.0	106.0
1990	117.0	–	124.0	109.0
1991	117.0	–	131.0	114.0

12. Netherlands

Table 2.12(i) National Accounts Statistics, at 1985 prices; Million Guilders

	Gov't Cons'n	Private Cons'n	Invest-ment	Exports	Imports	GDP
1973	52627	194710	82764	185180	183690	336800
1974	53788	201920	79451	189970	182140	350160
1975	55991	208580	75989	184020	174740	349840
1976	58290	219640	74333	202200	192420	367750
1977	60268	229740	81580	198620	197980	376270
1978	62611	239680	83639	205170	210430	385520
1979	64395	246820	82201	220360	223110	394660
1980	64760	246840	81430	223690	222130	398060
1981	66370	241830	73300	228280	209240	395500
1982	66660	238440	70160	227700	211440	389830
1983	67350	240050	71490	235250	219600	395200
1984	66830	241980	75200	252170	230500	407600
1985	67670	247720	80250	265540	245500	418180
1986	69330	255590	86550	274550	254340	426580
1987	70730	263580	87140	285820	269770	431100
1988	70720	266870	95680	308170	288660	442910
1989	71924	278960	100420	318003	298462	473304
1990	73406	290393	103999	335573	313097	491686
1991	74577	299831	104059	351122	324766	502707

Netherlands

Table 2.12(ii) Employment (1000s)

	Male Civilian	Female Civilian	Total Civilian	Wage & Salaried	Manufac-turing
1973	–	–	4664	4030	1203
1974	–	–	4667	4045	1203
1975	3364	1276	4640	4033	1160
1976	3354	1300	4654	4064	1108
1977	3365	1336	4701	4130	1092
1978	3378	1379	4757	4175	1092
1979	3400	1421	4821	4229	1074
1980	3445	1525	4970	4362	1067
1981	3454	1618	5072	4433	1062
1982	3370	1640	5010	4388	1029
1983	3287	1663	4950	4362	957
1984	3284	1696	4980	4386	975
1985	3334	1742	5076	4488	984
1986	3375	1760	5135	4562	988
1987	3670	2103	5773	5075	1106
1988	3713	2221	5934	5235	1109
1989	3786	2278	6065	5364	1152
1990	3864	2404	6268	5538	1185

Netherlands

Table 2.12(iii) Unemployment and Participation

	Unemployment			Participation Rate
	Total Rate %	Male Rate %	Female Rate %	%
1973	3.1	–	–	57.9
1974	3.7	–	–	57.5
1975	5.3	5.5	4.7	57.3
1976	5.6	5.8	5.3	56.8
1977	5.5	5.3	5.7	56.5
1978	5.4	5.1	6.3	56.4
1979	5.5	5.0	6.7	56.5
1980	6.2	5.7	7.1	57.7
1981	8.6	8.5	9.0	59.7
1982	11.6	11.7	11.3	60.2
1983	12.0	10.9	14.0	59.0
1984	12.2	11.2	14.0	58.8
1985	11.1	10.0	13.1	58.6
1986	10.5	9.2	12.9	58.5
1987	9.7	7.3	13.6	64.1
1988	9.3	7.3	12.5	65.2
1989	8.3	6.3	11.5	65.5
1990	7.5	5.5	10.7	66.5

Netherlands

Table 2.12(iv) Production and Prices

	Manufacturing Output (1985=100) (1985=100)	Hours worked in manufacturing	Hourly earnings (manufacturing)	Consumer Price Index
1973	80	43.0	44.4	50.5
1974	84	41.9	52.5	55.3
1975	78	41.2	60.0	61.0
1976	84	41.3	65.0	66.3
1977	85	41.2	71.4	70.6
1978	88	41.1	75.3	73.5
1979	91	41.1	78.7	76.6
1980	91	41.0	83.1	81.5
1981	91	40.8	87.8	87.0
1982	90	40.6	94.1	92.1
1983	90	40.5	96.1	94.6
1984	95	40.3	97.5	97.8
1985	100	40.3	100.0	100.0
1986	102	40.1	102.0	100.1
1987	103	39.9	103.0	99.4
1988	108	39.8	104.0	100.1
1989	113	39.8	106.0	101.2
1990	117	39.9	109.0	103.7
1991	119	–	113.0	107.7

13. Norway

Table 2.13(i) National Accounts Statistics, at 1985 prices; Million Kroner

	Gov't Cons'n	Private Cons'n	Invest-ment	Exports	Imports	GDP
1973	52900	161690	93021	137720	138320	305770
1974	55027	167920	97766	138660	144850	321650
1975	58559	176530	109420	142940	154920	335060
1976	62878	187260	120490	159030	174000	357880
1977	65979	200240	124880	164810	179980	370690
1978	69507	196980	110880	178630	155610	387520
1979	71973	203310	105370	183240	154530	407150
1980	75878	208080	103800	187080	159560	424280
1981	80539	210450	122400	189650	161930	428000
1982	83692	214170	108920	189380	167850	429430
1983	87583	217410	115260	203720	167820	449330
1984	89726	223310	127880	220450	183770	475140
1985	92653	245440	110040	235560	194600	500200
1986	94720	259180	136380	239230	213940	521110
1987	98961	257010	135740	247530	199730	538670
1988	99091	251180	138270	259520	194410	544570
1989	101560	242492	130331	282698	196786	531936
1990	103592	249411	95603	305454	201335	541349
1991	106003	248721	96571	324590	203948	551421

Norway

Table 2.13(ii) Employment (1000s)

	Male Civilian	Female Civilian	Total Civilian	Wage & Salaried	Manufac-turing
1973	1041	605	1646	1367	389
1974	1048	603	1651	1391	392
1975	1057	637	1694	1542	411
1976	1082	697	1779	1515	415
1977	1100	715	1815	1557	409
1978	1106	740	1846	1585	395
1979	1100	762	1862	1609	384
1980	1100	775	1875	1607	383
1981	1108	796	1904	1642	377
1982	1105	805	1910	1649	365
1983	1092	818	1910	1658	338
1984	1100	839	1939	1681	345
1985	1119	865	1984	1742	348
1986	1139	914	2053	1793	358
1987	1152	938	2090	1847	352
1988	1139	940	2079	1832	337
1989	1102	912	2014	1777	318
1990	1078	914	1992	1766	310

Norway

Table 2.13(iii) Unemployment and Participation

	Unemployment			Participation Rate
	Total Rate %	Male Rate %	Female Rate %	%
1973	1.6	1.0	2.4	68.7
1974	1.5	1.0	2.3	68.6
1975	2.3	1.9	2.9	70.7
1976	1.8	1.5	2.2	73.2
1977	1.5	1.0	2.2	74.1
1978	1.8	1.4	2.4	75.1
1979	1.9	1.6	2.4	75.6
1980	1.7	1.3	2.3	75.3
1981	2.1	1.6	2.7	76.1
1982	2.7	2.4	3.0	76.3
1983	3.5	3.3	3.8	76.5
1984	3.2	3.2	3.2	76.7
1985	2.6	2.2	3.1	77.5
1986	2.0	1.6	2.6	79.3
1987	2.1	1.8	2.5	80.3
1988	3.2	3.1	3.4	80.1
1989	4.9	5.1	4.7	78.7
1990	5.2	5.6	4.8	78.0

Norway

Table 2.13(iv) Production and Prices

	Manufacturing Output (1985=100) (1985=100)	Hours worked in manufacturing	Hourly earnings (manufacturing)	Consumer Price Index
1973	92	41.4	28.9	35.5
1974	97	40.6	34.0	38.8
1975	94	40.3	40.9	43.4
1976	94	39.3	47.8	47.3
1977	93	38.2	53.1	51.6
1978	92	38.0	57.3	55.8
1979	94	37.9	59.0	58.5
1980	94	38.3	64.8	64.9
1981	93	37.9	71.6	73.8
1982	93	37.7	79.7	82.1
1983	92	37.7	85.8	89.0
1984	95	37.7	92.9	94.6
1985	100	38.2	100.0	100.0
1986	102	38.4	110.3	107.2
1987	103	37.2	128.2	116.5
1988	102	37.7	135.5	124.3
1989	101	37.7	143.0	130.0
1990	101	37.0	151.0	135.0
1991	99	36.8	159.0	140.0

14. Portugal

Table 2.14(i) National Accounts Statistics, at 1985 prices; Million Escudos

	Gov't Cons'n	Private Cons'n	Invest-ment	Exports	Imports	GDP
1973	271920	2050200	907600	870100	1379200	2717700
1974	319000	2249900	844470	733420	1444900	2748700
1975	340120	2230000	749020	619080	1080500	2629200
1976	363930	2308000	755160	619080	1117200	2810600
1977	406870	2321900	845790	655600	1251300	2968100
1978	420340	2274400	898360	715210	1253500	3051700
1979	447590	2274400	886280	950980	1411200	3223800
1980	482970	2359400	961930	972060	1508800	3371700
1981	508220	2427800	1014900	928870	1544000	3426300
1982	526590	2485000	1037800	972240	1603700	3499500
1983	545990	2449300	963760	1104500	1505200	3493400
1984	546460	2377200	796200	1233000	1438300	3427700
1985	546900	2393200	767960	1315200	1458600	3523900
1986	586080	2527100	851440	1404100	1704900	3669900
1987	614560	2663100	979750	1525000	2045100	3862600
1988	647300	2838300	1126300	1680200	2374000	4014100
1989	665043	2932064	1189778	1903408	2591016	4221008
1990	674708	3088033	1260398	2084081	2852436	4405591
1991	694900	3248200	1291200	2107800	2993300	4500100

Portugal

Table 2.14(ii) Employment (1000s)

	Male Civilian	Female Civilian	Total Civilian	Wage & Salaried	Manufacturing
1973	–	–	3303	2532	818
1974	2227	1467	3694	2417	919
1975	2279	1445	3724	2451	931
1976	2332	1457	3789	2456	958
1977	2330	1454	3784	2410	918
1978	2338	1434	3772	2447	959
1979	2358	1496	3854	2496	982
1980	2438	1502	3940	2663	1026
1981	2371	1547	3918	2652	1009
1982	2380	1548	3928	2733	1016
1983	2492	1636	4128	2838	1027
1984	2446	1629	4075	2752	977
1985	2408	1649	4057	2746	969
1986	2423	1641	4064	2791	995
1987	2446	1725	4171	2830	1040
1988	2485	1795	4280	2954	1074
1989	2536	1841	4377	3058	1108
1990	2568	1906	4474	3144	1122

Portugal

Table 2.14(iii) Unemployment and Participation

	Unemployment			Participation Rate
	Total Rate %	Male Rate %	Female Rate %	%
1974	1.8	1.4	2.4	69.6
1975	4.6	4.1	5.2	69.9
1976	6.4	6.0	7.1	71.3
1977	7.5	5.9	10.0	71.4
1978	8.1	5.5	12.1	71.3
1979	8.2	4.9	12.9	71.9
1980	7.8	4.1	13.3	70.5
1981	7.6	4.2	12.3	69.4
1982	7.5	4.1	12.1	68.9
1983	7.9	4.8	12.2	71.9
1984	8.6	6.0	12.1	71.1
1985	8.7	6.4	11.7	70.5
1986	8.6	6.6	11.4	70.3
1987	7.1	5.4	9.4	70.7
1988	5.8	4.1	8.0	71.1
1989	5.0	3.3	7.2	71.8
1990	4.6	3.1	6.6	73.1

Portugal

Table 2.14(iv) Production and Prices

	Manufacturing Output (1985=100) (1985=100)	Hours worked in manufacturing	Hourly earnings (manufacturing)	Consumer Price Index
1973	61.7	44.7	7.2	8.4
1974	63.2	42.8	11.3	10.9
1975	60.0	41.8	16.3	13.1
1976	62.8	40.1	20.4	15.6
1977	70.1	39.8	23.9	19.9
1978	75.1	39.3	27.7	24.4
1979	79.9	40.7	33.6	30.2
1980	85.4	39.0	40.5	35.2
1981	88.8	38.8	49.1	42.3
1982	95.0	38.8	58.6	51.7
1983	97.4	38.6	68.4	64.9
1984	99.4	38.6	81.7	83.6
1985	100.0	38.8	100.0	100.0
1986	106.4	38.7	119.3	112.0
1987	109.5	38.9	137.0	122.0
1988	115.7	39.1	131.0	134.0
1989	120.0	–	148.0	151.0
1990	127.0	–	173.0	171.0
1991	125.0	–	200.0	190.0

15. Spain

Table 2.15(i) National Accounts Statistics, at 1985 prices; Billion Pesetas

	Gov't Cons'n	Private Cons'n	Invest-ment	Exports	Imports	GDP
1973	2236	15109	6080	3272	4499	22552
1974	2444	15873	6459	3240	4858	23750
1975	2571	16159	6167	3225	4817	23878
1976	2749	17055	6118	3387	5287	24659
1977	2857	17313	6060	3796	4994	25399
1978	3012	17476	5895	4201	4943	25767
1979	3138	17696	5637	4438	5505	25731
1980	3269	17797	5674	4539	5688	26050
1981	3330	17691	5489	4920	5447	25985
1982	3492	17723	5517	5155	5661	26301
1983	3629	17784	5377	5678	5626	26776
1984	3733	17715	5065	6344	5568	27258
1985	3907	18138	5275	6518	5914	27889
1986	4130	18792	5802	6602	6889	28803
1987	4489	19817	6650	6990	8295	30400
1988	4715	20713	7581	7432	9553	31905
1989	5384	22032	8813	7490	10835	33877
1990	5612	22857	9421	7730	11681	35100
1991	5900	23512	9574	8382	12774	35391

Spain

Table 2.15(ii) Employment (1000s)

	Male Civilian	Female Civilian	Total Civilian	Wage & Salaried	Manufac-turing
1973	9251	3600	12851	8638	3286
1974	9254	3670	12924	8767	3337
1975	9196	3496	12692	8864	3393
1976	8733	3582	12315	8545	3183
1977	8717	3536	12253	8564	3187
1978	8566	3476	12042	8417	3128
1979	8403	3442	11845	8254	3046
1980	8175	3320	11495	7986	2944
1981	7963	3193	11156	7729	2806
1982	7852	3191	11043	7676	2642
1983	7765	3223	10988	7599	2578
1984	7531	3143	10674	7276	2512
1985	7462	3105	10567	7267	2419
1986	7599	3216	10815	7608	2465
1987	7906	3477	11383	7946	2594
1988	8109	3671	11780	8320	2644
1989	8394	3866	12260	8843	2738
1990	8519	4059	12578	9234	2809

Spain

Table 2.15(iii) Unemployment and Participation

	Unemployment			Participation Rate
	Total Rate %	Male Rate %	Female Rate %	%
1973	2.7	2.8	2.6	62.7
1974	3.2	3.2	3.4	62.8
1975	4.7	4.9	4.2	62.0
1976	4.9	4.9	5.1	60.1
1977	5.3	5.2	5.6	59.1
1978	7.1	6.7	8.0	58.3
1979	8.8	8.4	9.8	57.7
1980	11.6	11.1	12.8	57.1
1981	14.4	13.8	16.1	56.8
1982	16.3	15.3	18.7	56.7
1983	17.8	16.6	20.6	56.6
1984	20.7	19.6	23.2	56.2
1985	22.0	20.6	25.1	55.9
1986	21.6	19.8	25.3	56.2
1987	20.6	17.3	27.2	57.7
1988	19.5	15.3	27.4	58.4
1989	16.9	12.6	25.2	58.6
1990	15.9	11.7	23.9	58.8

Spain

Table 2.15(iv) Production and Prices

	Manufacturing Output (1985=100) (1985=100)	Hours worked in manufacturing	Hourly earnings (manufacturing)	Consumer Price Index
1973	88.4	42.4	11.1	17.7
1974	96.8	42.0	14.0	20.5
1975	87.4	41.0	18.6	24.0
1976	91.5	39.9	24.1	28.2
1977	96.5	39.4	27.5	35.1
1978	98.4	38.8	35.1	42.0
1979	98.5	38.3	42.9	48.6
1980	98.9	38.5	50.5	56.2
1981	97.0	37.8	61.3	64.3
1982	95.2	38.0	70.7	73.6
1983	97.7	37.4	81.0	82.6
1984	98.3	36.5	91.1	91.9
1985	100.0	36.3	100.0	100.0
1986	103.7	36.7	111.0	108.8
1987	109.5	35.4	119.0	114.5
1988	113.0	35.8	127.0	120.0
1989	118.0	36.8	128.0	128.2
1990	118.0	36.7	137.0	136.8
1991	116.0	36.6	145.0	144.9

16. Sweden

Table 2.16(i) National Accounts Statistics, at 1985 prices; Million Kronor

	Gov't Cons'n	Private Cons'n	Invest-ment	Exports	Imports	GDP
1973	170120	388460	154400	206470	218950	695470
1974	175360	401580	149720	217430	240730	717710
1975	183560	412820	154350	197240	232380	736030
1976	190040	429970	157220	205760	253310	743820
1977	195690	425510	152590	208760	243800	731950
1978	202150	422500	142150	225040	230450	744770
1979	211720	432700	148500	238850	257240	773370
1980	219840	433840	150610	237490	258390	791000
1981	225280	432280	141860	242510	243580	791260
1982	227310	436730	141600	256910	252980	800050
1983	228900	427310	143930	282770	255060	814540
1984	234140	435260	152940	301840	269890	846980
1985	239160	447930	163780	306600	291190	865790
1986	242860	471060	164840	316380	304910	885470
1987	246140	492580	177400	328830	326770	911430
1988	248720	504730	188780	339830	345570	932740
1989	251225	511983	209783	348770	366534	952881
1990	258386	510507	208701	353921	370516	959952
1991	258988	515608	191344	346251	348824	942402

Sweden

Table 2.16(ii) Employment (1000s)

	Male Civilian	Female Civilian	Total Civilian	Wage & Salaried	Manufacturing
1973	2295	1584	3879	3521	1066
1974	2315	1647	3962	3609	1120
1975	2342	1720	4062	3715	1138
1976	2338	1750	4088	3752	1100
1977	2314	1785	4099	3770	1060
1978	2297	1818	4115	3783	1023
1979	2315	1865	4180	3843	1026
1980	2327	1905	4232	3895	1026
1981	2286	1938	4224	3890	984
1982	2273	1947	4220	3877	946
1983	2258	1966	4224	3891	941
1984	2261	1994	4255	3931	953
1985	2276	2023	4299	3986	968
1986	2238	2031	4269	3989	976
1987	2256	2081	4337	3940	960
1988	2287	2112	4399	4005	966
1989	2326	2140	4466	4059	978
1990	2346	2162	4508	4105	952

Sweden

Table 2.16(iii) Unemployment and Participation

	Unemployment			Participation Rate
	Total Rate %	Male Rate %	Female Rate %	%
1973	2.5	2.2	2.8	75.5
1974	2.0	1.7	2.4	76.9
1975	1.6	1.3	2.1	78.5
1976	1.6	1.3	2.0	78.9
1977	1.8	1.5	2.2	79.2
1978	2.2	2.1	2.4	79.6
1979	2.1	1.9	2.3	80.5
1980	2.0	1.7	2.3	81.0
1981	2.5	2.3	2.6	81.0
1982	3.1	2.9	3.4	81.2
1983	3.5	3.4	3.5	81.3
1984	3.1	3.0	3.3	81.4
1985	2.8	2.8	2.9	82.0
1986	2.7	2.7	2.7	81.3
1987	1.9	1.9	1.9	81.7
1988	1.6	1.6	1.6	82.3
1989	1.3	1.3	1.4	82.9
1990	1.5	1.5	1.5	83.2

Sweden

Table 2.16(iv) Production and Prices

	Manufacturing Output (1985=100) (1985=100)	Hours worked in manufacturing	Hourly earnings (manufacturing)	Consumer Price Index
1973	92	32.3	32.3	32.7
1974	95	31.6	35.9	36.0
1975	94	38.4	41.2	39.5
1976	94	38.2	48.5	43.5
1977	88	37.9	51.8	48.5
1978	87	37.7	56.3	53.4
1979	92	37.6	60.6	57.2
1980	92	37.6	66.0	65.0
1981	90	37.4	73.0	72.9
1982	89	37.6	79.3	79.2
1983	94	37.7	85.0	86.2
1984	98	38.1	93.0	93.1
1985	100	38.3	100.0	100.0
1986	101	38.3	107.4	104.3
1987	107	38.4	114.4	108.7
1988	109	38.5	123.5	115.0
1989	109	38.5	136.0	122.3
1990	106	38.5	149.0	135.1
1991	97	38.4	155.0	147.8

17. Switzerland

Table 2.17(i) National Accounts Statistics, at 1985 prices; Million Swiss Francs

	Gov't Cons'n	Private Cons'n	Invest-ment	Exports	Imports	GDP
1973	24690	125490	51372	59613	59244	208400
1974	25109	124880	49187	60227	58666	211430
1975	25272	121230	42508	56271	49660	196030
1976	25971	122530	38041	61507	56143	193280
1977	26076	126240	38657	67483	61337	197980
1978	26600	129040	41016	69991	68039	198790
1979	26880	130680	43107	71717	72701	203750
1980	27136	134120	47383	75353	77935	213120
1981	27800	134730	48519	78855	76950	216220
1982	28044	134730	47227	76507	74935	213780
1983	29104	136880	49239	77239	78255	215220
1984	29453	138980	51294	82163	83793	218990
1985	30420	141020	54200	89015	88065	227950
1986	31608	144950	58823	89369	94306	234370
1987	32409	147770	63307	90934	99461	239100
1988	33189	151330	67765	95858	104790	246810
1989	34883	154556	71060	100920	110314	255687
1990	36519	156893	72888	103969	113524	261564
1991	37530	159205	71101	103291	111581	261283

Switzerland

Table 2.17(ii) Employment (1000s)

	Male Civilian	Female Civilian	Total Civilian	Wage & Salaried	Manufacturing
1973	2152	1125	3277	2526	1153
1974	2143	1130	3273	2513	1145
1975	2035	1082	3117	2379	1053
1976	1969	1055	3024	2301	990
1977	1967	1069	3036	2305	984
1978	1978	1089	3067	2319	990
1979	1991	1109	3100	2336	987
1980	2026	1144	3170	2379	1005
1981	2041	1170	3211	2409	1010
1982	2021	1169	3190	2520	977
1983	1991	1158	3149	2488	942
1984	1982	1160	3142	2482	933
1985	2122	1245	3367	2505	1198
1986	2142	1256	3398	2543	865
1987	2160	1280	3440	–	864
1988	2176	1305	3481	–	864
1989	2191	1328	3519	–	873
1990	2208	1355	3563	–	881

Switzerland

Table 2.17(iii) Unemployment and Participation

	Unemployment			Participation Rate
	Total Rate %	Male Rate %	Female Rate %	%
1973	0.1	0.1	0.1	77.7
1974	0.1	0.1	0.1	77.4
1975	0.4	0.5	0.3	74.8
1976	0.7	0.7	0.6	73.6
1977	0.4	0.4	0.4	73.6
1978	0.3	0.3	0.4	73.7
1979	0.3	0.3	0.4	73.8
1980	0.2	0.1	0.3	74.4
1981	0.2	0.2	0.3	75.1
1982	0.4	0.4	0.5	74.7
1983	0.9	0.9	0.9	74.5
1984	1.0	0.8	1.4	74.7
1985	0.9	0.7	1.1	75.5
1986	0.8	0.6	0.9	75.8
1987	0.7	0.6	0.9	76.1
1988	0.6	0.5	0.8	76.3
1989	0.5	0.4	0.6	76.5
1990	0.5	0.5	0.6	76.7

Switzerland

Table 2.17(iv) Production and Prices

	Manufacturing Output (1985=100) (1985=100)	Hours worked in manufacturing	Hourly earnings (manufacturing)	Consumer Price Index
1973	99	44.9	57.4	61.7
1974	100	44.8	64.7	67.8
1975	86	44.5	69.5	72.3
1976	88	44.4	70.6	73.5
1977	91	44.6	71.8	74.5
1978	92	44.4	74.3	75.3
1979	93	44.2	75.9	78.0
1980	98	43.8	79.8	81.1
1981	97	43.8	83.8	86.4
1982	92	43.7	89.0	91.2
1983	92	43.2	95.1	94.0
1984	95	43.1	97.1	96.7
1985	100	43.0	100.0	100.0
1986	104	42.6	103.1	100.8
1987	105	42.4	105.8	102.2
1988	112	41.9	109.0	104.1
1989	117	41.8	113.2	107.4
1990	120	41.6	119.8	113.2
1991	121	41.5	–	119.8

18. UK

Table 2.18(i) National Accounts Statistics, at 1985 prices; Million Pounds

	Gov't Cons'n	Private Cons'n	Invest-ment	Exports	Imports	GDP
1973	62459	179000	55818	70994	74447	301220
1974	63627	176370	54465	75904	75050	296050
1975	67176	175600	53383	73459	69847	293730
1976	68006	176340	54277	79890	73175	301830
1977	66880	175650	53307	85094	74224	308850
1978	68423	185580	54914	86473	77021	320050
1979	69899	193690	56450	89755	84463	329050
1980	71012	193790	53416	89621	81531	321690
1981	71213	193940	48298	88878	79213	317560
1982	71791	195740	50915	89713	83121	323030
1983	73221	204090	53476	91489	88360	334500
1984	73930	207770	58058	97517	97074	341600
1985	73908	215510	60343	103180	99399	354160
1986	75486	227550	61478	107460	106040	366460
1987	76378	239780	66894	113010	114180	383800
1988	76710	256260	75680	113820	128180	399660
1989	77216	271144	82997	117972	137933	414053
1990	79721	272927	80464	123775	139364	416206
1991	81963	267186	72462	124155	135103	406842

UK

Table 2.18(ii) Employment (1000s)

	Male Civilian	Female Civilian	Total Civilian	Wage & Salaried	Manufac-turing
1973	15432	9283	24715	22679	7979
1974	15291	9512	24803	22804	8030
1975	15150	9569	24719	22723	7654
1976	14963	9546	24509	22557	7411
1977	14891	9647	24538	22631	7461
1978	14932	9764	24696	22790	7427
1979	15073	10007	25080	23173	7395
1980	14941	10063	25004	22991	7081
1981	14256	9755	24011	21892	6365
1982	13905	9679	23584	21414	6005
1983	13653	9651	23304	21067	5664
1984	13885	10024	23909	21238	5579
1985	13978	10232	24210	21423	5561
1986	13860	10380	24240	21387	5430
1987	14026	10729	24755	21584	5395
1988	14439	11159	25598	22258	5469
1989	14771	11605	26376	22661	5478
1990	14822	11756	26578	22856	5416

UK

Table 2.18(iii) Unemployment and Participation

	Unemployment			Participation Rate
	Total Rate %	Male Rate %	Female Rate %	%
1973	2.2	2.9	0.9	73.0
1974	2.1	2.8	0.8	73.1
1975	3.2	4.3	1.4	73.6
1976	4.8	6.1	2.8	73.9
1977	5.2	6.3	3.4	73.9
1978	5.1	6.1	3.5	73.9
1979	4.6	5.5	3.3	74.3
1980	5.6	6.6	4.2	74.4
1981	9.0	10.9	6.0	73.7
1982	10.4	12.6	7.0	73.1
1983	11.2	13.3	8.0	72.4
1984	11.1	13.0	8.3	73.5
1985	11.7	13.3	8.7	74.6
1986	11.6	13.5	8.9	74.5
1987	10.4	12.4	7.6	74.9
1988	8.3	10.0	6.0	75.5
1989	6.1	7.7	4.0	75.9
1990	5.5	7.1	3.3	75.8

Table 2.18(iv) Production and Prices

	Manufacturing Output (1985=100) (1985=100)	Hours worked in manufacturing	Hourly earnings (manufacturing)	Consumer Price Index
1973	111.2	42.5	22.6	25.1
1974	108.2	41.9	27.5	29.1
1975	102.2	41.0	34.8	36.1
1976	103.2	41.7	39.3	42.1
1977	105.3	41.7	42.5	48.7
1978	106.3	41.7	48.9	52.8
1979	106.3	41.4	57.0	59.8
1980	97.1	40.6	66.8	70.6
1981	91.3	40.7	73.7	79.0
1982	91.3	41.0	80.3	85.8
1983	94.2	41.5	86.5	89.8
1984	98.1	41.7	92.6	94.3
1985	100.0	41.8	100.0	100.0
1986	101.0	41.6	108.0	103.4
1987	106.8	42.2	116.0	107.7
1988	114.0	42.4	126.0	113.0
1989	119.0	42.2	137.0	121.8
1990	118.0	41.6	150.0	133.4
1991	112.0	–	162.0	141.2

3. Industry: Performance and Policies

Malcolm Sawyer

This chapter has two basic concerns. The first is to describe some of the major trends in industrial performance in European countries in terms of measures such as productivity growth, employment generation and profitability. The second concern is to outline some of the major elements in the industrial policies pursued in European countries.

The term industry is often used to signify manufacturing, public utilities, mining and construction, and many policies labelled industrial policies are largely concerned with those industries. In contrast, agricultural price support policies would not usually be seen as industrial policies. However, in this chapter industry is interpreted broadly to cover all types of production whether of goods or services. Indeed, the distribution of economic activity between different industrial sectors is a particular theme of the first part of this chapter.

1. Performance

There are many relevant dimensions to industrial performance, but space and data availability constrain the range of indicators which we can report. Some significant indicators (e.g. research and development) are covered in other chapters.

The sectoral composition of employment and output can be seen as relevant for a variety of reasons. Sectors vary in terms of significant characteristics such as capital intensity, scope for technological changes, productivity growth etc. Some have seen the manufacturing sector as the "engine of growth" with a relatively high productivity growth and as a generator of technical change. Some sectors (most evidently manufacturing) are much more important in terms of tradable commodities than other sectors (notably personal services). This would suggest that prices and profits in some sectors are much more constrained by international competition than those in other sectors. Further, since many economies are constrained by their balance of trade position, the size and growth of their traded goods sector is relevant to their overall growth and prosperity. This suggests that the changing sectoral composition of employment and output is of some significance for the overall operation of an economy.

2. Employment

The shifts in the sectoral composition of employment can be seen from Table 3.1 which provides statistics on the composition of employment at the beginning (1974), the middle (1981) and the end (1991) of the period on which this book focuses. The overall pattern is not unexpected as it indicates a general decline in the employment shares of the primary industries (ISIC 1 and 2) and of the secondary industries (ISIC 3, 4 and 5) and the consequent expansion of the employment share of the tertiary sector (ISIC 6, 7, 8 and 9). For the countries taken together, the share of employment in the primary sector falls by 4.5 percentage points over the period 1974 to 1991, which is equivalent to nearly 40 per cent of the initial employment share. Employment in manufacturing falls by over 7 percentage points which is equivalent to a quarter of its initial share (and the other parts of the secondary sector lost just over one percentage point). In contrast, the tertiary sector adds 12.5 percentage points, thereby adding over a quarter to its employment share.

The decline in the employment share of the primary sector is universal amongst the countries considered here, even for those such as the UK with a very small employment share initially. The declining in the employment share accounted for by manufacturing is almost universal (Portugal being the exception with a rise 0.1 per cent). However, there are very marked differences between countries with particularly large declines of over ten percentage points in Belgium, Luxembourg, Switzerland and the United Kingdom.

During the period from 1974 to 1991, there was an increase in employment for the countries included in Table 3.1 of over 9 million (with around 5 million of the increase in the decade after 1981). These statistics refer to the numbers in work, whether part-time or full-time, and it is likely that much of the increase was in part-time employment. However, there were declines in the absolute numbers employed in the primary sector (of the order of over 6 million) and in the secondary sector of nearly 8.5 million, whilst the tertiary sector expanded by 24 million jobs. These changes in the absolute levels of employment are almost universal. All countries experience falls in employment in the primary sector and increases in the tertiary sector. The picture for the secondary sector is more mixed with increases in employment in that sector in Austria, Greece, Iceland, Netherlands and Portugal

The overall growth in employment has been accompanied by a significant shift between male and female employment. Indeed for the nine countries for which data are available for the full period (i.e. those reported in Table 3.2 apart from Greece for which data are not available for 1974), male employment fell by nearly 1.9 million and female employment rose by over 7.2 million. The decline in male employment was particularly pronounced in Belgium, Spain (where total employment also declined) and the United

Kingdom. There was little change in male employment in Sweden and increases, generally relatively small, in the remaining countries. Female employment rose in all the countries for which data are available.

The general rise in female employment is illustrated in Table 3.2 which gives female employment as a proportion of the total for all activities and for each sector. The proportion rose in all countries. The table also reveals the very substantial differences in female involvement in employment between sectors. In one sense part of the increase in the female proportion can be attributed to the relative decline of the primary and secondary sectors which tend to employ a lower proportion of females than the tertiary sectors.

3. Output

Table 3.3 provides the shares in production (as measured by gross domestic product) for the nine sectors used previously. The coverage of countries is rather limited here, due to the lack of sectoral GDP break-downs for many countries. The final column of Table 3.3 provides the trend growth rate of output in each sector over the period of 1974 to 1991 (or 1990).

The output shares of each sector are, not surprisingly, not dissimilar to the corresponding employment shares. In most countries, the agricultural sector has continued to grow, though generally at a slower rate than overall output. Although employment has generally declined in manufacturing, there is a positive rate of growth of output in that sector, albeit often at a slower rate than the overall rate of growth. However, there are some substantial inter-country differences with manufacturing output growing at least as fast as total output in a number of countries. The growth of output in the tertiary sectors tends to outpace the overall rate of growth. Although the rate of output growth has been calculated as the trend rate over the relevant period, it may be sensitive to the precise period used. A relatively high rate of growth may be calculated if the beginning of the period was a time of recession and the end of the period one of boom, and comparisons between countries and between sectors may be made rather misleading by different countries/sectors being at different stages of the business cycle. In general, both 1974 and 1991 were times when economies were in the downswing of the business cycle.

The trend labour productivity record for each of the nine sectors for the countries under review and for which data are available is given in Table 3.4.[1] With the previous mentioned caveats in mind over the influence of the choice of start and end dates, it can first be remarked that there are very substantial variations between sectors in each country. The sector which stands out as recording rapid productivity growth is agriculture. In some countries, this growth of productivity may arise from the release of surplus labour from the agricultural sector, though in others it is likely to arise from

[1]No data was available for Italy.

large increases in non-labour inputs. Although the manufacturing sector is often identified with relatively rapid productivity growth, this is not fully confirmed in Table 3.4. Whilst for five countries productivity growth in manufacturing is faster than the overall average, the reverse holds in three others. It is well known that the growth of productivity generally slowed after 1973, as can be seen from the final line of Table 3.4.

The relative levels of labour productivity across the whole of the private sector can be gauged from Table 3.5. Productivity is measured as GDP (in the business sector) divided by the number of employees in that sector: thus no account is taken of variations in the average hours worked. The exchange rates used in these calculations are purchasing power parity rates which seek to take account of differences in price levels. The productivity figures are expressed relative to the OECD average.

4. Profitability

Table 3.6 provides information on movements in the profit share for a range of countries. Data limitations are particularly severe in this area (and even more so for the rate of profit which we will discuss shortly). It will be seen that the figures refer to a range of sectors, reducing comparability between countries: it is also the case that we have to sometimes use gross (of depreciation) profit shares and at other times net. Furthermore, there are substantial revisions to profit figures and in one case two overlapping series are provided. Thus relatively little should be read into the differences between countries and we focus here on the movements over time of the profit share figures.

The profit share is likely to be affected by the state of the business cycle, and this will be particularly so for the net profit share (since depreciation will be a larger deduction out of profits in times of recession than in times of boom). The degree of market power possessed by firms and the pressure on real wages from workers are important influences on the profit share.

The general pattern which emerges is for the profit share to decline in the mid-1970s and then to recover thereafter.

The measurement of the rate of profit faces difficulties in both measuring profits and the capital stock. Profit figures are influenced by accounting conventions on the treatment of costs and revenues. The valuation of the capital stock presents numerous difficulties. Capital equipment will have been acquired at different times and at different prices and have been subject to depreciation and scrapping. The recorded depreciation is likely to reflect tax laws and accounting conventions rather than economic depreciation. The figures on the rate of profit are rather limited and restricted to six countries. It is difficult to discern any common pattern on the movements in the rate of profit.

5. Foreign direct investment

The growth of international trade (even relative to income levels) and the general increasing globalisation of economic activity has been a notable feature of the post-war period. The focus of these paragraphs is on the growth of transnational corporations (TNCs). In a recent report, the United Nations argued that "[t]ransnational corporations have become central organizers of economic activities in an increasingly integrated world economy" (United Nations, 1992, p.1). "During the 1980s, world FDI [foreign direct investment] flows grew faster than world-wide domestic investment and domestic output and, to the extent that greenfield investments followed the same trend, output by foreign firms has contributed an increasing share to that output. Foreign direct investment, domestic output and domestic investment grew at similar rates during the 1970s. During the early 1980s, the rate of growth of FDI began to diverge from that of domestic output and domestic investment and since 1985 the rate of growth of FDI has accelerated, outpacing that of the other two. During the period 1985–1990, global FDI grew almost four times as fast as domestic output and more than twice as fast as domestic investment" (United Nations, 1992, p.51).

The data in Table 3.7 have their own limitations, and specifically relate to direct investment. Two important omissions are any influence of contractual arrangements (for example where a local firm contracts to produce the product of a multi-national enterprise) and of turnkey agreements. Hence, the figures in Table 3.7 tend to underestimate the influence of transnational corporations. The pattern of a rising influence of transnational corporations is evident over the two decades to which the data relate.

Table 3.8 provides data on both inward and outward flows of direct investment for many European economies. It is readily apparent that there are substantial cross-flows, which is particularly noticeable for the UK. The general increase in foreign direct investment can also be seen, even allowing for these figures being in current prices.

6. Policies

Industrial performance is influenced by most, if not all, public policies. Within the sphere of economic policies those which are regarded as macro-economic are likely to influence performance: for example, deflationary policies depress investment and thereby the long-term productive capacity. However, we limit our discussion to those policies which are generally labelled industrial: in other words those which are clearly geared towards changing, directly or indirectly, the performance of particular industrial sectors. One set of policies which are usually seen to involve changing industrial structure in order to influence performance comes under the heading of competition policy (including policies on monopolies, mergers and restrictive practices). Another set of policies in a similar vein – but one which concerns ownership rather than structure – is that of nationalisation and privatisation. These two sets of policies are considered below. We start with other policies which are generally labelled industrial policies and which generally involve some form of subsidy to specific activities (e.g. research and development expenditure) or to specific sectors.

The OECD groups policies under eight headings of industrial support policies, which are:[2]

- sectoral programmes aimed at improving a country''s competitiveness in a given sector;
- schemes of exceptional recourse for bailing-out companies in difficulty;
- programmes dedicated to the strengthening of research and development expenditures and capabilities;
- improving general investment behaviour by diminishing general capital costs;
- supporting regional development in areas with adjustment difficulties and remoteness handicaps;
- support for small and medium-sized enterprises;
- aid for employment and training activities inside companies;
- support for exports and international investment.

An indication of the magnitude (in terms of costs) of industrial support policies is given in Table 3.9, though the coverage of countries here is limited to members of the European Union. The figures indicate a wide variation in the degree of financial support which is given. Table 3.10 provides an indication of the scale of industrial policies in terms of the number of programmes operated and the net cost to government. The programmes surveyed are financed in a number of ways including subsidised loans, equity capital infusions, and tax concessions. The majority of the programmes are funded and administered by central government but some are undertaken by regional and local authorities and some by partially off-budget institutions.

7. Competition policy

Competition policy is generally based on the tenet that competition amongst independent firms has beneficial effects on industrial performance but that competition has to some degree to be promoted and protected. Some actions by firms (notably agreements between firms over price and market shares, mergers and acquisitions) are seen as possibly harmful for competition. Further, competition may be promoted through limitations on the activities of firms with large market shares (often labelled monopolists), and on rather infrequent occasions through the reduction of market shares. The broad

[2]From OECD (1992) p. 16.

heading of competition policy can encompass policies on monopolies (or more accurately on firms with relatively large market shares), mergers and restrictive practices. It can also cover policies on anti-competitive behaviour. All the countries covered by this chapter have some form of competition policy. Regular surveys of the evolution of competition policy are published by the Commission of the European Community (in the Annual Report on Competition) and by the OECD (in the annual publication on Competition Policy in OECD Countries).

Most of the countries with which this chapter is concerned are members of the European Union, and increasingly their competition and other industrial policies are determined by that membership. Articles 85 and 86 of the Treaty of Rome cover, so far as inter-state trade is affected, cartels and restrictive trade practices, and monopoly respectively. The implementation of this competition policy lies with the European Commission to take cases before the European Court of Justice. Article 85 covers agreements, decisions and concerted practices which may affect trade between member states and which have the effect of restricting or distorting competition, with agreements and practices which fix prices, limit production, share out markets between firms or which charge discriminatory prices being specifically mentioned. Firms do not have to register restrictive trade agreements though there are incentives to do so. Article 86 deals with the abuse of market dominance rather than with monopoly per se and with those abuses which affect trade between member states. In the Article, the abuses specifically mentioned include:

(a) directly or indirectly imposing unfair purchase, prices or trading conditions;
(b) limiting production, markets or technical developments;
(c) applying dissimilar conditions to equivalent transactions.

Since late 1990, the European Commission has had jurisdiction over "concentrations with a Community dimension", which are those where "the aggregate worldwide turnover of all parties concerned is more than ECU 5 billions; and the aggregate Community-wide turnover of each of at least two of the parties concerned is more than ECU 250 million; unless each of the parties achieves more than two thirds of its aggregate Community-wide turnover within one and the same member state" (Office of Fair Trading, Mergers, HMSO, 1991). National authorities may not apply their own competition laws to these mergers except in very limited circumstances.

8. Privatisation and Nationalisation: Recent Developments[3]

We conclude this chapter with a survey of recent developments in nationalisation and privatisation policies on a country by country basis. The

[3] The information in this section has been gathered from OECD reports on individual countries and from annual reports of the OECD on industrial policy.

level of public ownership in 1989 is indicated in Table 3.11. It is readily apparent that in most of these European countries, there was extensive public ownership in the public utilities (post office, telecommunications, gas, electricity), in many forms of public transport (airlines, railways) and in coal, steel and shipbuilding. Table 3.12 provides a different measure of the scale of public enterprises, and it can be readily seen that there is considerable variation between countries.

Much of the public ownership indicated in Table 3.11 was in place by 1950, and the succeeding thirty years had seen relatively little political debate over ownership. There had been some further nationalisation, often in response to the financial distress of privately owned firms. In the past decade or so, the question of ownership has again come to the fore in a number of European countries, notably Britain. Privatisation[4] has featured on a number of political agendas. But in some countries there has been no privatisation though there has often been an extensive restructuring of the nationalised companies.

In this section we describe some of the major policy initiatives in the area of privatisation and nationalisation.

(a) Austria

Nationalised industries within the group ÖIAG (state holding company) play a significant role in the Austrian economy, and in 1987 accounted for 17 per cent of Austrian exports (21 per cent in 1980) and 3.5 per cent of dependent employment. The share of the nationalised sector exceeds 90 per cent of employees in the iron and steel and oil industries, and is more than one third in mining, non-ferrous metals and foundries. In other important branches of industry, such as mechanical engineering, iron and metal products, and in the chemical and electrical industries, the employment share exceeds 10 per cent. One third of all Austrian foreign investment in 1991 was made by the state-holding company. By the late 1980s, the nationalised industries were recording increasingly large losses and a focus of the new government's supply side politics was the revitalisation of these industries through the restructuring of various companies, reductions in the federal share in several state-owned firms, and the privatisation of certain companies. Before 1988, some partial privatisations yielded 5 billion Austrian schillings, and included 15 per cent of Austrian's mineral oil company OMV and 18 per cent of the share of ÖIAG in Siemens Austria. During the 1980s, the ÖIAG companies were regrouped according to their activities into seven functional holdings: mining, machinery and plant engineering, electronics, steel, non-ferrous metals, oil, and chemicals.

[4] Privatisation is used here in the sense of the sale of publicly-owned assets to private owners. It does not include policies such as deregulation, liberalisation, or contracting-out of services from the public sector which are sometimes included under the term.

Asset sales by the Federal government in the period 1987–1989 yielded nearly 20 billion schillings. The sales included the complete sale of the National Mint (sold to the Austrian National Bank) and of some small electricity companies, and the partial sale of the Austrian Electricity Company and Austrian Airlines.

(b) Belgium

There have been moves to give greater autonomy to public enterprises and to depoliticise their activities. A three- to five-year management contract and explicitly defined social mission is negotiated with each corporation. But there have not been any significant privatisations.

(c) Denmark

The major state-owned enterprises are found in postal, telecommunications, transport and energy sectors, and their combined turnover is equivalent to 5 to 6 per cent of GDP. Five major publicly-owned enterprises changed their status from non-incorporated into state-owned limited-liability companies. An insurance company (Statsanstalten for Livsforsikring) was sold to a private company. There has also been the sale of part of the equity in Copenhagen Airport, Postal Giro and TeleDenmark.

(d) Finland

State ownership is relatively high in Finland, with state owned companies in the manufacturing sector producing 21 per cent value added, employing 14 per cent of the labour force, and accounting for 30 per cent of manufacturing investment in 1989. State ownership is particularly prevalent in the steel industry and in engineering/chemical industries. State-owned companies generally operate in an autonomous manner. There has been some partial privatisation but with the government retaining a controlling majority stake. Public enterprises are dominant in energy production and communications. To date, the state has not divested itself of majority holdings in any leading industrial firm.

(e) France

There was a substantial increase in the size of public ownership in 1982, and this has been followed by some privatisations since 1986.

The public sector expanded with waves of nationalisation in 1982, then slimmed down following the privatisation policies of 1986–87. Since then the policy has been to effect no divestments nor extensions of the public sector. Certain measures have been taken, however, which have shifted the frontier dividing the public from the private sector. The authorities decreed that minority interests in public corporations could be sold, provided that the change includes an industrial, financial or commercial co-operation agreement with the purchaser. In 1988 government holdings covered 2,000 enterprises employing 1.4 million workers which is equivalent to 11 per cent of those in independent employment. The share of the corporate public sector in the economy is estimated at around 12 per cent.

Legislation was passed to allow private firms, national or foreign, to take minority stakes in nationalised companies. In 1992 the government reduced its stake in the oil company Elf, and ceded 12.4 per cent of the capital of the oil concern Total. In October the government announced the sale of equity in the chemicals firm Rhône Poulenc. The incoming conservative government indicated in April 1993 its intention to begin a major programme of privatisations.

(f) Germany

There are two very distinct aspects to privatisation in Germany. The first part relates to a rather modest set of privatisations which have occurred in the former West Germany, and those are discussed first in this section. The second part covers the much more extensive privatisation programme of assets in the former East Germany, following reunification in 1990.

The government which has been in power since 1982 adopted the general policy that public ownership in industry should be limited to cases where a clear public interest existed and where no other means were available to achieve the desired objectives. Any privatisation should be undertaken in a gradual manner. By 1987, a number of government holdings and assets had been sold, notably its holdings in the giant conglomerate, VEBA. The sale of government shares in Volkswagen was delayed because of the 1987 stock market crisis, but in 1988 all federal government shares had been sold. In May 1988, the holding company VIAG (covering electricity, chemicals and aluminium) was fully privatised. Revenues from the 1984–88 privatisations amounted to DM 7 billion, and the number of firms with federal participation was reduced from 808 to 239. In terms of turnover, the reduction was from DM 110 billion to DM 14 billion, and for employment from 436,000 to 70,000 in 1988. In the summer of 1992, the government adopted a schedule for further reductions of state ownership. The new privatisations are set to be mainly in the service sector, particularly transport and telecommunications. Major projects include Telekom, Lufthansa, Gesellschaft für Nebenbetriebe (holding company), German Federal Railways and ports. In 1992, the Berliner Industriebank was sold and the Deutsche Airbus GmbH was fully privatised through the sale by the government of its remaining 20 per cent share.

The process of selling public sector assets is not a new one, and has been under way for 25 years. However, Länder and local authorities are important shareholders in regional banks, residential construction firms, public utilities (electricity & gas), traffic (airports), and transportation companies, and there has been little privatisation at that level of government.

The task of privatising the state-owned industries of the former GDR was given to the Treuhand. These companies were some 13,000 in number and employed nearly five million workers. Within two and half years, some 12,000 have been sold. The privatised firms are contractually obliged to create jobs for 1.4m people. The Treuhand finished most of its privatisation business by 1994. Some activities continue however, such as the monitoring of the employment and investment promises by privatised firms. Other continuing tasks include the further sales of real estate.

(g) Greece

The state-owned companies account for a relatively large proportion of the firms in many branches of the economy, especially banking and manufacturing, and there was extensive nationalisation, notably of the largest firms in sectors such as textiles and cement in the 1980s . Employment in the state controlled business sectors is estimated at over 15 per cent of total dependent employment.

The government announced a substantial privatisation programme in 1990, but the programme only really got underway in 1992. By the end of 1991 the proceeds from the sale of public enterprises had reached only 2.5 billion drachmas. In March 1992 the cement company AGET Heracles, the largest European cement exporter, was partly privatised; and in April the sale of the loss making Eleusis shipyard was agreed. In 1992, of the 124 firms available for liquidation or privatisation, 67 were liquidated, 26 were sold, and 31 remained to be privatised or liquidated in the near future. Revenues from the sales totalled 145.3 billion drachmas. The sale of two public refineries, planned for 1993, will complete the sale of the large public sector firms.

(h) Ireland

The state-owned enterprise sector is large in Ireland, accounting for approximately 10 per cent of GNP and for 7 per cent of total civilian employment. The energy, steel, transport and communications sectors are ones in which the government has a large ownership stake, and it also owns two banks and has a minority stake in an insurance company. The changes introduced in the 1980s were undertaken largely for financial reasons, when it was decided that the government could no longer support publicly owned companies in difficulty (steel, peat development, Irish shipping, fertiliser, sugar). There has been only limited privatisations. Those sales of state shareholdings that have taken place have been motivated primarily by the commercial interests of the company in question. The B&I Shipping Co. was privatised in 1992. In the case of sales relating to the Irish Sugar Co. and Irish Life, the companies had indicated a preference for such a course; there is, however, no long term policy of privatisation.

(i) Italy

Public ownership is relatively extensive in Italy.[5] All the major public utilities are state-owned at both the national and (with a few exceptions) local level. There are state holdings in a range of sectors, including mining, manufacturing and financial services. In 1987, public enterprises accounted for an estimated 19 per cent of value added, 24 per cent of gross fixed capital formation and 16 per cent of employment of the non-agricultural sector. The state owns 12 of the 20 largest Italian firms (ranked by net sales) and 18 of the largest 50. Public banks account for around 60 per cent of banking sector employment and 80 per cent of total deposits. The state is active in both acquiring and selling enterprises. In the decade ending in 1992, 231 enterprises were acquired and 195 sold, and the companies acquired tended to be somewhat larger than those sold. There are two major public holding companies, IRI and ENI, which along with an agency under liquidation, EFIM, control firms employing over half a million people in 1991. Another holding company, GEPI, has operated to aid small- and medium-sized firms in financial difficulties. There have been some significant sales including Alfa Romeo by IRI in 1986, of SIR fine chemicals by Comitatio SIR in 1987, of Lanerossi textiles by ENI in 1987 and Sopal food processing company by EFIM in 1990.

In the past few years, a number of measures have been taken by the government to lay the ground work for privatisations. These have included a law to provide the legal basis for turning a range of public enterprises into joint-stock corporations, and another to streamline the procedures for privatisation. In July 1992, the government liquidated EFIM which involved the sale of most of its subsidiaries. The financial plans for IRI and ENI include the receipt of 12 trillion lira from privatisation proceeds for IRI in the years 1993 and 1994, and over 9 trillion lira for ENI over the three year period 1993–95.

(j) Netherlands

There has been some limited sales of government owned stakes in companies. The government has sold 36.6 per cent of shares in Volvo Car BV, the Dutch car manufacturer, to Mitsubishi. The state remains the owner of 33.3 per cent of the stock. The government also sold its stake of 46 per cent in Vredestein NV, a tyre producer, to a private investment company. In 1993, there was the sale of the government's 32 per cent stake in the Fokker aeronautics firm to the German DASA, the aircraft subsidiary of Mercedes-Benz.

[5] The recent OECD Economic Survey of Italy (OECD, 1994) on which this section particularly draws contains much information on the size of the Italian public sector.

(k) Norway

The state has extensive ownership interests in companies within the mining, petroleum, and manufacturing sectors, but has no overall privatisation programme for state-owned companies. One recent extensive of public ownership has been the establishment in 1989 of a 49 per cent state-owned venture company, Norsk Vekst A/S.

(l) Portugal

A range of enterprises were nationalised in the mid-1970s, following the overthrow of the Salazar dictatorship, and the 1976 Constitution ruled out privatisation. This was amended in June 1989 to provide the basis for 100 per cent privatisation of public enterprises. Previously a law had been passed to permit the change of public enterprises into corporations in which the state retained 51 per cent of total equity. In the first phase of partial privatisation, the government selected some profitable enterprises: a brewery company, a medium sized bank and two insurance companies. However in the first year of the 1990s, there were a series of partial and total privatisation of publicly owned companies in competition with others. These included (figures in parenthesis refer to proceeds of sales):

- Companh de Seguros Tranquilidade [sale of 51 per cent of equity]: fourth largest Portuguese insurance company (18.9 billion escudos)
- Centralcer: brewery (34.6 billion escudos)
- Banco Português do Atlantico [33 per cent and later 17.6 per cent of equity sold] (49.8 billion escudos and 50.6 billion escudos respectively)
- Socieda Financeira Portuguesa (16.5 billion escudos)
- Diario de Noticias: newspaper (9 billion escudos)
- BESCL (40 per cent and later further 60 per cent): bank (60.9 billion escudos and 89 billion escudos respectively)
- Mundicel Confiança: insurance company (33.4 billion escudos)
- Petrogal [25 per cent of equity]: largest oil company (40.8 billion escudos)
- Imperio: insurance company (25.5 billion escudos)
- Credito Predial Português (40.8 billion escudos)

The cumulative revenues from the sale of state holdings in 25 enterprises by the end of 1992 had amounted to the equivalent of 6 per cent of GDP. Receipts of a similar magnitude are expected in the three years to the end of 1995.

(m) Spain

The thrust of policy in the context of publicly owned enterprises has been at improving the balance-sheet position of public firms, notably the INI group (a public holding company with majority participation in many industrial and service companies). By 1988, INI had moved into over-all profit after recording substantial losses during most of the 1980s. Many companies of the INI group were sold, and this included some which had been reporting large losses. Whilst there was on balance a reduction in the number of firms in the INI group, there were (partial) purchases of some companies offsetting the sales. There has also been some sales (e.g. ENDESA, electricity supply) of a proportion of the equity in the companies owned by INI.

(n) Sweden

The incoming conservative government announced a privatisation programme for state-owned companies in 1991. The privatisation programme includes those firms that used to be owned by the state-owned management company Fortia, such as Procordia, LKAB (mines), ASSI (pulp and paper), SSAB (steel), Vattenfall (electricity), Domanverjet (forests), and Nordbanken. In 1993, the government has begun to implement the authorisation given by parliament to sell the state's share in 35 wholly or partly owned companies. Certificates have been issued and sold for purchase of the government holding (42 per cent) in the SSAB steel concern and the state has sold or reduced its holdings in a number of smaller firms. In addition, as a first step towards privatisation, a number of public utilities (e.g. electricity) and the forestry service have been converted to limited liability companies.

(o) United Kingdom

The most extensive privatisation programme has been that carried out by the British government The list of the main companies privatised is given in Table 3.13, along with the estimates of the proceeds from those sales.

Table 3.1 Employment by major industrial sectors in selected years for European economies

Sector	Austria			Belgium			Denmark			Finland		
	1974	1981	1991	1974	1981	1991	1974	1981	1991	1974	1981	1991
1	13.01	10.27	7.39	3.91	3.19	2.66	9.70	7.40	5.76	16.31	13.05	8.51
2	1.13	0.49	0.35	1.04	0.79	0.19	0.13	0.09	0.08	–	–	0.17
3	30.35	29.73	27.00	31.68	24.70	20.92	23.75	21.49	20.69	27.63	27.21	20.23
4	1.07	1.13	1.16	0.90	0.93	0.81	0.60	0.68	0.77	–	–	1.20
5	8.67	8.68	8.58	7.98	7.32	6.59	8.03	7.32	6.46	8.43	7.92	7.69
6	16.11	17.58	19.09	16.10	16.36	17.28	14.69	14.34	14.73	15.77	13.95	15.42
7	6.70	6.41	6.47	7.22	7.77	7.03	7.13	6.94	7.04	6.94	7.87	7.52
8	4.54	5.15	6.70	5.49	6.39	9.12	6.15	6.68	9.24	4.46	5.56	8.55
9	18.41	20.56	23.27	25.67	32.55	35.40	29.82	35.06	35.23	20.46	24.43	30.71

Sector	France			Germany			Greece			Iceland		
	1974	1981	1991	1974	1981	1991	1974	1981	1990	1974	1981	1991
1	10.66	8.45	5.77	7.01	5.16	3.35	–	30.68	23.91	16.06	12.43	10.64
2	0.87	0.63	0.37	–	0.94	0.64	–	0.54	0.62	0.00	0.00	0.00
3	28.31	25.10	20.92	46.66	33.33	31.18	–	19.29	19.37	22.06	23.78	17.02
4	0.80	0.91	0.93	–	0.82	0.90	–	0.85	1.00	0.54	0.90	1.42
5	9.35	8.54	7.26	46.32	7.87	6.49	–	8.30	6.78	11.88	9.82	7.80
6	15.60	16.20	17.35	–	15.56	16.65	–	14.99	17.59	14.03	13.15	18.44
7	6.01	6.22	6.45	–	5.94	5.91	–	7.76	6.70	8.24	7.03	6.38
8	6.19	7.64	10.22	–	6.08	8.50	–	3.31	4.95	4.71	5.86	7.80
9	22.20	26.32	30.73	–	24.31	26.38	–	14.28	19.10	22.48	27.03	30.50

Sector	Ireland			Italy			Luxembourg			Netherlands			Norway		
	1974	1981	1991	1974	1981	1991	1974	1981	1990	1975	1981	1991	1974	1981	1991
1	22.78	17.47	13.89	17.54	13.42	8.51	7.23	5.13	3.28	5.67	4.87	4.58	10.61	8.36	5.90
2	0.93	0.98	0.63	–	1.09	1.06	–	–	–	0.17	0.16	0.22	0.61	0.68	1.07
3	21.66	21.12	19.93	39.26	26.19	22.10	32.92	26.27	19.80	25.00	20.94	18.27	23.76	19.83	14.95
4	1.31	1.25	1.26	–	–	–	0.90	0.89	0.74	0.93	0.89	0.69	1.09	1.10	1.07
5	8.68	9.00	7.21	43.20	10.28	9.14	11.04	10.06	9.95	8.79	7.93	6.53	8.91	7.68	6.61
6	44.63	16.67	18.03	–	19.23	21.77	47.90	57.66	66.23	17.22	17.53	17.79	16.67	17.36	18.00
7	–	6.24	5.86	–	5.65	5.37	–	–	–	6.12	6.33	6.30	9.88	9.15	8.24
8	–	6.15	8.57	–	2.75	4.68	–	–	–	7.50	9.23	10.66	4.36	5.21	7.78

Sector	Portugal			Spain			Switzerland			United Kingdom		
	1974	1981	1991	1974	1981	1991	1974	1981	1991	1974	1981	1991
1	34.93	25.96	17.35	23.17	18.79	10.67	7.45	6.57	5.53	2.82	2.66	2.27
2	0.49	0.54	0.30	0.77	0.84	0.60	0.21	0.00	0.08	1.44	1.46	0.72
3	24.91	25.75	24.99	25.82	25.03	21.65	34.96	37.86	24.41	32.38	26.51	20.13
4	0.49	0.56	1.17	0.62	0.77	0.69	0.67	–	0.62	1.40	1.46	1.09
5	7.91	10.16	8.27	9.90	8.65	10.11	8.43	55.57	9.33	6.82	6.36	6.72
6	11.14	12.40	15.81	16.94	18.03	20.61	18.17	–	20.51	18.04	19.60	20.09
7	4.15	3.85	4.69	5.32	5.80	5.77	5.68	–	6.15	6.33	6.36	5.97
8	1.68	2.27	4.73	2.92	3.57	5.82	7.11	–	10.76	6.52	7.92	12.34
9	14.31	18.50	22.69	14.55	18.54	24.06	17.31	–	22.61	24.24	27.68	30.67

List of sectors:
1. Agriculture, hunting, forestry and fishing
2. Mining and Quarrying
3. Manufacturing
4. Electricity, gas and water
5. Construction
6. Wholesale and retail trade, restaurants and hotels
7. Transport, storage and communication
8. Financing, insurance, real estate and business services
9. Community, social and personal services

Table 3.2 Female employment as percentage of total by industrial sector for selected years

		Belgium			Finland			Germany			Greece			Italy		
All		1974	1981	1991	1974	1981	1991	1974	1981	1991	1974	1981	1990	1974	1981	1991
Activities		34.1	36.3	40.9	46.4	47.3	48.7	38.1	39.4	41.4	-	31.4	35.2	29.2	32.4	35.3
	1	22.4	22.1	27.6	43.7	39.7	36.4	52.7	49.2	43.3	-	42.6	44.7	33.6	35.4	36.1
	2	2.6	3.6	0	-	-	-	-	4.8	8.7	-	-	8.7	-	9.1	8.4
	3	26.7	23.3	23.6	35.6	36.6	34.2	26.1	29.9	28.7	-	28.6	30.3	22.2	32.2	32.4
	4	6.1	9.1	10.0	-	-	21.4	-	13.8	16.8	-	13.3	13.5	-	-	-
	5	3.8	4.6	6.2	9.1	10.3	9.5	-	9.3	11.9	-	0.7	1.6	-	3.7	5.4
	6	47.7	48.5	49.8	64.0	59.8	56.6	-	55.6	55.5	-	31.9	38.1	-	33.6	36.9
	7	12.1	13.5	17.8	27.9	27.2	26.9	-	21.6	25.4	-	9.9	11.2	-	11.6	14.5
	8	35.8	37.6	42.3	64.7	65.4	55.3	47.9	48.7	48.2	-	33.3	40.2	33-.7	29.3	40.6
	9	54.0	55.3	59.5	67.4	70.8	72.3	-	53.9	57.6	-	41.9	47.0	-	50.3	50.4

		Norway			Spain			Sweden			Switzerland			U.K.		
All		1974	1981	1991	1974	1981	1991	1974	1981	1991	1974	1981	1991	1974	1981	1991
Activities		36.5	41.8	46.3	28.4	28.8	32.8	41.6	45.9	48.1	34.5	36.6	38.3	38.4	40.6	44.7
	1	29.1	29.6	25.9	25.5	26.6	26.9	24.2	26.2	26.6	24.2	29.6	29.4	20.7	18.8	23.5
	2	-	7.7	19.1	-	2.1	3.9	10.0	7.1	9.1	-	-	-	4.2	5.4	10.6
	3	21.9	23.3	25.5	20.2	21.7	22.9	25.9	26.8	27.6	23.3	21.9	28.1	30.5	28.5	29.3
	4	-	14.3	23.8	-	5.8	8.1	12.9	18.9	16.2	-	-	13.6	18.4	20.3	23.5
	5	2.7	6.2	7.7	-	2.3	3.6	6.5	8.3	8.3	-	-	6.9	5.5	7.9	9.4
	6	52.7	52.7	55.8	-	40.5	43.0	52.0	52.3	50.6	-	-	54.0	51.8	52.2	53.9
	7	17.8	24.1	29.0	-	9.4	11.8	25.1	27.0	31.8	-	-	24.7	16.5	18.6	21.8
	8	44.4	45.5	43.8	37.8	21.8	31.2	46.7	46.8	44.8	46.5	47.4	40.2	43.8	45.5	47.1
	9	64.3	64.6	-	-	51.0	54.7	68.1	70.6	71.9	-	-	53.8	57.6	60.3	62.8

Table 3.3 Shares in GDP by sector and trend growth rates

	Output Shares					Output Shares					Output Shares			
Austria	1974	1981	1991	Trend	Belgium	1974	1981	1990	Trend	Denmark	1974	1981	1990	Trend
1	4.3	4.1	3.5	1.6	1	2.9	2.6	2.2	1.9	1	7.5	7.8	8.1	3.3
2	0.8	0.7	0.4	−1.0	2	0.6	0.4	0.1	−9.7	2	0.1	0.4	4.9	31.1
3	34.4	33.1	33.0	2.5	3	27.5	27.1	28.9	2.5	3	24.7	25.4	22.1	1.8
4	3.4	3.7	3.5	2.7	4	2.1	3.3	3.1	3.5	4	1.3	1.7	1.8	4.4
5	11.8	9.6	8.1	−0.1	5	9.5	7.9	7.1	−1.2	5	11.8	8.2	5.9	−0.9
6	20.0	19.8	20.6	2.6	6	23.5	21.3	17.7	−0.1	6	18.0	18.0	18.1	2.1
7	6.1	6.8	7.7	3.9	7	10.5	9.4	10.0	1.9	7	10.2	10.7	12.0	2.8
8	15.1	17.9	18.7	3.8	8	5.1	6.9	7.8	5.0	8	20.0	21.1	21.7	2.7
9	4.2	4.3	4.7	3.3	9	18.2	21.1	23.2	3.4	9	6.4	6.6	5.4	1.0
Total				2.5	Total				2.2	Total				2.3
Finland	1974	1981	1990	Trend	France	1974	1981	1990	Trend	Germany	1974	1981	1990	Trend
1	11.4	10.4	8.0	0.7	1	7.7	5.3	5.2	2.3	1	2.4	2.1	2.1	1.7
2	0.4	0.5	0.5	4.1	2	1.0	1.0	0.7	−1.1	2	1.8	1.2	0.7	−2.9
3	29.0	30.3	27.2	3.3	3	38.7	30.1	26.1	1.0	3	41.7	38.8	35.4	1.2
4	2.8	3.4	3.7	4.3	4	4.7	2.5	3.1	5.9	4	3.0	3.3	3.2	2.6
5	11.7	9.8	8.5	1.3	5	11.4	8.6	7.7	0.4	5	8.1	7.1	5.7	−0.1
6	15.1	13.8	13.6	2.9	6	26.0	17.9	17.6	1.8	6	12.5	12.2	11.8	1.5
7	9.1	10.0	10.7	3.5	7	13.8	7.5	9.3	4.6	7	5.9	6.7	7.3	3.6
8	15.2	17.3	22.9	5.4	8	34.0	21.6	23.0	3.6	8	12.6	14.6	15.6	3.7
9	4.7	4.5	4.9	3.4	9	10.8	5.5	7.3	5.2	9	11.9	14.0	18.2	4.9
Total				3.3	Total				2.3	Total				2.2

Greece	1974	1981	1990	Trend	Italy	1974	1981	1991	Trend	Norway	1974	1981	1990	Trend
1	18.2	15.7	12.5	0.7	1	5.7	5.4	4.6	1.2	1	5.2	4.4	3.5	2.5
2	1.6	1.6	2.1	4.3	2	0.0	0.0	0.0	–	2	2.9	19.2	36.5	16.0
3	22.8	23.4	20.4	1.5	3	28.2	28.0	28.2	2.7	3	31.2	19.3	13.4	0.0
4	2.6	3.7	5.2	6.1	4	6.0	6.2	5.2	1.6	4	4.9	4.7	3.9	4.2
5	7.5	6.4	6.1	-0.2	5	10.1	8.3	6.9	0.3	5	7.7	7.3	4.9	2.4
6	14.0	13.3	14.1	2.4	6	21.7	22.2	21.8	2.6	6	15.1	14.4	10.3	2.5
7	9.3	10.9	12.1	4.3	7	5.5	6.0	6.8	3.8	7	11.4	10.5	10.9	4.2
8	12.3	13.2	15.2	3.8	8	22.8	23.9	26.5		8	15.2	14.4	11.9	3.7
9	11.7	11.9	12.5	2.4	9					9	6.5	5.8	4.7	2.8
Total				2.3	Total				2.6	Total				3.7

a: Trend refers to trend growth rate of relevant sector as a share of GDP
Source: OECD *National Accounts*, various issues

Table 3.4 Productivity growth by sector (trend annual rate 1974–1991)

Sector	Austria	Belgium	Denmark	Finland	France	Germany[a]	Greece[b]	Norway
1	3.91	4.08	5.66	3.96	5.68	5.43	2.00	4.40
2	4.06	-2.50	31.58	-	3.73	-1.05	3.72	9.66
3	2.21	5.13	2.12	4.29	2.78	1.52	-0.18	1.79
4	1.37	4.14	1.84	-	4.56	0.33	2.97	2.18
5	-0.53	1.43	-0.25	1.07	2.08	1.31	3.94	1.50
6	0.71	-0.50	1.28	2.09	1.03	0.72	0.17	0.40
7	3.21	2.27	1.57	2.96	3.97	2.97	4.63	4.32
8	0.64	1.90	-1.65	0.98	0.61	-0.71	-1.46	-0.79
9	0.77	1.42	-0.90	0.31	3.08	3.96	-1.39	-1.18
Total	1.58	2.34	1.39	2.60	2.23	1.85	1.41	2.58

a: Figures for Germany are for 1980–1990
b: Figures for Greece are for 1981–1990

Table 3.5 Relative productivity in the business sector based on purchasing power parity (OECD average = 100 in each year)

	1975	1980	1985	1990
Austria	89	93	91	96
Belgium	102	110	113	117
Denmark	85	83	87	88
Finland	76	80	82	92
France	104	106	108	115
Germany	98	101	102	105
Greece	50	53	46	44
Iceland	71	83	76	81
Ireland	60	65	73	83
Italy	99	105	100	102
Netherlands	111	115	122	118
Norway	78	71	71	79
Portugal	40	46	42	43
Spain	82	89	94	96
Sweden	93	89	90	86
Switzerland	115	111	103	106
UK	88	85	90	90

Source: *OECD, Industrial Policy in OECD Countries*, Paris: OECD Table 17

Table 3.6 Profit shares in selected countries

	Belgium ITC Gross	Denmark M Gross	Denmark ITC Gross	France M Net	France M Gross	France ITC Net	France ITC Gross	Germany M Net	Germany M Gross	Germany ITC Net	Germany ITC Gross	Iceland M Gross	Iceland ITC Gross	Ireland ITC Gross	Ireland ITC Net
1974	36.0	21.4	31.5	-	-	27.8	36.7	21.9	30.3	22.5	31.8	-	-	31.2	-
1975	32.3	25.5	33.2	-	-	20.4	31.2	19.6	29.1	20.7	31.0	-	-	27.9	-
1976	31.5	25.4	31.8	-	-	20.9	31.6	21.3	30.2	22.8	32.5	25.5	35.4	27.7	-
1977	31.9	25.0	31.6	-	-	20.2	31.3	20.4	29.2	22.3	32.0	22.1	31.7	32.2	-
1978	32.4	24.7	31.3	-	-	19.7	31.0	19.8	28.8	22.5	32.0	15.2	28.2	34.2	-
1979	33.5	23.5	30.1	20.9	29.4	21.5	32.8	19.2	27.9	22.4	31.9	18.5	27.2	31.7	-
1980	32.0	25.9	31.2	15.0	24.9	18.0	30.4	14.1	23.8	18.6	29.0	17.9	29.5	29.2	21.1
1981	30.2	25.6	31.5	12.9	23.5	15.9	29.3	13.0	23.3	17.5	28.4	19.9	31.0	29.9	23.1
1982	33.3	27.8	34.1	12.9	23.7	15.3	29.1	12.7	23.3	17.2	28.5	15.9	32.2	35.6	27.7
1983	34.2	30.4	34.7	15.1	25.6	17.1	30.6	15.9	26.1	19.8	30.8	22.2	39.7	37.9	29.7
1984	34.7	31.7	35.6	15.3	25.9	18.3	31.7	16.2	26.3	20.3	31.1	28.5	44.0	41.8	32.7
1985	37.4	30.6	35.2	17.4	27.6	20.9	33.7	17.7	27.2	21.3	31.9	21.3	37.1	41.6	37.1
1986	35.9	29.2	34.4	22.3	31.7	24.0	36.2	20.1	28.9	22.5	32.6	29.6	41.1	43.8	36.7
1987	35.5	26.8	33.4	23.0	32.5	24.9	37.0	17.4	26.6	20.9	31.4	21.9	34.1	44.6	38.6
1988	38.1	29.6	35.1	27.5	36.2	27.5	39.0	18.1	27.2	21.3	31.6	21.3	34.3	46.3	39.6
1989	40.5	29.4	36.7	-	-	-	-	17.8	27.0	21.7	32.0	26.7	37.4	45.4	41.2
1990	40.0	30.7	38.8	-	-	-	-	17.8	26.8	21.5	31.6	29.2	39.9	-	40.4
1991	-	30.7	38.6	-	-	-	-	-	-	-	-	-	-	-	

	Italy ITC Gross	Netherlands ITC Net	Netherlands ITC Gross	Netherlands Non-financial Net	Netherlands Non-financial Gross	Netherlands Non-financial Gross	Norway ITC Net	Norway ITC Gross	Sweden M Gross	Sweden ITC Gross	UK ITC Net	UK ITC Gross	UK Non-financial Net	UK Non-financial Gross
1974		30.4	38.2	37.2	43.6	-	22.6	37.7	30.5	33.6	15.0	26.5	12.4	23.3
1975		26.4	35.8	35.1	42.2	-	19.3	35.0	26.7	30.7	11.5	23.9	9.5	21.1
1976	40.4	31.1	39.5	37.7	44.3	-	14.8	33.8	18.9	26.2	15.3	27.4	11.8	23.6
1977	40.7	30.6	39.1	37.0	43.8	-	10.1	32.0	14.5	23.7	20.7	32.1	18.0	28.9
1978	42.5	29.9	38.7	36.5	43.5	-	17.0	36.3	15.2	24.7	20.8	32.3	18.5	29.4
1979	43.1	29.7	38.7	35.8	43.0	-	28.8	43.7	21.3	29.0	22.2	31.4	16.8	28.1
1980	45.3	29.9	39.1	35.4	43.0	-	37.4	49.4	21.7	29.0	22.1	31.9	15.7	27.8
1981	44.4	32.7	42.0	37.6	45.2	-	38.4	50.8	19.3	27.5	24.0	33.9	16.2	28.9
1982	44.7	34.3	43.7	39.3	46.8	-	36.5	50.2	24.8	31.2	27.9	37.0	19.9	31.7
1983	44.7	36.2	45.5	40.9	48.2	-	40.3	52.9	29.0	33.8	31.3	39.8	22.8	34.0
1984	47.6	40.6	49.0	44.0	50.9	-	44.8	55.6	31.3	35.3	32.3	40.6	23.7	34.7
1985	48.0	42.0	50.1	44.7	51.4	-	44.2	54.8	30.0	34.1	33.3	41.2	25.4	35.9
1986	49.3	39.0	47.7	43.3	50.2	-	29.6	45.0	32.0	35.3	30.1	38.8	22.6	33.8
1987	48.9	33.7	43.7	41.0	48.4	39.7	25.8	42.9	30.7	34.4	32.1	40.3	24.5	35.0
1988	49.7	35.5	45.1	41.9	49.3	40.1	24.2	42.8	30.2	34.1	33.5	41.1	25.4	35.2
1989	49.1	36.2	46.0	43.0	50.4	41.5	34.6	50	30.1	34.5	32.5	40.3	23.9	34.0
1990	47.9	37.6	47.0	43.2	50.5	41.1	37.6	51.8	27.4	32.3	31.3	39.2	22.0	32.4
1991	46.9	-	-	-	-	40.8	37.8	52.8	23.1	30.0	-	-	20.5	31.3

Notes: M = Manufacturing, ITC = Industrial, transport and communications
Source: OECD, *National Accounts*, various issues.

Table 3.7 Statistics on Foreign Direct Investment

	FDI 1980–85	FDI 1986–90	FDI as Proportion of GDCF (Percent)				Ratio of stock of FDI to GDP
	annual average millions of dollars	annual average millions of dollars	1971–75	1976–80	1981–85	1986–89	1988
Austria	259	627.8	1.8	0.9	1.7	1.9	5.5
Belgium	1189	4792	7.1	5.8	7.6	14.9	-
Denmark	87	610.6	3.0	0.3	0.9	2.4	-
Finland	77	522.8	0.6	0.4	0.7	1.6	3.3
France	2343	7985.8	1.8	1.9	2.0	3.8	4.9
Germany	693	2450	2.1	0.8	0.6	1.2	5.6
Greece	500	763.6	1.0	5.4	6.0	7.8	-
Iceland	21	-5	4.4	1.3	3.0	-0.8	-
Ireland	198	64.4	3.8	6.7	4.0	1.0	-
Italy	968	3930.6	1.8	0.8	1.1	2.1	5.3
Netherlands	1648	5608.2	6.1	4.5	6.1	11.9	22.2
Norway	149	763.6	3.1	3.2	1.2	3.3	2.8
Portugal	178	1097.4	3.1	1.5	3.0	7.9	7.7
Spain	1724	7462.4	1.9	2.8	5.3	8.2	9.6
Sweden	283	1353.2	0.6	0.5	1.6	3.4	-
Switzerland	896	2519.8	-	-	3.9	4.1	-
UK	5163	20247	7.3	8.4	5.4	12.3	16.2

Notes: FDI = Foreign Direct Investment, GDCF = Gross Domestic Capital Formation
Source: United Nations (1992)

Table 3.8 Outward and inward direct investment flows (current US dollars in billions)

Country	Outward Flows		Inward Flows	
	1973–80	1981–91	1973–80	1981–91
Austria	0.5	5.4	1.2	3.6
Belgium	2.9	27.5	8.4	36.3
Denmark	0.7	8.1	1.0	5.0
Finland	0.5	13.2	0.3	2.6
France	13.0	106.3	15.7	54.5
Germany	22.3	107.8	10.9	20.6
Italy	3.0	34.7	4.6	27.5
Netherlands	18.0	64.5	1.6	1.3
Norway	0.9	10.8	2.6	4.3
Portugal	-	0.8	0.6	9.4
Spain	1.2	12.5	6.6	61.7
Sweden	4.2	52.8	0.7	14.0
Switzerland	-	36.4	-	14.4
UK	51.4	202.2	38.2	151.8

Notes: First figure for Portugal for inward direct investment refers to 1975–80; figures for Switzerland refer to 1983–91.

Source: OECD, *Industrial Policy in OECD Countries*, Paris: OECD Table 38

Table 3.9 State support in European Community countries

	Aid in Manufacturing as percent of value added	ECUs per employee
Belgium	4.4	1601
Denmark	2.0	770
France	3.7	1456
Germany	2.7	1135
Greece	15.5	3545
Ireland	6.1	2504
Italy	6.7	3136
Luxembourg	2.3	956
Netherlands	3.3	1458
Portugal	8.3	744
Spain	5.3	1528
United Kingdom	2.7	806

Source: Commission of the European Community: *Second Survey on State Aids in the European Community in the Manufacturing and Certain Other Sectors*, Brussels, 1990

Table 3.10 Number and relative costs of industrial policies

	1a	1b	2a	2b	3a	3b	4a	4b	5a	5b	6a	6b	7a	7b	8a	8b
Austria	2	0.6	4	51.0	15	11.0	9	4	23	19.0	4	4	3	3.0	9	6.0
Belgium	1	1.0	1	-	6	5.0	-	-	2	64.0	2	28	1	2.0	1	0.02
Denmark	1	38.0	-	-	9.	46.0	1	3	1	.9.0	2	0.8	-	-	2	11.0
Finland	3	5.0	3	1.0	5	11.0	8	52	11	3.0	1	0	1	7.0	3	21.0
France	8	14.0	2	0.4	8	17.0	8	4	3	0.15	6	2.0	9	16.0	5	46.0
Germany	10	18.0	*	*	11	12.0	20	39	9	9.0	16	6.0	1	0	2	16.0
Iceland	4	35.0	4	37.0	1	16.0	-	-	-	-	-	-	-	-	1	12.0
Ireland	-	-	1	n.a	2	11.0	8	53	2	12.0	-	-	5	23	3	1.0
Italy	7	10.0	3	0.1	4	1.0	14	80	8	n.a	6	2.0	5	0.9	3	6.0
Netherlands	5	13.0	2	0.1	6	56.0	3	20	6	9.0	3	2.0	-	-	7	2.0
Norway	7	26.0	6	12.0	3	11.0	10	18	8	15.0	3	4.0	1	2.0	3	13.0
Portugal	2	0.4	-	-	5	0.3	-	-	9	94.0	5	.04	6	5.0	3	0.1
Spain	10	64.0	-	-	7	9.0	4	-	4	19.0	8	1.0	2	5.0	4	2.0
Sweden	7	18.0	5	11.0	11	14.0	11	29	3	11.0	4	2.0	3	9.0	5	6.0
Switzerland	*	*	*	*	2	1.0	4	10	3	0.9	1	.4.0	3	4.0	3	72
U.K.	6	5.0	*	*	9	11.0	22	30	4	1.0	10	11.0	6	6.0	11	35
CEC	13	12	*	*	6	51	12	37	*	*	*	*	*	*	*	*

a: number of programes, b: percentage of net cost paid by government (1989) (the data on net cost are not available for all programmes)

1 = sectoral programmes; 2 = crisis programmes; 3 = research and development programmes; 4= regional development; 5= general investment aid; 6= support for small and medium-sized enterprises; 7= aid for employment and training activities inside companies; 8= support for exports and international investment

Figures for Belgium refer to 1988. In 1989 the only programmes with a net cost to central government were research and development programmes as Belgium evolved into a federally-structured country
CEC = Commission of the European Communities

Source; OECD, *Industrial Support Policies in OECD Countries, 1986–1989*, OECD: Paris

Table 3.11 Distribution of public enterprises by industry, 1989 (Percent of value added in each industry)

	Post Office	Telecom-munications	Electricity	Gas	Oil	Coal	Railways	Air transport	Road transport	Steel	Ship-building
Austria	100	100	100	100	100	100	100	100	100	100	–
Belgium	100	100	25	25	–	0	100	100	100	50	0
France	100	100	100	100	–	100	100	75	50	75	0
Germany	100	100	75	50	25	50	100	100	25	0	25
Italy	100	100	75	100	–	–	100	100	25	75	75
Netherlands	100	100	75	75	–	–	100	75	50	25	0
Spain	100	50	40	75	–	50	100	100	0	50	75
Sweden	100	100	50	100	–	–	100	50	25	75	75
Switzerland	100	100	100	100	–	–	100	25	0	0	–
UK	100	0	100	25	25	100	100	0	0	75	50

- indicates that there is no such industry in the country concerned

Source: OECD, *Industrial Policy in OECD Countries, 1992,* OECD, Paris Table 7

Table 3.12 Relative size of public enterprises

	1982	1985	1988
Belgium	12	11	10
France	23	24	18
Germany	14	13	12
Italy	20	20	20
Netherlands	9	9	10
Spain	12	12	10
United Kingdom	16	13	7

Note: The relative size is measured by the average share of value added, capital formation and employment of public enterprises in the respective aggregate values

Source: Public Enterprise European Center as reported in OECD, *Economic Survey*, Italy, Paris: OECD

Table 3.13 Privatisation in United Kingdom

(i) Proceeds from the sale of public assets (£ billions at 1989/90 prices)

1979/80	0.8	1980/81	0.4	1981/82	0.8	1982/83	0.7
1983/84	1.6	1984/85	2.7	1985/86	3.4	1986/87	5.4
1987/88	5.9	1988/89	7.5	1989/90	4.2	1991/92	4.9

Source: *Public Expenditure Analyses to 1993/94*, HMSO Cmnd. No. 1520

(ii) Main Asset Sales by British Government 1979–1993

Sale of shares:

Amersham International
Associated British Ports
British Aerospace
British Airports Authority
British Airways
British Gas
British Steel
British Telecom
Britoil
Cable and Wireless
Enterprise Oil
Jaguar Cars
Electricity companies and Regional electricity boards
Rolls-Royce
Regional Water Companies (12 in number)

Other Sales:

Royal Ordnance and Rover Cars to British Aerospace
Sealink sold to British Ferries
National Freight sold to consortium of managers, employees and company pensioners
National Bus Company (sold as 72 separate companies)
Girobank sold to Alliance and Leicester Building Society
British Shipbuilders (warship yards)
Sale of minority shareholdings in British Sugar, British Petroleum, ICL, Ferranti and British Technology Group
Sale of property etc. of Crown Agents Holdings, Forestry Commission, New Town Development Corporation

4. Labour Markets: Diversity in Restructuring

Peter Nolan and David Harvie

The labour markets of Europe are diverse in their structure and effects, yet they are commonly discussed in the aggregate and contrasted with the labour markets of, for example, the United States and Japan. Many commentators have argued that the central European economies are characterised by 'rigid' labour markets which have seriously impaired their economic performance. The return in the 1980s of mass unemployment, and what many judge to be a sharp deterioration in the relative competitiveness of many European businesses, are thus linked to a debilitating disorder known as 'Eurosclerosis'. It is said to be especially acute in the central European and Nordic countries, and is thought to be the product of unwarranted institutional rigidities in the hiring, deployment, remuneration and disposal of the services of labour. This chapter looks at the data on some of the critical outcomes of labour market processes and institutions in Europe and considers whether or not the Eurosclerosis thesis is firmly rooted.

The first section describes the changing structure of employment, by broad sector and gender, while the second examines trends in employment and unemployment and situates the European record in terms of that of the United States and Japan. The third section reviews the data on wages, labour costs and productivity and highlights some of the formidable statistical and conceptual problems involved in making comparisons between countries. The fourth section draws out some of the critical areas of contrasting experience and suggests that notions of labour market homogeneity in Europe are as unhelpful as they are misleading. The diverse patterns of labour market restructuring and their associated consequences are highlighted by a brief discussion of recent developments in Britain and Germany.

1. Employment structure

The advanced economies of Western Europe, in common with the United States and Japan, have experienced important changes in the sectoral composition of employment. The relative shares of agriculture and industry have declined, sometimes quite dramatically, while employment in services has expanded very rapidly. The changes are described in Tables 4.1, 4.2 and 4.3.

Table 4.1 reveals that in 1973 agriculture accounted for a very small proportion of total civilian employment in the more mature economies of the United Kingdom, Belgium, Germany and the Netherlands. But it remained an important source of paid employment in Greece (36.8 per cent), Spain (24.3 per cent), Ireland (24.1 per cent), and Italy (18.3 per cent), while in France it absorbed more than 10 per cent of the working population. By 1991, however, the share of agriculture in total employment had greatly diminished in each of the above countries, as illustrated by Spain (10.7 per cent) and Ireland (13.8 per cent).

The changing pattern of industrial employment is shown in Table 4.2. Industry in this context embraces the manufacturing, construction and extractive industries, and it should be noted that while all the countries included in the table have experienced a decline in industrial employment, the change in relative shares between extractive, construction and manufacturing is quite different, with some countries, notably Britain, experiencing a particularly sharp contraction in manufacturing employment.

The reduction in the relative shares of agricultural and industrial employment is mirrored by a dramatic increase in service sector employment. Many service sector jobs, particularly those in the private sector, are part-time. They are commonly filled by women, and characterised by low pay, irregular hours and inferior conditions (limited job security, for example). The growth of service sector employment is to be expected in mature economies, characterised by rapid advances in productivity in agriculture, manufacturing and extractive industries. But it is helpful to distinguish those economies in which service sector employment growth has coincided with industrial output growth, from those economies in which services have grown relatively at the expense of industrial output. This distinction lies at the heart of the debate about de-industrialisation, as discussed below, and is especially pertinent to the case of Britain where seven in every ten employees are engaged in services.

The growth of service sector employment has been accompanied by a very significant increase in female participation rates, as indicated in Table 4.4, which charts the changes in the proportion of female to male civilian employment. It shows that the female employment ratio has grown in all countries, although the Nordic countries stand out as having ratios close to unity. In Britain the ratio has increased by 25 per cent over the period, so that four in every ten employees are female. But there remain important variations in the ways that women are incorporated into paid employment. In Britain most women work part-time, often in jobs offering fewer than sixteen and sometimes eight hours work. Elsewhere, notably Germany, women generally work longer hours, and hence gain access to equivalent employment rights to their full-time male colleagues. These points are taken up in section four.

2. Employment and unemployment

Comparative statistics on the levels and rates of change of employment and unemployment are fraught with difficulties. How should unemployment be defined, and what constitutes paid employment? Should the figures include the self-employed, those engaged by the armed forces, or only those involved in a direct relationship with an employer? Britain provides a graphic illustration of the difficulties that can arise. Since 1979 it is estimated that the definition of unemployment has been altered by the government on no fewer than 19 occasions. Accordingly, if the definitions of 1979 were applied to contemporary statistics, it is estimated that the current unemployment figure would be increased by approximately 1 million or 3 per cent (Sawyer, 1993). The OECD data, which underpins the following discussion, benefits from the application of standardised definitions and measurement procedures, but should be approached with caution nonetheless.

Table 4.5 shows that employment levels increased significantly in the western European countries between 1971 and 1991, in some cases – for example, Portugal and the Netherlands – by as much as 25 per cent. Employment in Spain, which has remained constant at a little over 12.5 million employees, is the notable exception, although the pattern is uneven across countries. Sweden has the best record, starting the period with a 2.5 per cent unemployment rate and finishing at 2.7 per cent (see Table 4.6). In Britain, Italy and France unemployment in the 1980s has often been above 10 per cent. Some commentators, for example Burton (1987) and Minford (1990), allege that Sweden's apparently impressive record actually masks 'a form of hidden long-term unemployment' in the public sector, but in making such claims these writers present little supporting evidence and merely assume that the growth of state employment is sub-optimal with respect to the level that might obtain in a perfectly competitive economy with minimal state intervention.

For Europe as a whole, the upward trend in unemployment is described in Table 4.7. The coincidence of rising levels of employment and unemployment is indicative of rising participation rates and the generation of insufficient new job opportunities to fully absorb the available supply of labour power. It is this imbalance which has led some economists to complain that the 'spontaneous forces', which might have served to more rapidly promote European employment levels and balance demand with supply, have been inhibited by the combined effects of systems of voluntary and statutory employment regulation and social welfare programmes.

In comparison to the United States and Japan, Europe's unemployment record over the past decade has been poor, as proponents of the Eurosclerosis thesis have stressed. Advocates of this perspective usually draw a sharp contrast between Central Europe and the situation in Britain and the United States, where, it is said, such constraints have been progressively eroded by the liberalisation of markets under the Thatcher, Reagan and Bush administrations of the 1980s. The deregulation of labour markets and a tougher approach to unions, which characterised the labour market policies of these administrations are said to have promoted record levels of employment growth (particularly in services), the renewal of manufacturing and the restoration of competitive advantage (Minford, 1990). Yet such broad brush comparisons tend to be misleading in a number of critical respects.

A closer examination of the evidence for the United States suggests that the conventional wisdom is misleading on at least three counts. First, unregulated labour markets and weak unionism do not correlate with low unemployment. Union membership decline pre-dated the Reagan presidency, as did the retreat from social welfarism, yet throughout the 1970s unemployment in the United States actually exceeded the European average (see Table 4.7). More crucially, the employment gains after 1986 were secured primarily through the proliferation of low wage, low productivity, part-time service sector jobs in personal and recreation services (Appelbaum & Schettkat, 1991). Since such sectors have never been associated with a strong union presence, or significant state regulation, it is clearly implausible to attribute recent employment gains to unions' declining fortunes and the retreat of the state.

Second, Freeman (1988) has exposed major weaknesses in the research evidence purporting to show that unemployment is higher and economic growth lower in highly unionised states. After controlling for previously omitted variables, Freeman found 'no consistent relation between union density and the proportion of the working-age population that is employed'. Indeed, 'the economies of several unionised states such as New York or Massachusetts performed better than those of weakly unionised states such as Texas or the Carolinas' (Freeman, 1988: 707).

Third, evidence of the increasing salience of low wage, low productivity employment throughout the economy, including manufacturing, and the stagnation of per capita incomes since the mid-1980s, strongly suggests that employment growth in the United States has been secured at the expense of technological dynamism and greater industrial efficiency (Harrison and Bluestone, 1990). The comparative data on trends in manufacturing trade certainly support this interpretation. Between 1984 and 1987 the United States share of total OECD exports of high technology, high value added manufactured goods fell from 25 to 21 per cent. By contrast, the four largest industrial countries of Europe (France, Germany, Italy and the UK) increased their share from 32 to 35 per cent (Hughes, 1993).

A more disturbing picture of Europe's comparative record emerges when Japan, rather than the United States, is chosen as the relevant reference point. Industrial productivity in Japan has increased by leaps and bounds since the 1960s, averaging 5.1 per cent over the past three decades, and more than 7 per cent annually in manufacturing. Nevertheless, as Table 4.7 indicates, the rate of unemployment has remained very low, averaging around 2.5 per cent throughout the 1980s. With manufacturing output growing more or less in line with productivity, there has been no immediate pressure for a massive labour 'shake-out' similar to that experienced in the Unites States and the leading European countries in the 1980s.

Rapid growth of exports to other OECD countries helped sustain the expansion of industrial output and employment. In 1970, Japan and Britain each held approximately 11 per cent shares of total world trade in manufactures, but by 1990 Japan's share was twice that of Britain's. Moreover, in contrast to the United States, which has experienced a declining share of exports in high technology products, Japan's share of these expanding markets has grown rapidly. The result is that Japan enjoys a substantial trade surplus in high and medium technology products. Tables 4.7 and 4.8 show the consequences for levels of employment. What emerges is a record of rapid manufacturing employment decline in Europe, with 15 per cent of the workforce displaced between 1979 and 1990, while in Japan the corresponding figure was a mere 2 per cent.

The rate of manufacturing employment decline in Europe has been uneven, and most pronounced in Britain. Since 1979, for example, employment has shrunk from a little over 7 million to 4 million; and since 1960 it has almost halved. By contrast, in Germany roughly a third of total civilian employees continue to work in manufacturing. Japan has a smaller share at around a quarter of the workforce, but it has increased as a proportion of total employment since 1960.

The sharp contraction of employment in British manufacturing may, of course, be a symptom of success rather than failure, the product of a history of rapid productivity growth. If productivity grows faster than output, then the level of employment must eventually fall. Such an account would be misleading for the British economy, however, for it has achieved quite modest advances in productivity and particularly so in comparison with Germany and Japan. The central problem has been Britain's poor record of manufacturing output growth, which has remained more or less static since the early 1970s. Between 1979–1981 it fell by a staggering 20 per cent: thereafter the recovery of output merely served to re-establish the levels achieved in previous peak years. The level achieved in 1974, for example, was not surpassed until 1989.

Britain's peculiar trajectory has been characterised as a process of 'negative' deindustrialisation. According to Rowthorn and Wells (1987), 'a dynamic manufacturing sector may be shedding labour, yet at the same time, contributing to the creation of employment in the economy as steady increases in industrial production lay the material foundation for a prosperous and expanding service sector'. This is the case of 'positive' deindustrialisation and is exemplified by the German experience (see Appelbaum & Schettkay, 1991; and the discussion below). But Britain's experience has been different: manufacturing output and employment changes have been conditioned by internal weaknesses (lack of investment and competitiveness) and by adverse shifts in the pattern of demand. On the one hand, the pattern of domestic demand has shifted in favour of commodities produced overseas; on the other hand, manufacturers located in Britain have experienced increasing difficulties in maintaining their share of international markets (see Nolan & Walsh, 1995).

As noted above, however, advocates of the Eurosclerosis thesis contend that the process of negative deindustrialisation in Britain has been checked in recent years. By contrast the economies of Continental Europe are said to be experiencing continuing relative decline because of the high costs of employment and poor productivity record which have characterised their recent development. The next section assesses these claims against the empirical evidence.

3. Labour costs and productivity

The ranking of countries in terms of their relative international competitiveness has become increasingly common in recent years, yet the underlying methodological basis for such comparisons remains controversial. Nations do not compete with one another in international markets, nor is there a straightforward correspondence between the competitive strategies of, for example, multinational companies and the economic performance and prosperity of their host countries. Be that as it may, it is difficult to envisage that the current focus on the nation state as the basic unit of analysis for studies of competitive performance will change, particularly given the prospect of continuing shifts and transformations in the hierarchy of economic relationships within and between the advanced and developing economies.

Broadly speaking, the research literature on international competitiveness falls into two main categories: detailed historical case studies of specific industries, which aim to elucidate the structural and strategic sources of national competitiveness (e.g. Porter, 1990); and quantitative time-series studies of a range of performance indicators (most usually unemployment, inflation, the balance of trade and relative unit labour costs). The focus here is on relative unit labour costs, that is the relationship between employment costs (wages and other indirect charges) and the productivity of labour, expressed in terms of a common currency.

The limitations of this concept, as a measure of international competitiveness, should be recorded. First, unit labour costs make no allowance for the impact of non-price variables (for example, marketing and design) on production and competitiveness. While acknowledging the potential importance of such factors, most analysts concede that they are intrinsically difficult to quantify and hence push them to one side (see Hooper & Larin, 1989). Second, by definition, unit labour costs do not allow for variations in the cost, quality and quantity of capital. The operating assumption is that labour is the most important non-traded variable in production. Third, as elaborated below, the construction of consistent comparative time-series data on labour costs and productivity over time and place, and in the face of continuous exchange rate movements, is far from straightforward.

Theoretically, this procedure raises profound questions about the appropriate method of aggregation: is like being compared with like and what accounting units should be used to sum together heterogeneous units of labour and output? Parallelling in important ways the aggregation problems highlighted by the Cambridge 'capital' controversies in the 1960s and 1970s, the issues in respect of labour have scarcely been addressed, still less resolved. What is the appropriate method for summing labour services of different qualities and productivities? Total factor productivity studies (see Nolan, 1989, for a discussion) draw upon earnings data to capture quality differences under the usual neo-classical assumption that labour markets are competitive and wages reflect marginal productivities. By contrast, studies of relative unit labour costs take as their denominator a relatively crude *extensive* measure of labour input, either total numbers employed or total employee hours. Such measures do not attempt to adjust for quality or variations in the intensity of effort per worker hour. But, as Muellbauer (1986) has shown, such variations may be a significant source of measurement error. Output per employee hour may, for example, be biased upwards by the failure to allow for any increases in labour utilisation, or, what amounts to the same thing, increases in labour input.

More attention has been given to the problem of generating consistent output values across countries, given the possibility that prices for a particular set of commodities may vary significantly. Such variations would introduce distortions into output measures when those commodities are valued in a common currency, the US dollar for example, at market exchange rates. The real value of output in one country as compared to another may be seriously inflated or deflated, depending upon the nature of the initial discrepancy in prices. The recent studies on relative unit labour costs have sought to address this problem by developing purchasing power parity (PPP) exchange rates to convert outputs into common currency units. For an individual commodity, the PPP represents the exchange rate necessary to purchase the same quantity of that commodity in another country. The data presented in Tables 4.10 and 4.11 are based on PPP, and hence remain free from the more serious distortions common in official output series.

Table 4.9 presents standardised cross country data on relative levels of compensation in manufacturing, as compiled by the U.S. Bureau of Labor. The figures are formed by summing total hourly earnings and other non-wage costs, such as social insurance charges. The Table shows that the United Kingdom became a centre for relatively cheap labour in the early 1960s. Immediately after the Second World War the United Kingdom was a relatively high wage economy, but by 1970 only Japan of the leading capitalist countries had lower total labour costs. By contrast Germany, Belgium and the Netherlands emerged from the post-war reconstruction years as high labour cost countries. France and Italy occupied the middle ground, while Spain and Portugal (not shown in the Table) took up the low ground. By the early 1990s, the United Kingdom's relative standing was more akin to Spain than to France and Italy. Germany had become the highest labour cost country, while the United States – which had been at the top of the international league table for most of the period – assumed a middle range position alongside Japan.

The relatively low costs of labour in Britain, Spain and more recently the United States would suggest that these countries possess a significant competive advantage, especially in labour intensive production. But, as indicated above, relative unit labour costs are the relevant measure and these are determined in part by the productivity of labour. Table 4.10 provides the relevant information on relative productivity levels in manufacturing for five countries and is standardised for purchasing power parity rations (see above). The data reveal a substantial and enduring shortfall in productivity levels in the United Kingdom, as compared to the United States, the Netherlands, France and Germany. The differential with the United States opened up early on this century, but as the Table reveals the gap with workers in Europe developed much later, in the 1950s and 1960s, as other countries achieved much higher productivity growth rates following the reconstruction of their industries after 1945.

Table 4.11 combines the information on total hourly labour costs and labour productivity levels. It shows that the existence of low labour costs in a particular country is not necessarily reflected in low relative unit labour costs. The United Kingdom is the clearest example. Although labour costs are lower in the United Kingdom than in the other leading economies, Table 4.11 indicates that unit labour costs were higher in the United Kingdom in the 1980s than elsewhere, with Germany as the notable exception. For the United Kingdom the underlying problem is low relative levels of productivity. For Germany, in contrast, high levels of total hourly compensation have served to erode that country's once pre-eminent competitive advantage.

4. Labour markets and industrial performance

The approach of the Single Market gave employers a renewed impetus to achieve cost-cutting changes in production. In consequence, the past decade has been characterised by major shifts and transformations in work organisation; in the nature, scope and boundaries of internal labour markets; and in the substantive content and character of industrial relations. It is not possible to do justice here to the complexity and unevenness of the change process, but some of the impacts on trade union membership, collective bargaining and patterns of industrial conflict can be briefly highlighted.

Table 4.12 thus reports for selected years since 1970 the changes in union density (the total number of union members expressed as a proportion of potential membership). The figures reveal a steep decline in the Netherlands, Spain, Portugal and France, and overall reductions in 10 of the 18 countries.

But there have been significant increases in union density in Belgium, Denmark, Finland and Sweden which testify to the continuing resilience of unionism in parts of Continental Europe. The attempts by employers to redefine the character of the employment relationship and the scope and agenda of collective bargaining, notwithstanding the continuing salience of unionism, is to some extent revealed by Table 4.13. This shows that the incidence of industrial disputes has fallen in virtually all cases. Spain is the notable exception.

The diversity of labour market restructuring strategies is particularly striking in respect of collective bargaining. Fragmentation and de-collectivisation processes have for example been most pronounced in Britain. Indeed, the latest survey evidence, as interpreted by Brown (1993), points to 'a substantial contraction in the coverage of collective agreements, the narrowing in the scope of collective bargaining, the decline in the depth of union involvement and the erosion of unions' organisational security' (Brown, 1993: 189). The coverage of collective agreements, which encompassed three quarters of all employees in 1973, has fallen drastically and in 1990 influenced the wages and conditions of less than half the workforce. Elsewhere, in Germany, Italy and Sweden, for example, the drive for enhanced workforce flexibility and productivity has been pursued while maintaining broadly intact the framework of collective labour market and industrial relations institutions elaborated in the previous expansionary phase. What have been the employment consequences of these differing patterns of labour market restructuring?

Figure 4.1 describes the relationship between changes in unemployment and union density for the major OECD countries, between 1980 and 1988. It reveals that heavily unionised countries, like Sweden and Finland, have out-performed Britain, the Netherlands and France where unionism has shown a marked decline. In short the proposition, advanced with such force in recent years, that unionism is an unwarranted rigidity in the labour market which necessarily inhibits employment growth is not supported by this evidence. Quite the opposite in fact: the inverse relationship between unionism and unemployment which is highlighted for many countries points to the urgent need for a more subtle analysis of the complex connections between labour market institutions, industrial restructuring and employment outcomes.

The diverse experiences of Britain and West Germany are cited below in an attempt to unravel the relevant relationships. In important respects these countries occupy near polar positions in terms of the spectrum of labour market adjustment policies that have been pursued within Europe in the 1980s.

Britain

Since 1979 successive Conservative governments have sought to help spur the process of industrial renewal by placing the reform of the labour market and industrial relations system centre stage. The erosion of trade union 'power and privileges' has been seen as an essential precondition for employment growth.

Accordingly a complex set of legislative reforms have been introduced, roughly on a two year cycle, with the clear intention of eroding the 'social power of unions' and increasing 'managerial control of industrial relations'. Among other things, the new laws have undermined the closed shop, outlawed secondary picketing and sympathetic strikes, introduced compulsory pre-strike ballots and narrowed the purposes for which 'legitimate' industrial action could be taken. These tough anti-union laws have been accompanied by further measures to deregulate the labour market and free employers from the 'rigid' collective structures of employment regulation which had prevailed prior to 1979. What have been their employment consequences and have they succeeded in boosting labour productivity?

The evolution of Britain's employment structure since 1979 parallels in important respects developments in the United States under Reagan and Bush. Key elements include the rapid growth of low paid, part-time service sector jobs, particularly after 1985, and the accelerating decline of manufacturing and industrial employment. In 1979, more than 7 million employees worked in manufacturing – approximately a third of the labour force – yet now the figure is closer to 4 million.

A decade of poor, often negative, annual rates of productivity growth in the 1970s gave way to more rapid advances in the 1980s. The apparent improvement has been widely attributed to the Thatcher governments' policies, and was initially judged to be indicative of a new sustainable high growth trajectory (for example, see Crafts, 1988). Compared with the record of the 1970s, there was indeed an improvement, but the argument about government policies is unconvincing: productivity rises for the economy as a whole, including services and primary industries, were quite modest, rising annually by only 2.3 per cent between 1979–1988, which is broadly in line with international experience. Moreover as one recent commentator noted: 'if the Thatcher revolution boosted productivity by bashing unions, cutting taxes and privatising nationalised industries, why were the effects limited to manufacturing?' (Gordon, 1992: 425)

But even the record for manufacturing looks less impressive when judged against Britain's own experience in the 1960s. According to one recent study (Darby and Wren-Lewis, 1988), productivity growth in the 1980s returned to the trend established in the 1960s: it was the performance of the 1970s that was out of step. And, as Table 4.8 shows, the gains in the 1980s were insufficient to close the gap with other leading economies. The result, as far as cost competitiveness is concerned, is to leave industries in Britain at a substantial disadvantage. Unit labour costs – total labour costs divided by the productivity of labour – are relatively high despite Britain's low labour costs.

The massive shake-out of labour from industry has been interpreted by some writers as the inevitable consequence of years of managerial neglect and the consequent proliferation of output restrictions by labour. A period of labour 'dis-hoarding' thus was accordingly thought long overdue. Against this view stands the compelling evidence of the wholesale destruction of large sections of manufacturing industry, much of which was toppled by the sharp intensification of liquidity constraints in the early 1980s rather than underlying structural deficiencies (Oulton, 1987). The much vaunted productivity 'miracle' of the 1980s – which in any case never extended to private services where growth has averaged little more than one per cent per annum – derived primarily from the application of more intensive work regimes – which may or may not prove sustainable – and piecemeal changes in work organisation and production technique (Nolan, 1989b).

Within the broader international context, Britain's role as a specialist producer of relatively low wage, low technology, low value added products appears to have been entrenched. The restructuring of labour market institutions, particularly the weakening of the collective institutions of labour, may have served to consolidate these adverse trends (Nolan, 1989a). The availability of a relatively cheap, easily disposable and segmented workforce in Britain has entrenched a particular pattern of foreign direct investment, skewed towards low skill, low productivity activities, which has served to reproduce and amplify long-standing structural weaknesses.

Germany

The form and consequences of restructuring in (West) Germany offer a striking contrast. Flexibility and sustainable productivity gains have been sought without a major employers' offensive on collective institutions. In contrast to Britain, bargaining between unions and employers in Germany is still concentrated at industry level and generally serves the purpose of setting a 'floor' to wages and conditions. The agreements which emerge from such multi-employer bargaining arrangements tend to be set with a view to the performance and productivity of the average enterprise in each sector, but in more profitable companies negotiations at works council level may lift pay above the average level. Flexibility is thus possible within a system in which collective agreements and regulations remain dominant.

Industrial performance in Germany, prior to unification, was arguably the strongest of all the European economies. Employment in manufacturing industry remains relatively high, certainly by British standards, at around 32 per cent of the total employed workforce, which is only slightly down from a mid-1970s peak of 35 per cent. Productivity levels exceed Britain's by an average of 22 per cent, which is only slightly lower than the comparable figure for 1968 (25 per cent), and the most recent authoritative research (O'Mahony, 1992) attributes the differential to variations in levels of human and physical capital. The differential was found to be most pronounced in the engineering sector, and least apparent in relatively low-technology, low-skill industries such as food and drink and textiles, in which Britain retains a strong international presence and remains attractive as a site of low-wage production for transnationals.

Streeck's compelling account of the connections between the labour market, the pattern of industrial restructuring and the performance consequences represents a powerful challenge to the conventional account of the sources of Eurosclerosis. In particular, he argues that the high-quality, high value-added production systems – what he terms 'diversified quality production' – emerged in Germany precisely because of the existence of powerful and binding 'institutional constraints'.

Especially significant, according to Streeck, was the presence of strong workplace trade unions with the organisational capacities to force companies to pursue a strategy of continuous modernisation and improvement. Other vital ingredients which he lists include: a system of 'rigid' wage determination, which forced employers to 'adapt their product range to non-price competitive product markets capable of sustaining a high wage level'; a legally enforceable system of employment protection that promotes internal flexibility and a commitment to invest in training and retraining; and a 'set of binding rules' compelling employers to consult with their employees 'and seek their consent above and beyond what many or most would on their own find expedient' (1986: 22–3; 1991: 52–3).

Proponents of the Eurosclerosis thesis would condemn the above system of rules and constrains as a fetter on economic efficiency. Streeck, by contrast, argues that their net effect has been to induce 'a virtuous circle of upmarket industrial restructuring' (1991: 54). By blocking 'quick-fix' solutions and low-wage routes to profitability, this framework of rules and institutions has 'forced, induced and enabled' management to embark on more demanding design, production and marketing strategies.

Streeck's account is buttressed by Appelbaum and Schettkat's comparative study of employment dynamics and labour force restructuring in Germany and the United States. 'The picture that emerges, of a very rapid and dynamic restructuring of the West German economy, is quite different from the usual view and raises serious questions about the hypothesis that labour market structures in West Germany are too rigid' (Appelbaum and Schettkat, 1991: 156). The relatively dynamic German production system has not only proved compatible with high levels of employment in manufacturing – a feature which marks it off from the experience of all other European countries – it has also helped facilitate the growth of service sector employment.

In terms of the growth rate of service sector jobs, Germany's record is more or less comparable to that of the United States, the latter having been dubbed a 'job creating machine'. But the character of service sector jobs is diffferent in the two countries. In the United States the growth of services has spawned millions of 'small', insecure and poorly paid part-time jobs, particularly in personal services. In Germany, however, 'just 6.6 per cent of wage and salary earners [in services] were on schedules of less than 21 hours in 1987': the remaining 93.4 per cent qualified for full entitlement to the German social insurance system (Appelbaum and Schettkat, 1991: 153).

Germany's record also contrasts with that of Britain's, which like the United States, has experienced a rapid expansion of service sector employment by creating millions of small (i.e. fewer than 8 hours), lowly paid, insecure jobs (Casey, 1991).

5. Conclusion

Several themes emerge from the foregoing discussion. The labour markets of Europe do not exhibit the same structural characteristics, no more than they have identical performance records, whether in respect of employment, unemployment, productivity, labour costs or industrial restructuring. Diversity is very much in evidence. At one extreme is the British economy, which has been subject to extensive deregulation by successive governments since 1979. This economy has been shown to be characterised by low labour costs, low productivity and structural adjustments which have dramatically eroded employment in manufacturing while giving rise to the rapid growth of low value added and hence poorly remunerated service sector jobs. Unemployment in Britain has been above the European average for most of the past two decades, yet proponents of the Eurosclerosis thesis hold up the British case as an exemplar of what deregulation policies can supposedly deliver in terms of dynamic growth.

Germany and Sweden stand at the other end of the European spectrum. Sweden, as indicated, has the best employment record, while Germany has consistently out-performed the rest of Europe in sustaining a high level of manufacturing employment. Yet both countries have been held to be suffering the symptoms of economic sclerosis. The above analysis has questioned the value of such broad brush generalisations and has sought to highlight the diverse and uneven effects of labour market institutions and restructuring.

Bibliography

Appelbaum, E. & Schettkat, R. (1991), 'Employment and industrial restructuring in the United States and West Germany', in Matzner, E. & Streeck, W. (eds), *Beyond Keynesianism: The Socioeconomics of Production and Full Employment*, Aldershot: Edward Elgar.

Ark, B. van (1990), 'Comparative Levels of manufacturing productivity in postwar Europe: measurement and comparisons', *Oxford Bulletin of Economic Statistics*, 53, 4.

Boyer, R. (1988), 'Europe at the crossroads', in Boyer, R. (ed.), *The Search for Labour Market Flexibility: European Economies in Transition*, Oxford: Clarendon Press.

Brown, W. (1993), 'The contraction of collective bargaining', *British Journal of Industrial Relations*, 31, 2.

Burton, J. (1987), *Workfare*, Employment Research Institute, University of Birmingham.

Calmfors, L. & Driffill, J. (1989), 'Bargaining structure, corporatism and macroeconomic performance', *Economic Policy*.

Casey, B. (1991), 'Survey evidence on trends in non-standard employment', Pollert, A. (ed.), *Farewell to Flexibility*, Oxford: Blackwell.

Crafts, N. (1988), 'The Assessment: British economic growth over the long run', *Oxford Review of Economic Policy*, 4, 1.

Darby, J. and Wren Lewis, S. (1988), *Trends in Manufacturing Labour Productivity*, National Institute of Economic and Social Research Discussion Paper, 145.

Freeman, R. (1988), 'Union Density and Economic Performance: an analysis of US States', *European Economic Review*, 32.

Gordon, R. (1992), 'Discussion Note on Nick Crafts: Productivity Growth Reconsidered', *Economic Policy*, 15, 4, pp. 414-425.

Harrison, B. & Bluestone, B. (1990), 'Wage polarisation in the US and the "flexibility" debate', *Cambridge Journal of Economics*, 14, 3.

Hooper P. & Larin, K.A. (1989), 'International Comparisons of Labor Costs in Manufacturing', *Review of Income and Wealth*, Series 35 no.4.

Hughes, K. (ed.) (1993), *European Competitiveness,* Cambridge: Cambridge University Press.

Marsden, D. & Silvestre, J.J. (1992), 'Pay and European Integration', in Marsden, D. (ed.), *Pay and Employment in the New Europe*, Aldershot: Edward Elgar.

Minford, P. (1990), 'Corporatism, the natural rate and productivity', in Philpott, J. (ed.), *Trade Unions and the Economy: Into the 1990s*, Employment Institute.

Muellbauer, J. (1986), 'The assessment: productivity and competitiveness in British manufacturing', *Oxford Review of Economic Policy,* 2, 3.

Nolan, P. (1989a), 'Walking on water? Performance and industrial relations under Thatcher', *Industrial Relations Journal*, 20, 2.

Nolan, P. (1989b), 'The productivity miracle?', in Green, F. (ed.), *The Restructuring of the UK Economy,* Brighton: Harvester.

Nolan, P. and Walsh, J. (1995), 'The structure of the economy and labour market', in Edwards, P. (ed.), *Industrial Relations: Theory and Practice in Britain*, Oxford, Blackwell.

OECD (1992), *Historical Statistics 1960–1990*, Paris.

OECD (1992), *Employment Outlook*, Paris.

O'Mahony (1992), 'Productivity Levels in British and German Manufacturing Industry', *National Institute Economic Review*, (February).

Oulton, N. (1987), 'Plant closures and the productivity "miracle" in manufacturing', *National Institute Economic Review*, (August).

Porter, M. (1990), *The Competitive Advantage of Nations*, London: Macmillan.

Rowthorn, R. and Wells, J. (1987), *De-industrialisation and Foreign Trade*, Cambridge, Cambridge University Press.

Sawyer, M. (1993) 'Unemployment and the Dismal Science', in Pitt, G. (ed.), *University of Leeds Review*, vol. 36.

Streeck, W. (1986), 'Industrial Relations and industrial restructuring in the motor industry', Industrial Relations Research Unit, University of Warwick.

Streeck, W. (1991), 'On the institutional conditions of diversified quality production', in Matzner, E. & Streeck, W. (eds), *Beyond Keynesianism: The Socioeconomics of Production and Full Employment*. Aldershot: Edward Elgar.

United States Department of Labor, Bureau of Labor Statistics, International Comparisons of Hourly Compensation Costs for Production Workers in Manufacturing, 1992, Report 844, April 1993.

Figure 4.1 Changes in unemployment and union density, 1980-88 (percentage points)

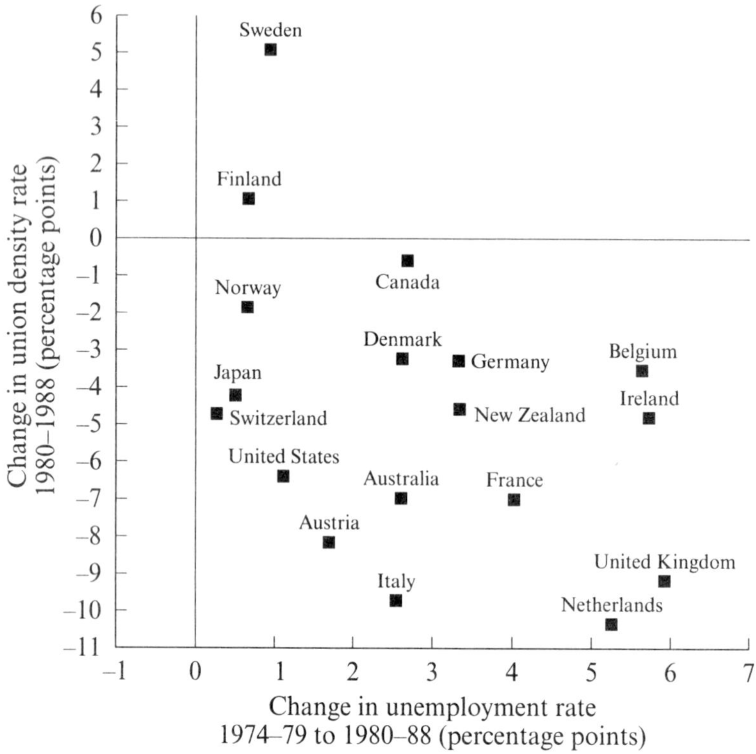

Source: OECD *Employment Outlook*, July 1992, Chart 4.2.

Table 4.1 ***Civilian employment by sector: agriculture (percentage share of total civilian employment)***

	1973	1974	1976	1977	1978	1979	1980	1981	1982	1983	1984	1986	1987	1988	1989	1990	1991
Austria	11.8	11.4	12.4	11.8	10.9	10.7	10.5	10.3	10.0	9.9	9.4	8.7	8.6	8.1	8.0	7.9	7.4
Belgium	4.0	3.8	3.6	3.5	3.4	3.3	3.2	3.2	3.1	3.2	3.1	3.0	3.0	2.8	2.8	2.7	2.6
Denmark	9.5	9.6	8.3	7.8	7.9	7.2	7.1	7.3	7.5	7.4	6.7	5.9	5.7	5.8	5.7	5.6	5.7
Finland	17.1	16.3	16.2	15.1	14.4	13.8	13.5	13.0	13.2	12.7	12.2	11.0	10.4	9.8	8.9	8.4	8.5
France	11.2	10.6	9.9	9.5	9.2	9.0	8.7	8.4	8.2	7.9	7.8	7.3	7.0	6.7	6.4	6.0	5.8
Germany	7.3	7.0	6.4	6.0	5.8	5.4	5.3	5.2	5.0	5.0	4.8	4.4	4.2	4.0	3.8	3.5	3.4
Greece	36.8	36.0	34.2	33.2	32.0	30.8	30.3	30.7	28.9	29.9	29.4	28.5	27.0	26.6	25.3	23.9	22.6
Iceland	16.1	16.1	14.9	14.3	13.9	13.5	13.2	12.4	12.2	11.9	11.3	10.8	10.5	10.2	10.3	10.3	10.7
Ireland	24.1	22.8	22.1	21.3	20.6	19.6	18.3	17.3	17.0	17.0	16.7	15.7	15.3	15.4	15.1	15.0	13.8
Italy	18.3	17.5	16.5	15.8	15.5	14.9	14.3	13.4	12.4	21.4	11.9	10.9	10.5	9.9	9.3	8.8	8.5
Luxembourg	7.9	7.2	6.7	6.4	6.2	5.8	5.4	5.1	4.9	4.7	4.7	4.2	3.9	3.7	3.4	3.3	–
Netherlands	5.8	5.7	5.6	5.3	5.4	5.3	4.9	4.9	5.0	5.0	5.0	4.8	4.9	4.8	4.7	4.6	4.5
Norway	11.5	10.6	9.4	9.1	8.7	8.6	8.5	8.4	8.1	7.7	7.4	7.4	6.7	6.4	6.6	6.5	5.9
Portugal	27.2	34.9	33.9	32.9	31.3	30.5	27.3	26.0	25.2	23.2	23.8	21.9	22.2	20.7	19.0	17.8	17.3
Spain	24.3	23.2	22.1	21.1	20.8	20.0	19.3	18.8	18.6	18.7	18.5	16.2	15.1	14.4	13.0	11.8	10.7
Sweden	7.1	6.7	6.2	6.1	6.1	5.8	5.6	5.6	5.6	5.4	5.1	4.2	3.9	3.8	3.6	3.3	32.0
Switzerland	7.5	7.5	7.8	7.6	7.3	7.2	6.9	6.6	6.4	6.4	6.2	5.9	5.9	5.7	5.6	5.6	5.5
UK	3.0	2.8	2.8	2.8	2.8	2.7	2.6	2.7	2.7	2.7	2.6	2.5	2.4	2.3	2.1	2.1	2.2

Source: OECD, 1993, Table 7.0 pp. 42–3

Table 4.2 Civilian employment by sector: industry (percentage share of total civilian employment)

	1973	1974	1976	1977	1978	1979	1980	1981	1982	1983	1984	1986	1987	1988	1989	1990	1991
Austria	42.8	42.3	40.1	40.6	40.6	40.5	40.3	40.0	39.9	38.8	38.1	37.8	37.7	37.4	37.0	36.8	36.9
Belgium	41.2	41.0	38.7	37.7	36.5	35.5	34.7	33.3	32.2	31.4	30.8	29.6	28.9	28.3	28.5	28.3	28.1
Denmark	33.8	32.3	33.5	32.6	31.9	32.5	30.4	29.3	28.3	28.4	26.8	28.2	28.2	27.2	27.4	27.5	27.7
Finland	35.7	36.0	34.8	34.9	34.6	34.7	34.6	35.0	33.8	33.2	32.6	32.0	31.2	30.6	31.0	31.0	29.2
France	39.5	39.4	38.0	37.5	36.8	36.3	35.9	35.2	34.6	33.8	32.9	31.4	30.8	30.3	30.1	29.9	29.5
Germany	44.8	46.7	44.9	44.6	44.3	44.2	43.7	43.0	42.1	41.4	41.1	40.8	40.4	39.9	39.8	39.8	39.2
Greece	27.6	27.8	28.7	29.2	29.7	30.0	30.2	29.0	29.2	28.6	27.8	28.1	28.0	27.2	27.5	27.7	27.5
Iceland	35.0	34.5	35.3	35.3	35.0	35.1	35.4	34.5	34.2	34.3	34.2	32.1	31.7	30.2	30.1	29.8	26.4
Ireland	31.7	32.6	31.0	31.5	32.0	32.3	32.5	32.1	31.3	29.7	29.2	28.7	27.9	27.8	28.4	28.6	28.9
Italy	39.2	39.3	38.4	38.5	38.1	37.8	37.9	37.6	37.1	36.1	34.5	33.1	32.6	32.4	32.4	32.7	32.3
Luxembourg	44.4	44.9	42.0	41.0	39.2	38.5	38.1	37.2	36.4	35.4	34.7	33.5	32.9	31.9	31.2	30.5	–
Netherlands	36.5	35.9	33.6	33.0	33.0	32.5	31.4	29.9	28.7	28.1	28.3	26.8	26.8	26.4	26.5	26.3	25.5
Norway	34.0	34.3	33.3	32.5	31.7	30.3	29.7	29.3	28.6	27.4	27.6	27.1	27.0	26.4	25.3	24.8	23.7
Portugal	34.6	33.8	33.5	33.1	34.8	35.0	36.6	37.0	37.5	35.3	34.1	34.1	34.9	35.1	35.3	34.8	33.9
Spain	36.7	37.2	36.9	37.3	37.1	36.6	36.1	35.3	34.1	33.5	32.7	32.0	32.3	32.5	32.9	33.4	33.1
Sweden	36.8	37.0	35.4	34.3	33.0	32.5	32.2	31.3	30.3	29.9	29.8	30.1	29.8	29.5	29.4	29.1	28.2
Switzerland	44.8	44.3	40.9	40.4	40.1	39.7	38.1	37.9	36.9	36.0	35.7	35.7	35.3	35.1	35.1	35.0	34.4
UK	42.3	42.0	39.6	39.4	39.1	38.7	37.7	35.8	34.6	33.4	32.3	30.8	30.2	29.7	29.4	28.8	27.8

Source: OECD, 1993, Table 7.0 pp. 42–3

Table 4.3 ***Civilian employment by sector: services (percentage share of total civilian employment)***

	1973	1974	1976	1977	1978	1979	1980	1981	1982	1983	1984	1986	1987	1988	1989	1990	1991
Austria	45.4	46.3	47.5	47.6	48.5	48.8	49.3	49.8	50.0	51.3	52.4	53.6	53.7	54.6	55.1	55.3	55.8
Belgium	54.7	55.2	57.7	58.8	60.1	61.2	62.1	63.6	64.7	65.4	66.1	67.4	68.2	68.9	68.8	69.0	69.3
Denmark	56.7	58.0	58.2	59.6	60.2	60.3	62.4	63.3	64.2	64.2	66.5	65.9	66.1	67.1	66.9	66.9	66.6
Finland	47.2	47.6	49.0	50.0	51.0	51.6	51.8	51.9	53.0	54.2	55.2	57.0	58.4	59.6	60.1	60.6	62.3
France	49.3	49.9	52.1	53.0	54.0	54.8	55.4	56.4	57.3	58.3	59.3	61.3	62.2	63.0	63.5	64.1	64.8
Germany	45.2	46.3	48.7	49.4	49.9	50.4	51.0	51.9	52.9	53.6	54.1	54.8	55.4	56.0	56.4	56.7	57.4
Greece	35.6	36.2	37.1	37.5	38.2	39.2	39.5	40.4	42.0	41.5	42.8	43.4	45.0	46.2	47.1	48.3	50.0
Iceland	48.9	49.4	49.9	50.4	51.1	51.4	51.4	53.1	53.6	53.8	54.5	57.0	57.8	59.6	59.6	59.8	62.9
Ireland	44.2	44.6	47.0	47.2	47.4	48.1	49.2	50.6	51.6	53.2	54.1	55.5	56.8	56.8	56.4	56.4	57.2
Italy	42.5	43.2	45.2	45.7	46.4	47.3	47.8	49.0	50.5	51.5	53.6	56.0	56.8	57.7	58.2	58.5	59.2
Luxembourg	47.7	47.9	51.3	52.7	54.6	55.7	56.5	57.7	58.7	59.9	60.6	62.3	63.2	64.5	65.4	66.2	–
Netherlands	57.6	58.4	60.8	61.7	61.6	62.2	63.6	65.2	66.3	66.9	66.8	68.4	68.3	68.8	68.8	69.1	69.9
Norway	54.4	55.1	57.2	58.4	59.5	61.1	61.9	62.4	63.4	64.9	65.0	65.6	66.3	67.1	68.1	68.8	70.4
Portugal	38.2	31.3	32.6	34.0	33.9	34.4	36.1	37.0	37.3	41.5	42.2	43.9	42.9	44.2	45.7	47.3	48.7
Spain	38.9	39.6	41.0	41.6	42.1	43.4	44.6	45.9	47.3	47.8	48.8	51.9	52.5	53.1	54.0	54.8	56.3
Sweden	56.1	56.3	58.3	59.6	60.9	61.7	62.2	63.1	64.1	64.7	65.1	65.7	66.3	66.7	67.0	67.5	68.5
Switzerland	47.6	48.3	51.4	52.0	52.6	53.2	55.0	55.6	56.6	57.6	58.1	58.4	58.8	59.2	59.3	59.5	60.1
UK	54.7	55.1	57.6	57.8	58.2	58.6	59.7	61.5	62.7	63.9	65.1	66.7	67.4	68.1	68.5	69.0	70.0

Source: OECD, 1993, Table 7.0 pp. 44–5

Table 4.4 Ratio of female to male civilian employment

	1973	1974	1976	1977	1978	1979	1980	1981	1982	1983	1984	1986	1987	1988	1989	1990	1991
Austria	0.62	0.63	0.62	0.62	0.63	0.63	0.62	0.63	0.62	0.62	0.66	0.66	0.67	0.68	0.68	0.69	0.69
Belgium	0.51	0.52	0.52	0.53	0.54	0.55	0.56	0.57	0.58	0.59	0.61	0.63	0.65	0.67	0.67	0.68	0.69
Denmark	0.70	0.71	0.69	0.69	0.71	0.76	-	0.81	0.83	0.83	0.83	0.83	0.85	0.84	0.84	0.86	0.86
Finland	0.86	0.87	0.88	0.90	0.90	0.89	0.88	0.90	0.91	0.92	0.92	0.93	0.93	0.93	0.92	0.92	0.95
France	0.59	0.59	0.62	0.63	0.64	0.65	0.65	0.66	0.67	0.68	0.70	0.72	0.72	0.73	0.73	0.74	0.75
Germany	0.61	0.62	0.63	0.63	0.64	0.64	0.64	0.65	0.65	0.65	0.65	0.66	0.66	0.67	0.68	0.69	0.71
Greece	–	–	–	0.43	0.43	0.42	0.42	0.46	0.44	0.49	0.49	0.52	0.52	0.54	0.54	0.54	–
Iceland	–	–	–	–	–	–	–	–	–	–	–	–	–	–	–	–	0.84
Ireland	0.37	0.38	0.39	0.39	0.39	0.40	0.41	0.42	0.44	0.45	0.45	0.46	0.49	0.48	0.49	0.50	0.51
Italy	0.40	0.41	0.43	0.45	0.45	0.46	0.47	0.48	0.48	0.49	0.49	0.51	0.52	0.52	0.53	0.54	0.55
Luxembourg	0.38	0.39	0.43	0.43	0.45	0.45	0.45	0.48	0.48	0.49	0.50	0.52	0.52	0.53	0.53	0.53	0.56
Netherlands	–	–	0.39	0.40	0.41	0.42	0.44	0.47	0.49	0.51	0.52	0.53	0.57	0.60	0.60	0.62	0.64
Norway	0.58	0.57	0.64	0.65	0.67	0.69	0.70	0.72	0.73	0.75	0.76	0.80	0.81	0.82	0.83	0.85	0.86
Portugal	–	0.66	0.63	0.62	0.61	0.63	0.62	0.65	0.65	0.66	0.67	0.68	0.71	0.72	0.73	0.74	0.77
Spain	0.39	0.40	0.42	0.41	0.41	0.41	0.41	0.40	0.41	0.42	0.42	0.42	0.44	0.45	0.46	0.48	0.49
Sweden	0.69	0.71	0.75	0.77	0.79	0.81	0.82	0.85	0.86	0.87	0.88	0.91	0.92	0.92	0.92	0.92	0.93
Switzerland	0.52	0.53	0.54	0.54	0.55	0.56	0.57	0.58	0.58	0.58	0.59	0.59	0.59	0.60	0.61	0.61	0.62
UK	0.60	0.62	0.64	0.65	0.65	0.67	0.67	0.68	0.69	0.71	0.72	0.75	0.76	0.77	0.79	0.79	0.81

Source: OECD, 1993, various tables

Table 4.5 Aggregate civilian employment (000s)

	1973	1974	1976	1977	1978	1979	1980	1981	1982	1983	1984	1986	1987	1988	1989	1990	1991
Aus	3160	3190	2947	2988	3015	3051	3070	3091	3189	3159	3235	3279	3297	3308	3342	3412	3482
Bel	3656	3715	3641	3627	3628	3660	3657	3585	3537	3502	3497	3541	3558	3610	3670	3726	3735
Den	2385	2355	2307	2321	2330	2439	2460	2369	2374	2389	2457	2630	2646	2660	2610	2638	2612
Fin	2154	2220	2268	2221	2190	2246	2318	2343	2367	2380	2403	2421	2414	2420	2460	2457	2330
Fr	20863	21059	21016	21188	21263	21305	21334	21203	21240	21168	20981	20955	21023	21196	21458	21683	21782
Ger	26649	26302	25442	25475	25689	26120	26528	26498	26193	25809	25869	26431	26626	26835	27237	27997	28533
Gr	3191	3195	3235	3262	3276	3311	3356	3531	3502	3540	3553	3601	3598	3658	3671	3719	3768
Ice	90	93	98	99	102	103	106	111	114	115	117	125	132	128	126	126	140
Ir	1057	1071	1050	1068	1095	1129	1141	1131	1133	1110	1090	1068	1074	1078	1076	1115	1113
It	19006	19392	19612	19791	19863	20057	20313	20361	20297	20350	20418	20614	20583	20815	20833	21215	21410
Lux	151	155	157	157	156	156	157	158	158	157	158	164	169	174	181	189	162
Neth	4670	4672	4654	4701	4757	4821	4970	5072	5010	4950	4980	5155	5773	5934	6065	6268	6444
Nor	1646	1651	1779	1815	1846	1862	1875	1904	1910	1910	1939	2053	2090	2079	2014	1992	1973
Port	3286	3694	3789	3784	3772	3854	3940	3918	3928	4128	4075	4064	4171	4280	4377	4474	4607
Sp	12608	12670	12476	12330	12096	11902	11550	11216	11098	11047	10748	10875	11384	11780	12260	12578	12608
Swe	3879	3962	4088	4099	4115	4180	4232	4225	4219	4224	4255	4269	4337	4399	4466	4508	4431
Swi	3277	3274	3024	3036	3057	3100	3166	3240	3256	3257	3288	3398	3440	3481	3518	3563	3560
UK	24715	24803	24509	24538	24697	25079	25004	24011	23584	23304	23909	24239	24755	25598	26376	26620	25726

Source: OECD, 1993, Table 6.0, pp. 34–5

Table 4.6 Unemployment as a proportion of total labour force

	1973	1974	1976	1977	1978	1979	1980	1981	1982	1983	1984	1986	1987	1988	1989	1990	1991
Austria	1.0	1.1	1.8	1.6	2.1	2.1	1.9	2.5	3.5	4.1	3.8	3.1	3.8	3.6	3.1	3.2	3.5
Belgium	2.4	2.5	5.9	6.7	7.2	7.5	7.9	10.2	11.9	13.2	13.2	11.6	11.3	10.3	9.3	8.7	9.3
Denmark	0.9	3.5	6.3	7.3	8.3	6.0	6.5	10.3	11.0	11.4	8.5	5.5	5.4	6.5	8.1	8.3	9.1
Finland	2.3	1.7	3.8	5.8	7.2	5.9	4.6	4.8	5.3	5.4	5.2	5.3	5.0	4.5	3.4	3.4	7.5
France	2.7	2.8	4.4	4.9	5.2	5.9	6.3	7.4	8.1	8.3	9.7	10.4	10.5	10.0	9.4	8.9	9.3
Germany	1.0	2.1	3.9	3.8	3.6	3.2	3.2	4.5	6.4	7.9	7.9	7.6	7.6	7.6	6.8	6.2	5.5
Greece	2.0	2.1	1.9	1.7	1.8	1.9	2.8	4.0	5.8	7.9	8.1	7.4	7.4	7.7	7.5	7.0	7.0
Iceland	1.1	1.1	1.0	0.0	0.0	0.0	0.0	0.0	0.9	0.9	0.8	0.8	0.8	0.8	1.6	1.6	2.1
Ireland	5.7	5.3	9.0	8.8	8.2	7.1	7.3	9.9	11.4	14.0	15.6	17.4	17.6	16.7	15.6	13.7	15.7
Italy	6.2	5.3	6.6	7.0	7.1	7.6	7.5	7.8	8.4	9.3	9.9	10.9	11.8	11.8	11.8	11.2	10.8
Luxembourg	–	–	0.6	0.6	0.6	0.6	0.6	1.3	1.3	1.9	1.9	1.2	1.7	1.7	1.1	1.0	1.2
Netherlands	2.2	2.7	5.5	5.3	5.3	5.4	6.0	8.5	11.3	11.8	11.9	10.3	9.6	9.2	8.3	7.5	7.0
Norway	1.5	1.5	1.7	1.4	1.8	2.0	1.6	2.0	2.6	3.4	3.1	2.0	2.1	3.2	4.9	5.2	5.5
Portugal	2.5	1.7	6.3	7.4	8.0	8.1	7.7	7.4	7.3	7.8	8.4	8.5	7.0	5.7	5.0	4.6	4.1
Spain	2.5	3.0	4.4	5.1	6.8	8.4	11.1	13.8	15.6	17.0	19.7	20.8	20.1	19.1	16.9	15.9	16.0
Sweden	2.5	2.0	1.6	1.8	2.2	2.1	2.0	2.5	3.1	3.5	3.1	2.7	1.9	1.6	1.3	1.5	2.7
Switzerland	–	–	0.7	0.4	0.3	0.3	0.2	0.2	0.4	0.9	1.1	0.8	0.7	0.6	0.5	0.6	1.2
UK	2.2	2.1	4.8	5.2	5.1	4.6	5.6	9.0	10.4	11.2	11.1	11.6	10.4	8.3	6.1	5.5	7.9

Source: OECD, 1993, Table 5.1 pp. 32–3

Table 4.7 Unemployment as a percentage of total labour force

	1960	1974	1980	1985	1990
EC	2.4	2.9	6.2	11.0	8.5
USA	5.4	5.5	7.0	7.1	5.4
Japan	1.7	1.4	2.0	2.6	2.1

Source: OECD *Historical Statistics 1960-1990*, Table 2.15

Table 4.8 Employment in manufacturing as a percentage of civilian employment 1960–1990

					Percentage change	
	1960	1974	1980	1990	1980–1990	1960–1990
USA	26.4	24.2	22.1	18.0	–19	–32
Japan	21.3	27.2	22.1	18.0	–2	+13
Germany	34.3	35.8	33.9	31.5	–7	–8
France	27.3	28.3	25.8	21.3	–17	–22
UK	38.4	34.6	30.2	22.5	–25	–41
Italy	24.2	28.0	26.8	21.1	–16	
Sweden	31.5	28.3	24.2	21.1	–9	
OECD Europe	27.3	28.0	25.9	22.1	–15	

Source: *OECD Historical Statistics 1960-1990*

Table 4.9 Manufacturing compensation per hour in current US dollars

Year	US	Germany	Japan	France	UK	Italy	Belgium	Netherlands
1960	2.66	0.85	0.26	0.82	0.84	0.63	0.81	0.67
1970	4.18	2.36	0.99	1.73	1.49	1.76	2.08	2.12
1971	3.39	2.81	1.18	1.94	1.73	2.12	2.46	2.56
1972	4.84	3.42	1.58	2.35	2.03	2.57	3.16	3.15
1973	5.26	4.67	2.19	3.09	2.26	3.20	4.15	4.31
1974	5.75	5.46	2.67	3.43	2.60	3.66	5.03	5.37
1975	6.36	6.35	3.05	4.60	3.32	4.65	6.41	6.58
1976	6.92	6.73	3.30	4.70	3.17	4.41	6.90	6.90
1977	7.59	7.86	4.02	5.21	3.40	5.10	8.29	8.02
1978	8.27	9.65	5.54	6.43	4.34	6.09	10.14	9.98
1979	9.02	11.29	5.49	7.69	5.61	7.12	11.84	11.41
1980	9.84	12.33	5.61	8.94	7.43	8.00	13.15	12.06
1981	10.84	10.53	6.18	8.02	7.20	7.39	11.31	9.91
1982	11.64	10.28	5.70	7.85	6.82	7.30	9.49	9.78
1983	12.10	10.23	6.13	7.74	6.39	7.61	9.07	9.49
1984	12.51	9.43	6.34	7.29	5.95	7.21	8.62	8.70
1985	12.96	9.56	6.47	7.52	6.19	7.40	8.95	8.70
1986	13.21	13.35	9.47	10.27	7.50	10.01	12.35	12.24
1987	13.46	16.83	11.34	12.36	9.07	12.33	15.08	15.11
1992	16.17	25.99	16.16	16.88	14.69	19.41	22.01	20.72

Source: US Bureau of Labor Statistics

Table 4.10 Gross Value Added per person-hour in Manufacturing in the Netherlands, France, Germany and the USA as a Percentage of the UK, 1960-88 (UK = 100.0)

Year	UK	Netherlands	France	Germany	USA
1960	100	98.5	80.7	105.3	242.5
1970	100	124.8	111.7	133.1	223.7
1971	100	129.8	113.9	130.0	227.7
1972	100	132.5	112.0	133.0	223.6
1973	100	135.3	112.8	133.3	219.9
1974	100	138.5	115.6	137.0	210.2
1975	100	142.4	119.8	141.9	216.7
1976	100	151.5	123.5	147.1	220.1
1977	100	156.5	130.7	152.1	226.6
1978	100	163.2	135.1	154.5	226.3
1979	100	169.1	141.8	161.6	225.6
1980	100	173.5	144.2	164.3	227.2
1981	100	167.9	139.0	157.5	217.1
1982	100	165.4	142.1	152.3	212.2
1983	100	163.0	135.3	149.3	208.7
1984	100	165.5	130.8	146.8	209.6
1985	100	161.7	130.5	148.2	212.7
1986	100	155.1	129.3	142.8	213.0
1987	100	146.0	125.8	137.9	208.4
1988	100	144.1	125.5	136.8	207.0

Source: Ark, B. van, 1990

Table 4.11 Manufacturing Unit Labour Costs (in US dollars)

Year	US	Germany	Japan	France	UK	Italy	Belgium	Netherlands
1960	28.9	18.8	13.8	21.3	22.1	15.4	21.6	17.0
1970	35.0	29.5	18.8	23.5	27.3	20.9	30.3	27.1
1971	35.6	33.8	21.1	25.0	30.2	24.4	33.8	31.1
1972	36.8	38.6	25.8	28.6	33.6	27.3	39.0	35.1
1973	38.1	49.5	32.4	35.5	34.8	30.4	46.3	43.4
1974	43.0	55.7	37.9	38.0	39.4	33.1	53.2	50.1
1975	46.3	62.8	42.8	49.1	51.5	44.0	65.2	62.7
1976	48.2	62.1	43.0	46.7	47.1	38.5	63.7	59.1
1977	51.4	70.0	49.4	49.3	50.0	44.0	72.9	65.9
1978	55.2	83.4	63.1	58.1	62.9	51.0	84.1	77.0
1979	60.2	93.0	58.8	66.3	80.5	55.6	93.1	83.4
1980	65.7	101.1	56.2	76.4	107.4	59.0	97.0	87.0
1981	70.8	84.5	59.7	66.5	99.0	51.1	78.0	69.6
1982	74.4	81.3	51.9	60.8	88.5	48.6	61.7	67.3
1983	73.1	76.5	53.0	58.5	76.4	47.4	53.8	61.1
1984	71.7	68.0	51.1	54.0	67.4	42.1	49.1	50.8
1985	71.2	66.3	49.4	54.3	67.7	42.1	49.5	49.1
1986	70.0	92.6	71.1	72.0	79.9	56.5	65.7	69.4
1987	69.0	115.1	81.8	83.9	90.4	67.4	77.9	85.3
1988	69.9	119.8	92.3	90.3	100.6	72.6	79.8	87.5

Source: Hooper P. and Larin K.A., 1989

Table 4.12 Union density[a]

	1970	1975	1980	1985	1988
Austria	59.8	56.1	53.8	48.6	45.7
Belgium	46.0	55.3	56.5	54.3	53.0
Denmark	60.0	67.4	76.5	78.3	73.2
Finland	51.4	67.4	69.8	68.6	71.3[b]
France	22.3	22.8	19.0	16.3	12.0
Germany	33.0	36.6	37.0	37.4	33.8
Greece[c]	–	35.8[d]	–	36.7	25.0
Iceland[c]	–	–	68.1[e]	–	78.3[b]
Ireland	53.1	55.2	57.0	56.0	52.4[f]
Italy	36.3	47.2	49.3	42.0	39.6
Luxembourg[c]	46.8	45.8	52.2[g]	–	49.7[b]
Netherlands	37.0	38.4	35.3	28.7	25.0
Norway	50.6	52.7	56.9	55.7	57.1[b]
Portugal[c]	59.0[h]	52.4	58.8[i]	51.6[j]	30.0
Spain[c]	–	30.4[k]	22.0[l]	16.0	–
Sweden	67.7	74.5	80.0	84.0	85.3
Switzerland	30.7	32.9	30.7	28.8	26.0[m]
United Kingdom	44.8	48.3	50.7	45.5	41.5

Notes: a: Calculated on the basis of employed membership unless otherwise indicated
b: 1989
c: Calculated on the basis of total recorded membership
d: 1977
e: 1979
f: 1987
g: 1981
h: 1969
i: Average 1979–84
j: Average 1985–86
k: Average 1974–79
l: 1981
m: 1987

Source: OECD, 1991, Table 4.1, p. 101

Table 4.13 Work-days not worked due to industrial disputes (in 000s)

	1973	1974	1976	1977	1978	1979	1980	1981	1982	1983	1984	1986	1987	1988	1989	1990	1991
Aus	160	7	1	0	10	1	17	4	0	1	1	3	5	-	3	9	58
Bel	872	580	897	664	1003	615	217	-	-	-	-	-	-	194	133	103	-
Den[a]	3901	184	210	230	129	173	187	652	93	79	132	93	137	97	53	98	70
Fin	2497	435	1238	2375	132	3172	1523	1442	208	720	1527	2788	131	180	204	935	458
Fr[b]	3915	3380	5011	3666	2200	3657	1686	1496	2327	1484	1347	1041	969	1242	901	694	666
Ger[c d]	563	1051	534	24	4281	483	128	58	15	41	5618	28	33	42	100	364	154
Gr[e]	-	-	-	1252	987	1679	2907	813	1431	555	562	1263	18	6541	9339	23	-
Ice	14	93	310	190	51	16	31	78	119	-	301	1	99	101	80	-	3
Ir	207	552	777	442	613	1465	412	434	434	319	386	309	264	143	50	223	85
It[f]	23419	19467	25	16566	10177	2730	16457	10527	19	98	61	40	32	23	31	36	-
Lux	-	-	-	-	-	-	-	-	-	-	-	-	-	-	-	-	-
Neth	584	7	14	247	6	309	57	24	215	118	29	39	58	9	24	207	96
Nor[g]	11	318	138	25	63	7	104	28	281	6	104	1031	13	83	17	139	3
Port[h i]	-	-	-	309	-	493	533	750	456	651	270	382	113	198	387	147	-
Sp[j]	1081	1749	12593	16642	11551	18917	6178	5154	2788	4417	6358	2428	5114	11839	3740	2613	4537
Swe	12	58	25	87	37	29	4479	209	2	37	31	683	15	797	410	770	22
Swi	-	3	20	5	5	2	6	0	1	4	1	0	-	1	0	4	0
UK[k]	7197	14750	3284	10142	9405	29474	11964	4266	5313	3754	27	1920	3546	3702	4128	1903	761

Notes: a) Excl. disputes in which less than 100 workdays lost. b) Excl.localised strikes (following a call to strike from within the establishment) in agriculture and public administration: prior to 1977 excludes all disputes in agriculture and public administration. c) The series relates to the territory of the Fed. Rep. of Germany before 3.10.1990. d) Incl. work stoppages lasting less than one day only if more than 100 work-days not worked. e) Computed on the basis of an average number of work-hours per day. f) Prior to 1983: days not worked computed on the basis of a 7-hour working day; from 1983: work-hours not worked. g) Excl. work stoppages lasting less than one day. h) Prior to 1986: strikes only. i) From 1986: excl. Madeira and the Azores; firms with less than 5 workers. j) From 1986: excl. Catalonia; from 1986: excl. the Basque country. k) Incl. disputes lasting than one day only if more than 100 working days lost: prior to 1983: excl. political strikes; from 1983: incl work stoppages involving less than 10 workers only if more than 100 work-days not worked .

Source: ILO, various years

5. Science and Technology, R&D and Innovation

Daniele Archibugi and Jonathan Michie[1]

It is generally considered that advances in science and technology are one of the main factors underlying countries' international competitiveness and growth of productivity, output and employment.[2] However, despite efforts made in recent years, economists have yet to produce sufficient evidence of how exactly this role is played. Related to this are the problems involved in attempting to collect reliable information about science and technology (S&T). 'Knowledge' is more difficult to measure quantitatively than are variables such as employment, income or trade. The measurement of technological change has received increasing attention since the 1970s, but a number of problems remain unresolved. To measure S&T we are forced to rely on proxies of time-series and/or cross-sectional variations in the phenomena we wish to measure (innovations in selected countries, industries, firms or technological fields). Technological indicators are the tip of the innovative iceberg; insofar as there is a clear relationship between the visible and hidden part of the iceberg, they may be useful measures.

This chapter looks at indicators which allow international comparisons to be made. Since the 1960s, a major effort has been made by international organizations such as the OECD and UNESCO to produce standard methodologies. Each of the resulting indicators do, however, have their drawbacks and differ in the closeness of their links with economic performance. Some of them, such as trade in high technology products, are a direct expression of the relationship between technology and economic performance. Others such as the resources devoted to scientific research or the number of articles in scientific journals are less directly linked to the economic process. Table 5.1 reports the strengths and weaknesses of the following five indicators reported in this chapter: resources devoted to R&D; the technology balance of payments (TBP); patenting; trade in high technology products; and bibliographic indicators.

---

[1] We are grateful to Mario Pianta and Giorgio Sirilli for their assistance in the preparation of the material reported in this chapter.

[2] On productivity, see Salter (1966), Nelson (1981), and Baumol *et al.* (1989). On employment see Freeman and Soete (1987). On international competitiveness see Soete (1981), Hughes (1986), and Fagerberg (1988). And on growth rates see Denison (1967), and Fagerberg (1987).

1. R&D

Information on the level or resources devoted to formal scientific and technological research activities is given by R&D data. This reports monetary values (the amount of financial resources spent) and human resources (the number of researchers and employees in the R&D sector) and also gives information on the scientific and technological activities performed in both the public and business sectors. This distinction is less relevant for the ex-planned economies, but is crucial for the OECD economies, where the resources for R&D come from both government and business.

Since the end of the 1960s international organizations – such as the OECD (OECD, 1981) and UNESCO (Sirilli, 1980) – have gathered data annually on expenditure and number of researchers broken down for countries and branches of economic activity (see Tables 5.2–5.5). While R&D data are available for most industrial countries in national currencies, to make international comparisons it is necessary to express these in a common measure. The OECD produces regular statistics on R&D expenditure expressed in constant dollars and Purchasing Power Parities (PPPs). An alternative is to calculate the ratio of R&D expenditure to Gross Domestic Product. Another method, avoiding such monetary adjustments, is to consider the human resources devoted to R&D. An effort to provide internationally comparable statistics by adjusting national sources has been made by the OECD, taking account of the fact that in some countries, such as Japan, a larger number of researchers work part-time than in other countries. Thus the R&D intensity of a country can be illustrated by the ratio between the number of researchers and the population or labour force. There are additional problems with comparisons beyond the OECD. Some of the ex-planned economies, for example, had substantial resources devoted to R&D, both in terms of researchers and as a proportion of GDP, but they were not strictly comparable with market economies since the linkage between the R&D system and the production process was much less direct.[3]

The US has a greater level of spending than that of the European Community and Japan combined, although the US share has decreased slightly (Table 5.2). The EC share fell from 31.4% to 27.9% of total OECD R&D, while Japan increased its share from 12.2% to 16.2%. (Japanese national sources tend to overestimate national expenditure in comparison to the other industrial economies; the OECD produces adjusted values which have been used here). Within the EC the share of the three largest R&D spenders – Germany,[4] France and the UK fell, and a similar fall is found for

[3] Different problems are encountered when comparing OECD economies with developing countries. Some developing countries report very low, if any, expenditure on R&D. Although this might be due partly to shortcomings in data collection, the majority of under-developed countries do not perform a significant amount of R&D. Of course, this does not imply that they do not have any technological capabilities, but only that R&D is not the appropriate indicator to measure the technological differential between developed and developing economies.

[4] The data reported here refer to the Federal Republic of Germany before unification. Data for the ex-GDR are not included.

the Netherlands and Belgium. Italy and Spain increased their shares, followed by Portugal and Greece. Outside the EC, Sweden, Norway and Finland show an increasing share of OECD R&D expenditure, while Switzerland is losing ground.

Resources devoted to R&D in absolute terms will obviously depend on the country's size and income. In order to obtain comparable information on the R&D effort of each country, Table 5.3 reports the ratio of R&D expenditure to Gross Domestic Product.

The EC as a whole has an R&D intensity, at 1.9% of GDP, substantially lower than the other two major industrial areas. Within the EC, a wide range of R&D intensities can be found. Only Germany has an R&D intensity comparable to the US and slightly above Japan. The two other largest spenders - France and the UK - devote about 2.3% of GDP to R&D (as do the Netherlands). Belgium, Denmark and Italy spend between one and two per cent of their GDP on R&D; Ireland, Spain, Portugal and Greece devote less than 1%. Two other European countries - Sweden and Switzerland - emerge amongst the most R&D intensive economies.

An important qualification of the R&D data is provided by the ratio of *civilian* R&D to GDP, shown (for 1987) in the last column of Table 5.3. As several studies have shown, military R&D is less likely to produce benefits in terms of improved national competitiveness and economic performance (see Rosenberg, 1982, 1986 and Pianta, 1988). The R&D intensity of the US is considerably lower if military R&D is excluded, and the same applies to a lesser degree for the UK and France. The highest civilian R&D intensity is found, amongst the largest spenders, in Germany and Japan, as well as in Sweden and the Netherlands.

Table 5.4 reports the average annual growth rates of R&D expenditure in real terms, showing strong growth between 1975 and 1989 in all countries. The growth rate achieved by Japan (7.4%) is substantially higher than that of the US (4.6%) and the EC (4.1%). The slowest growth occurred in European countries such as the UK, the Netherlands and Switzerland. The fastest growth rates were achieved, with the notable exception of Japan, by economies with a low R&D intensity, such as Spain, Portugal and Italy. Since countries with a low R&D intensity have generally grown faster than average, the variability of R&D intensity across OECD economies was reduced. In the same table, the growth rates of four sub-periods are shown. The highest growth was in the 1983–85 period, while in more recent years a slow-down is evident.

Although some data for the latest years are still preliminary, we appear to be entering a period of slower growth of R&D spending, in particular in the US and the UK. If confirmed, this trend would have major implications for S&T policy; the search for innovation might shift from R&D to more selective efforts for improving the comparative advantage of nations.

Innovative activities are located not only in the R&D laboratories, but also in the wider economic and social systems, involving education, managerial skills, and the diffusion of knowledge. Thus, innovative activities outside the R&D laboratories may be growing at the expenses of those carried out inside them. International agreements among firms and public research institutions may also act as a substitute for greater domestic R&D expenditure. Thus each country may try to appropriate the results of its innovations in external markets, moving from 'more R&D' to 'R&D more exploitable globally'.

Table 5.5 reports the breakdown by source of funds and the sector in which the R&D is undertaken for OECD countries in 1987. Countries where companies fund a large part of R&D would be expected to produce research results which are more directly related to the companies' activity and are more likely to be proprietary in nature. The R&D funded by the public sector, on the other hand, is generally aimed at improving national economic performance and at furthering the advancement of knowledge. In some cases, such as Switzerland, Japan and Germany, the business sector contributes more than half of the national R&D resources, but in the majority of countries its contribution is lower. In the US the business sector funds half of total R&D, but it performs more than 70%, the difference being due to government funded military and space programmes. A similar pattern is followed in Europe by France. The share of foreign funded R&D is particularly high in the UK, where it is close to 10%, reflecting the importance of research laboratories established by foreign firms.

However, the resources devoted to R&D do not represent the total amount devoted to innovation (see Rosenberg, 1976). In all sectors, and overwhelmingly in engineering, a large proportion of innovative activity takes place outside research laboratories, for example in design and planning, or in the production plants themselves. Small and medium sized firms do not have formal R&D departments but they do undertake occasional research activities (see Kleinknecht, 1987, Archibugi *et al.*, 1987). More recently, R&D has failed to take into account a fundamental part of technological change, namely that connected with software. Moreover, there is no guarantee that allotting a certain amount of resources to R&D will produce a uniform rate of innovation. Economic organisations may receive different benefits from the same level of resources devoted to R&D because of their market power, economies of scale, economies of scope, and so on. Because of the high level of uncertainty present in scientific and technological research, a linear relationship between inputs and outputs is even less likely to be present here than in other areas of economic life.

2. The technology balance of payments (TBP)

The technology balance of payments (TBP) measures transactions between firms and sectors of different countries (see Madeuf, 1984). The OECD collects statistics on the international financial flows related to technological transactions, giving an idea of the openness of a country and its dependence on technology created abroad, on the one hand, and of the internationalization of the home-produced technology on the other. Table 5.6 reports trade in technology for the OECD countries in 1988. The country with the largest surplus is the United States. Both the EC as a whole and Japan have considerable deficits.

Unlike R&D data, the TBP refers in the first instance to technology transfers with a commercial objective and thus excludes non-commercial inventive and innovative activities, such as the majority of those carried out by the public sector. Also, while R&D is more a proxy of inventive than of innovative activity, the TBP accounts for technologies sold or bought for commercial purposes, and is therefore directly linked to firms' innovative strategies. However, the TBP, by definition, provides no indication of resources devoted to innovative activity, only of the amount of technological activity internationally transferred. In other words, all those technologies which are not the object of commercial transaction are excluded. Among these are, for example, the technologies used exclusively within the producing firm, which do not therefore involve direct payments between different organizations, the technology created by non-profit organizations, and so on. Finally, the TBP does not, by definition, regard the flows of technology transferred within a country.

3. Patent statistics

Increasing emphasis is being put on patenting as a technological indicator (see the surveys by Basberg, 1987, Pavitt, 1988, Griliches, 1990 and Archibugi, 1992). Patent statistics are available in almost all industrialized countries and in many developing countries, broken down for the country of origin of the invention for which the patent is requested and for the technological category of the invention, for very detailed technological sectors. Statistics on patents are collected for administrative reasons; however they are a valuable source of information on the spatial, temporal and sectoral distribution of inventions.

A patent is a right the state grants to an inventor in return for the publication of his or her invention. It gives the inventor exclusive rights over the commercial exploitation of the invention for a limited period and with certain conditions. Patents are the outcome of the part of S&T activities which have a proprietary nature and are likely to generate business applications. In other words, patents are more likely to reflect technological rather than scientific activities. The legal provisions concerning the application for and the granting and protection of the patent vary considerably from country to country, although there has been a certain harmonisation over the last few years. The strengths of patenting data include the following: first, patents represent the outcome of the inventive process, and more specifically of those inventions which are expected to have a business impact. Second, obtaining patent protection is time consuming and costly; it is therefore likely that applications are presented only for those innovations which are expected to provide benefits which compensate the costs involved in obtaining patent protection. And third, patent applications are accurately broken down by technological classes by independent external examiners;

this provides internationally comparable information on sectoral patenting up to the five digit level of disaggregation.

However, there are limitations of patenting as a technology indicator: first, not all inventions are patented; often firms protect their innovations by industrial secrecy or other appropriability methods. Second, not all inventions are technically patentable; this is the case for software, which is playing an increasingly important role in technological advance. Third, the propensity to patent (that is the amount of patents registered for each unit of inventive and innovative activity, see Scherer, 1983) varies greatly across technological areas. While in pharmaceuticals, for example, a large part of the outcome of the inventions are codified in patent applications, in other equally S&T intensive fields, such as nuclear technology, only a minority of inventions are actually patented. Fourth, firms have a different propensity to patent in each national market, according to their business expectations regarding the possibility of exploiting their inventions. The size of national markets and the level of integration in international trade affects the number of foreign patent applications received by each country. Moreover, each patent office receives an over-represented number of applications by domestic inventors and firms. And fifth, in spite of the international patent agreements among the majority of industrial countries, each national patent office has its own institutional characteristics; the attractiveness for applicants of any patent institution depends on the nature, costs length and effectiveness of the protection accorded.

Table 5.7 reports the share of patents registered during the 1980s in five patent offices: the European Patent Office, Japan, Germany, France and the US, according to the country of origin of the applicant. The data are aggregated over several years to avoid random fluctuations. Each patent office receives applications from both national and foreign investors, although the proportion varies significantly from country to country. Countries with low S&T budgets have generally a restricted internal market, and are not particularly attractive to foreign inventors. In large countries there are a great number of foreign applications. The institutions which receive a large number of foreign patents are also those which are better suited to providing international comparisons on countries' technological activities. The technical importance of patents and their economic impact varies widely, and the absolute numbers of patents registered do not provide entirely reliable information on the quality and impact of patented innovations. It is well known that the quality and impact of patents are highly skewed; while few patents have an important economic impact, many of them are never used. Several attempts have been made to obtain information on the quality and impact of single patents. Schankerman and Pakes (1986), for example, took into account the money spent on renewal fees to assess the value of each patent. Another method of obtaining information on the impact of a patent is to consider the number of times a patent is cited in subsequent patents. A well cited patented invention is likely to be associated with important innovations.

The European Patent Office (EPO) was founded in 1978 by 13 European countries: Austria, Belgium, France, Federal Germany, Greece, Italy, Liechtenstein, Luxembourg, the Netherlands, Spain, Sweden, Switzerland and the UK. Nine of these countries are also EC members. This patent office is the only one in the world to be truly international, since a single application can potentially be extended in all the 13 member countries. Total applications at the EPO have grown from 11,000 in 1979 to nearly 50,000 in 1989, 48% of which came from EC countries, while 55% came from EPO member countries.

The US has the largest share of patents, at 26%. Although the US ranks first, its share of patents in the European market underestimates the US technological potential as measured by inventions registered in the US domestic market. The share of Germany at the EPO is close to that of the US at 23%. Third comes Japan, which, even in the European market, has a 16% share, much higher than France (9%) or the UK (7%). The share of patents held by European countries at the EPO is obviously larger than their share in the US. However, the ranking of the shares held by European countries in both institutions is very similar, as the European and the US markets have similar economic attractions for all. The most notable exceptions are the UK, whose share of patents is greater than France in the US but smaller at the EPO, and Sweden, which ranks 6th among countries in the US, but is overtaken by the Netherlands at the EPO. Both the UK and Sweden are countries with close trade and cultural links with the US.

The institutional nature of the Japanese Patent Office is substantially different from those of the other advanced countries, since it asks inventors to split into several applications the different technical aspects related to the same invention. It differs also in the procedures adopted to evaluate applications as indicated by the fact that only one third of the applications receive a patent.[5] Applications in the Japanese patent system are mainly the outcome of national inventors and firms, which account for nearly 90% of the applications and for more than 83% of the patents granted.

In France and Germany the average number of patent applications directly filed at the national offices has been steadily eroded by the growth of the applications at the EPO. However, the EPO did not erode the number of domestic applications, and this allows the differences between domestic and foreign patenting for France and Federal Germany to be considered. Table 5.7 shows that domestic investors account for 71% of the applications in Germany and for 56% in France. In France, the US share is higher than the Japanese one, while in Germany the share of Japanese patents is higher than that of the US.

[5] In the US almost two thirds of applications are granted a patent and at the EPO more than 80%.

Table 5.8 reports some basic data on the changing pattern of patenting activity in advanced countries. The average growth rates of domestic patents during the 1980s (that is patents registered by residents in their own country) is reported in column 1, showing that the number of patent applications has not grown significantly. In 8 countries a negative rate of change has occurred, while in another three countries growth rates below 2% have taken place. This steady pattern in domestic patenting should be compared to the rates of change of R&D inputs shown above. In spite of the slow-down after 1985, R&D expenditure grew at a faster rate than domestic patents. Some authors (for example Evenson, 1984) have related the slow-down in domestic patent applications to a decreasing productivity of scientific and technological research. The decrease of domestic patents, however, is also likely to be related to an awareness by the applicants of the opportunities offered by the patent system; the slow or negative growth rate is generally associated with a decreasing number of applications presented by individual inventors, which have, on average, a lower probability of becoming actual innovations.

The greater the resources devoted to S&T, the more we might expect firms to try to appropriate the benefits of their innovations in several markets. Thus, the total number of foreign patents (that is patent applications filed by foreign applications in a given country) has significantly increased in all OECD countries (column 2 of Table 5.8). Although applications registered by foreigners in each country have grown, differences across countries have emerged. In many small and medium sized European countries - including Greece, Austria and Spain - a double-figure growth rate has occurred. Markets at the periphery of international competition seem to become the targets for companies expanding their activities, and many firms with a largely domestic orientation will face an increasing challenge from foreign competitors. Japan is again a significant exception: the extensive penetration by Japanese firms of Western technology markets has not been paralleled by an equally widespread presence of Western companies in the Japanese market: the growth rate of foreign patent applications has been relatively moderate, and much below the growth rate of domestic applications.

Information on the internationalization of technology markets is provided by the share of external applications (that is the applications presented by firms and inventors of each country in other countries), reported in column 3 of Table 5.8. All countries show rapidly growing efforts to patent abroad to earn returns from their inventions in foreign markets. Among the largest countries Japan ranks first. The divergent trends in the growth rates of domestic and foreign patent applications suggest that the reduction in the volume of domestic applications has principally affected those inventions with less certain business potential. This evidence is consistent with the findings of research which shows that, although the number of patents granted in selected European countries has declined, the money spent on renewal fees has not.

Columns 4 and 5 of Table 5.8 report the ratio of external to domestic patents for 1979 and 1988. This has increased considerably in all countries. Two different factors have contributed to this: a rise in the average number of countries in which each patent extended abroad is registered and an increase in the number of patents which are extended abroad. While there is a general trend towards the internationalization of patenting, significant cross-country differences do emerge. In 1988, the ratio was particularly high for R&D intensive small and medium sized countries, such as the Netherlands (7.9), Switzerland (7.6), Belgium (7.0), Sweden (6.5) and Denmark (6.4). Countries which have a small internal market are to some extent forced to appropriate the results of their innovations in foreign markets. Larger countries, on the other hand, have a weaker propensity to extend their patented inventions abroad. The US and the UK have a lower ratio than the other advanced countries. Japan is the only OECD country, besides Greece, which has a ratio below unity: for any three domestic applications, there is only one application abroad. This result is partly an institutional artefact, since the Japanese patent system does not allow the same application to include different technical aspects of the same invention, inducing inventors to multiply their applications in the domestic market. However, it also indicates Japan's as yet unexploited technological potential.

Table 5.9 reports the world's patents by geographical area, broken down by domestic (that is the applications presented by residents in their own country) and foreign applications (that is applications presented by foreigners in a given country). Total national applications are the sum of the two, i.e. the number of applications received by each patent office. Table 5.9 shows how innovative potential is highly concentrated in the OECD countries, while developing countries produce a very low share of world innovations.

We assume that it is an advantage to hold a higher share of patents in sectors which are growing faster than average. To assess the position of individual countries, we report two measures of the relationship between the number of patents in the fast growing classes and the overall number of patents granted to each country: first, the share of patents held by each country in the 'fast growing' quartile, and second, a specialization index (calculated for the aggregate of the fast growing classes), that is the ratio of the country's share of patents in the fast growing classes to its share of total patents. The results are reported in Table 5.10.

It is worth remembering that not all inventions or innovations are patentable. There are many inventions and innovations for which it is not possible to get a patent. One typical case is the Coca-Cola formula, but the same is true of software, as well as almost all organizational innovations. Also, not all inventions or innovations are actually patented. Firms often feel that their inventions and innovations are better protected by secrecy than by patents.[6] Shepherd (1979) has argued that:

---

[6] On the effectiveness of the various appropriability methods see Wyatt *et al.*, 1985, and Levin *et al.*, 1987.

> patents are a notoriously weak measure. Most of the eighty thousand patents issued each yearare worthless and are never used. Many are of moderate value, and a few are bonanzas. Still others have a negative social value. They are used as 'blocking' patents to stop innovation, or they are simply developed to keep the competition out.

However, this should not be taken as negating the usefulness of patents as technological indicators: first, while it is true that many patents are never used, the same applied to R&D expenditure – many R&D projects do not become actual innovations. Second, while it is also true that the economic impact of patents is highly skewed (see Napolitano and Sirilli, 1990), this is due to the uneven economic impact of inventive and innovative activities. Third, the negative social value of patents reflects the nature of the innovative activity itself. Finally, it is also true that patents are often used in firms' competitive strategies, but this does not prevent them from representing a technological capability of the firm.

Although countries have subscribed to many agreements on industrial property rights which should give equal rights to the patented inventions of each country, there are still basic differences across countries on the costs, form of examination, time of registration and legal protection accorded by patent laws. This implies that the propensity to register and, above all, to extend abroad a patent is affected by the existing legislation and practice in each country. The propensity to extend a patent abroad is also affected by economic, cultural and linguistic factors. Firms and individual inventors have an interest in extending their patentable inventions in those countries where there is a stronger economic partnership (measured, for example, by trade flows). A comparison between, say, the Italian and German technological capacity may therefore be made by considering the patents extended by these two countries in a third country which is equally significant to them, for example the United States.[7]

4. Trade in High Technology Products

The analysis of trade in terms of products grouped according to technological content raises a number of issues over how to distinguish the high, medium and low technology products. In most studies the technological intensity of products is obtained by relating a variable of innovativeness to one referring to economic activity. In general the variables used are research and development expenditures on the one hand and turnover or value added on the other. Products for which a large share of the revenue or value added is invested in R&D are defined as high technology products; when the ratio falls below a threshold value the products are considered of intermediate technological level, and below a lower threshold the rest are taken as low

---

[7] Many empirical studies have been devoted to the determinants of the propensity to patent (see for example Scherer, 1983, Levin *et al.*, 1987, Wyatt *et al.*, 1985, Winter, 1989).

technology products. This approach has a number of limitations: research intensity and technological intensity are not necessarily equivalent concepts; the data on which the intensity ratios are based are not uniform; the choice of threshold values for high, medium and low technology is arbitrary; product groups are generally too broad, and the technological intensity can vary greatly within them; and the intensity ratios take no account of technologies indirectly acquired with machinery and materials. Moreover, they are intrinsically static (taking no account of the accumulation of scientific and technological know-how over time). However, three broad categories which reflect R&D intensity relative to production are identified in Table 5.11. Highly R&D intensive industries are aerospace, computers, electronics, pharmaceuticals, scientific instruments and electrical machinery. As Table 5.11 shows, these sectors account for a growing proportion of manufactures exported by all OECD countries, and Table 5.12 shows countries' shares of these exports.

An alternative approach to high technology products has recently been proposed (see Amendola and Perrucci, 1991). Instead of relying on the R&D intensity of each industry, high technology products were identified according to the classification made by independent experts and engineers. Nearly 250 product classes were included in the high technology category. This 'bottom-up' approach leads to a somewhat more restrictive classification of high-technology, and has almost halved the share of high-technology products in the total volume of international trade.

Table 5.13 reports the data for the EC member countries broken down by 8 main sectors. Germany emerges as the European leader in technology markets, with very high shares in sectors such as automated machine tools (64.5%) and electrical and electronic instruments (40.6%).

5. Bibliometric indicators

Finally, 'scientific' activities can be proxied using bibliometric indicators. Publication of research results is one of the main aims of scientific activity, but teaching and other activities of applied research, not leading to scientific publications, are also important parts of the scientific enterprise. In order to describe and investigate the characteristics of scientific activity, a variety of bibliometric indicators have been developed, aiming at measuring the quantifiable aspects of scientific literature. These indicators, developed from a growing number of databases, have been used as output indicators of scientific activity in countries, sectors and institutions. A large literature has described the nature of scientific publications and citations. The main indicators of scientific activity are the number of papers, and the number of citations they receive from other papers.

While the number of citations a paper has received is a useful indicator of its impact on the scientific literature, it is not an adequate measure of the quality of scientific work. Several factors, including the constraints of dominant scientific paradigms, the underestimate of applied studies and the lack of content evaluation, limit the reliability of this indicator, which tends to reduce the complexity of scientific research (see Lindsey, 1989). Particular caution is therefore needed in the evaluation of citation data.

The available bibliometric databases consider a subset of world publications, selected in a variety of possible ways. The database used for this chapter was developed by CHI Research, using data from the Science Citation Index of the Institute for Scientific Information. Articles, notes and reviews published by a number of important international journals are considered. A first database includes bibliometric data from 1973 to 1984 drawn from a constant set of 2100 scientific and technical journals, which were selected in 1973. A second database includes data from 1981 on, based on a set of 3081 journals chosen in 1981. Annual data for all countries on the number of publications, the number of citations received from later papers, and the citations to previous papers are available in both databases; all these indicators refer to publications appearing in the fixed journal set.

It should be stressed that this database, however large, represents only a subset of the world's scientific literature (and the same applies to any other existing database). The database is dominated by English-language journals and in the SCI database biomedical sciences are highly represented because it was originally developed to provide information on publications in these areas. To avoid annual fluctuations in the data, and to ensure a substantial number of cases even in the most disaggregated sectoral distribution, the 1973 journal set annual data series has been grouped into two periods, 1973–78 and 1979–84. The data of the 1981 journal set have been grouped in a single period of 1981–86 for the same reasons. An analysis of the changes over time in the patterns on scientific activity is therefore possible for the first database. Three sets of data for number of papers and number of citations are used in this analysis: 1973–78 data based on the 1973 journal set; 1979–84 data based on the 1973 journal set; and 1981–86 data based on the 1981 journal set. The percent distribution among countries of world papers and paper citations in the three databases is shown in Table 5.14, together with the average number of citations per paper.

These data provide an overview of the relative importance and pattern of change of the countries considered; national shares, however, reflect the characteristics of the database, where English language journals account for a disproportionate share of all publications. The US accounts for 37.1% of all papers and 52.6% of the citations included in the database in both the 1973–79 and the 1979–84 periods. In the second database, the US shares fall slightly to 35.8% and 50.6%. EC countries show a remarkably stable pattern, with about 26% of all papers and 25% of citations in all periods; the largest contribution comes from the UK, whose share fell from around 9.1% in 1973–78 to 8.3% in 1981–86; Germany and France show a slight fall in the number of papers and an increase in their share of citations; Italy, starting from a very low level, increases. Japan, on the other hand, expands its share of world papers from 5.6% in 1973–78 to 7.3% in 1981–86, and its citations grow from 4.2% to 5.8%. The remaining OECD countries have a generally stable pattern. The US has the most cited papers in all periods, but it is followed closely by Switzerland (especially in the latest data), Sweden, Denmark, the UK and the Netherlands. The EC aggregate is further behind, but over time it moves closer to the world average.

The fall in British scientific output has been the subject of much debate, including over the appropriateness of the database used here to assess countries' positions (see Martin *et al.*, 1987, Leydersdorff, 1988, Braun *et al.*, 1989 and Irvine and Martin, 1989). Recent analyses seem, however, to confirm the validity of the CHI Research data base for international comparisons.

Bibliography

Amendola, G. and Perrucci, A. (1991), 'European Patterns of Specialization in High-Technology Products: A New Approach', mimeo.

Archibugi, D. (1989), *The Sectoral Structure of Innovative Activities in Italy. Results and Methodology,* Ph.D. thesis, University of Sussex, Brighton.

Archibugi, D. (1992), 'Patents as Indicator of Technological Innovation', *Science and Public Policy,* vol. 17, no. 6.

Archibugi, D., Cesaratto, S. and Sirilli, G. (1987), 'Innovative Activity, R&D and Patenting: The Evidence of the Survey on Innovation Diffusion in Italy', *Science Technology Industry Review,* No. 2, pp. 135-150.

Archibugi, D. and Michie, J. (1994), 'The Globalisation of Technology: A New Taxonomy', *Cambridge Journal of Economics*, forthcoming.

Archibugi, D. and Pianta, M. (1992), *The Technological Specialization of Advanced Countries,* Dordrecht: Kluwer, and Commission of the European Communities.

Basberg, B. (1987), 'Patents and the Measurement of Technological Change: a Survey of the Literature', *Research Policy,* vol. 16, nos. 2–4, pp. 131–141.

Baumol, W.J., Blackman, B.S.A. and Wolff, E.N. (1989), *Productivity and American Leadership: The Long View,* MIT Press, Cambridge (Mass.).

Braun, T., Glanzel, W. and Schubert, A. (1989), 'Assessing Assessments of British Science: Some Facts and Figures to Accept or Decline', *Scientometrics,* vol. 15, nos. 3–4, pp. 165–170.

Cantwell, J. (1989), *Technological Innovation and Multinational Corporations,* Basil Blackwell, Oxford.

Chi Research - Computer Horizons (1989a), *Technological Activity and Impact Indicators Database,* (Tape Data 1975 through 1988), Haddon Heights data user manual.

Chi Research - Computer Horizons (1989b), *Science Literature Indicators SP 2 Subfield Citation Tape 1973–1984 and 1981–1986,* Haddon Heights, data user manual.

Denison, E.F. (1967), *Why Growth Rates Differ*, Brookings Institute, Washington, D.C.

Dosi, G., Freeman, C., Nelson, R., Silverberg, G. and Soete, L. (eds) (1988), *Technical Change and Economic Theory*, Frances Pinter, London.

European Patent Office (various years), *Annual Report*, EPO, Munich.

Evenson, R.E. (1984), 'International Invention: Implications for Technology Market Analysis', in Griliches (ed.), 1984.

Evenson, R.E. (1989), *Patented Data: Evidence for Declining R&D Potency?*, Yale University, New Haven.

Fagerberg, J. (1987), 'A Technology Gap Approach to Why Growth Rates Differ', in Freeman, C. (ed.) (1987).

Fagerberg, J. (1988), 'International Competitiveness', *Economic Journal*, vol. 98, pp. 355–374.

Freeman, C. (1982), *The Economics of Industrial Innovation*, Frances Pinter, London.

Freeman, C. (1987), *Technology Policy and Economic Performance. Lessons from Japan*, Frances Pinter, London.

Freeman, C. (ed.) (1987), *Output Measurement in Science and Technology*, North-Holland, Amsterdam.

Freeman, C. and Lundvall, B.A. (eds) (1988), *Small Countries Facing the Technological Revolution*, Frances Pinter, London.

Freeman, C. and Soete, L. (eds) (1987), *Technical Change and Full Employment*, Basil Blackwell, Oxford.

Garfield, E. (1979), *Citation Indexing; Its Theory and Application in Science, Technology, and Humanities*, Wiley, New York.

Griliches, Z. (ed.) (1984), *R&D, Patents and Productivity*, University of Chicago Press, Chicago.

Griliches, Z. (1990), 'Patent Statistics as Economic Indicators: A Survey', *Journal of Economic Literature*, vol. 28, no. 4, pp. 1661–1797.

Grupp, H. (1989), *The Measurement of Technical Performance in the Framework of R&D Intensity, Patents, and Trade Indicators*, FhG, Karlsruhe, mimeo.

Grupp, H. (1990), 'The Concept of Entropy in Scientometrics and Innovation Research', *Scientometrics*, vol. 18.

Hood, N. and J.-E. Vahlne (eds) (1987), *Strategies in Global Competition*, Croom Helm, London, New York, Sydney.

Hughes, K. (1986), *Technology and Exports*, Cambridge University Press, Cambridge.

Irvine, J. and Martin, B.R. (1989), 'International Comparison of Scientific Performance Revisited', *Scientometrics*, vol. 15, nos. 5–6, pp. 369-392.

Kleinknecht, A. (1987), 'Measuring R&D in Small Firms: How Much Are We Missing?', *Journal of Industrial Economics*, vol. 35, pp. 253–256.

Levin, R.C., Klevorick, A.K., Nelson, R.R. and Winter, S.G. (1987), 'Appropriating the Returns from Industrial Research and Development', *Brookings Papers on Economic Activity*, no. 3.

Leydersdorff, L. (1988), 'Problems with the Measurement of National Scientific Performance', *Science and Public Policy,* vol. 15, no. 3, pp. 149–152.

Lindsey, D. (1989), 'Using Citation Counts as a Measure of Quality in Science. Measuring What's Measurable Rather Than What's Valid', *Scientometrics,* vol. 15.

Lundvall, B.A. (1985), *Product Innovation and User-Producer Interaction,* Industrial Development Research Series, no. 31, Aalborg, Aalborg University Centre.

Madeuf, B. (1984), 'International Technology Transfers and International Technology Payments: Definitions, Measurement and Firms' Behaviour', *Research Policy,* vol. 13, pp. 125–140.

Martin, B., Irvine, J. and Hicks, D. (1987), 'The continuing decline of British science', *Nature,* vol. 330, 12 November.

Napolitano, G. and Sirilli, G. (1990), 'The Patent System and the Exploitation of Inventions: Results of a Statistical Survey Conducted in Italy', *Technovation,* vol. 10, no. 1.

Narin, F. and Noma, E. (1985), 'Is Technology becoming Science?', *Scientometrics,* vol. 7.

Narin, F. and Olivastro, D. (1987a), *Identifying Areas of Strength and Excellence in U.K. Technology,* Department of Trade and Industry, London.

Narin, F. and Olivastro, D. (1987b), *Identifying Areas of Strength and Excellence in F.R.G. Technology,* Bundesministerium für Forschung und Technologie, Bonn.

Narin, F. and Olivastro, D. (1988a), *Identifying Areas of Leading Edge Japanese Science and Technology,* National Science Foundation, Washington D.C.

Narin, F. and Olivastro, D. (1988b), *Technology Indicators based on Patents and Patent Citations,* in Van Raan, 1988.

Nelson, R. (1981), 'Research on Productivity Growth and Productivity Differences: Dead Ends and New Departures', *Journal of Economic Literature,* vol. 19, no. 3, pp. 1029–1064.

OECD (various years), *Main Science and Technology Indicators,* Paris.

OECD (1981), *The Measurement of Scientific and Technical Activities – Frascati Manual,* Paris.

OECD (1985a), *Science and Technology Policy Outlook,* Paris.

OECD (1985b), *The Semiconductor Industry Trade Related Issues,* Paris.

OECD (1990), *Report of the Technology and Economic Program,* Paris.

Patel, P. and Pavitt, K. (1987a), 'Is Western Europe Losing the Technological Race?', *Research Policy*, vol. 16, pp. 59–85.

Patel, P. and Pavitt, K. (1987b), *The Technological Activities of the U.K.: A Fresh Look,* British Association for the Advancement of Science.

Patel, P. and Pavitt, K. (1989a), *Do Large Firms Control the World's Technology?,* SPRU, Brighton.

Patel, P. and Pavitt, K. (1989b), Technological Activities in FR Germany and the UK: Differences and Determinants, *National Westminster Bank Quarterly Review*, May, pp. 27–42.

Patel, P. and Soete, L. (1988), *International Comparisons of Activity in Fast-Growing Patent Fields,* SPRU, Brighton.

Pavitt, K. (1984), 'Sectoral Patterns of Technical Change: Towards a Taxonomy and a Theory', *Research Policy*, no. 13, pp. 343–373.

Pavitt, K. (1987), 'International Patterns of Technological Accumulation', in Hood and Vahlne (eds).

Pavitt, K. (1988), 'Uses and Abuses of Patent Statistics', in Van Raan (ed.), 1988.

Pavitt, K. and Patel, P. (1989), *Technological Accumulation in France: What the Patenting Statistics Show,* SPRU, Brighton.

Pianta, M. (1988), *New Technologies Across the Atlantic: US Leadership or European Autonomy?,* Harvest-Wheatsheaf, The United Nations University, Hemel Hempstead, Tokyo.

Porter, M. (1990), *The Competitive Advantage of Nations,* MacMillan, New York.

Posner, M. (1961), 'International Trade and Technical Change', *Oxford Economic Papers*, vol. 13, pp. 323–341.

Price, D.J. De Solla (1986), *Little Science, Big Science...and Beyond,* Columbia University Press, New York.

Rosenberg, N. (1976), *Perspectives on Technology,* Cambridge University Press, Cambridge.

Rosenberg, N. (1982), *Inside the Black Box: Technology and Economics,* Cambridge University Press, Cambridge.

Rosenberg, N. (1986), *Civilian 'Spillovers' from Military R&D Spend: the American Experience since World War II,* Stanford University.

Salter, W.E.G. (1966), *Productivity and Technical Change,* Cambridge University Press, Cambridge.

Schankerman, M. and Pakes, A. (1986), 'Estimates of the Value of Patent Rights in European Countries During the Post-1950 period', *Economic Journal,* vol. 96, pp. 1077–1083.

Scherer, F.M. (1983), 'The Propensity to Patent', *International Journal of Industrial Organization,* vol. 1, pp. 107–128.

Scherer, F.M. (1984), *Innovation and Growth. Schumpeterian Perspectives,* The Mit Press, Cambridge, Mass.

Schmoch, U. and Grupp, H. (1989), 'Patent between Corporate Strategy and Technology Output: An Approach to the Synoptic Evaluation of US, European and West German Patent Data', in Van Raan *et al.* (eds).

Shepherd, W.G. (1979), *The Economics of Industrial Organization,* Prentice-Hall, Englewood Cliffs.

Sirilli, G. (1980), *Conceptual and Methodological Problems in the Development of Science and Technology Indicators,* UNESCO, Paris.

Sirilli, G. (1987), 'Patents and Inventors: An Empirical Study', *Research Policy,* vol. 16, pp. 157–174.

Soete, L. (1981), 'A General Test of the Technology Gap Trade Theory', *Weltwirschaftliches Archiv,* vol. 117, pp. 638–660.

Soete, L. (1987), 'The Impact of Technological Innovation on International Trade Patterns: The Evidence Reconsidered', *Research Policy*, vol. 16, no. 2–4, pp. 101–130.

Soete, L. (1988), 'Technical Change and International Implications for Small Countries', in Freeman and Lundvall (eds).

Soete, L. and Wyatt, S. (1983), 'The Use of Foreign Patenting as an Internationally Comparable Science and Technology Indicator', *Scientometrics,* vol. 5, pp. 31–54.

Trajtenberg, M. (1990), *Economic Analysis of Product Innovation – The Case of CT Scanners,* Harvard University Press, Cambridge, Mass.

Van Raan, A.F.J. (ed.) (1988), *Handbook of Quantitative Studies of Science and Technology,* Elsevier, Amsterdam.

Van Raan, A.F.J., Nederhof, A.J. and Moed, H.F. (eds) (1989), *Science and Technology indicators: Their Use in Science Policy and Their Role in Science Studies,* DSWO Press, Leiden.

Van Raan, A.F.J. and Tijssen R.J.W. (1990), *An Overview of Quantitative Science and Technology Indicators Based on Bibliometric Methods,* Paper to OECD Conference, Paris, 2–5 July.

Walsh, V. (1984), 'Invention and Innovation in the Chemical Industry: Demand Pull or Discovery Push?', *Research Policy,* Vol. 13, no. 4.

Weil, V. and Snapper, W.J. (eds) (1989), *Owning Scientific and Technical Information,* Rutgers University Press, New Brunswick and London.

Wheal, P.R. and McNally, R.M. (1986), 'Patent Trend Analysis. The case of Microgenetic Engineering', *Futures,* October.

Winter, S. (1989), 'Patents in Complex Contexts: Incentives and Effectiveness', in Weil and Snapper (eds).

Wyatt, S., Bertin, G. and Pavitt, K. (1985), 'Patents and Multinational Corporations: Results from Questionnaires', *World Patent Information,* vol. 7, pp. 196–212.

Table 5.1 Proxy measures of scientific and technological activity

Measure	Strengths	Weaknesses
Research and Development	* Regular data collection * Sectoral uniformity across industries * Internationally comparable	* Monetary adjustments required for international comparability * Underestimates innovation in small firms * Excludes design, software and production engineering
Technology balance of payments (TBP)	*Measure of 'disembodied' technology *Indirect measure of technological level	*Excludes technology transfers with no financial counterpart *Influenced by intra-firm policies of MNEs *Influenced by tax systems and exchange controls
Patenting	*Regular data collection *Detailed breakdown for technological fields *Internationally comparable *Direct measure of technological output	*National systems are biased by domestic inventors *Not all inventions are patented *Not all inventions are patentable *Differences in the propensity to patent across sectors
Trade in	*Measure of 'technological sophistication'	*Products identified according to R&D

high-tech products	of traded goods *Detailed breakdown of data *Indirect measure of technological level	intensities *Arbitrariness of thresholds used to distinguish between high, medium and low technology *Technological intensity vary greatly within groups of products
Bibliographic indicators: **(1) Scientific Papers**	*Detailed breakdown for scientific disciplines *Internationally comparable *Direct measure of scientific output	*Databases include a sub-set of world publications *Differences in the propensity to publish across disciplines *Language barriers
(2) Scientific citations	*Measure of impact of scientific literature	*differences in the number of citations across time and sectors

Table 5.2 Gross Domestic Expenditure on R&D
(% distribution within the OECD in 1975, 1981, 1987 and R&D expenditure in 1988 in millions of US dollars at 1988 prices and purchasing power parity exchange rates).

	Percentage distribution			**$m**
Countries	**1975**	**1981**	**1987**	**1988**
United States	49.63	48.27	49.02	137816
Japan[a]	12.18	14.62	16.22	47649
EC 12	31.36	30.22	27.91	78950
W. Germany	9.64	9.46	8.75	24626
France	6.68	6.70	6.16	17528
United Kingdom	8.17	7.54	6.10	16184[b]
Italy	2.80	2.85	3.14	10004
Netherlands	2.02	1.63	1.57	4365
Belgium	0.85	0.85	0.74	2056
Denmark	0.36	0.34	0.37	973[b]
Spain	0.65	0.61	0.79	2437
Ireland	0.10	0.09	0.10	270
Portugal	0.08	0.10	0.10	255[c]
Greece	0.02	0.07	0.09	252
Switzerland	1.41	1.14	1.02	2866[c]
Sweden	1.18	1.25	1.34	3533[b]
Austria	0.43	0.50	0.44	1258
Canada	2.23	2.37	2.26	6322
Australia	0.92	0.94	0.98	2625[b]
Finland	0.28	0.33	0.41	1204
Norway	0.37	0.36	0.40	1194[b]
TOTAL OECD	**100.00**	**100.00**	**100.00**	**283417**

Notes: Missing values have been estimated from the regression line over the 1975–89 period.
a) Data for Japan are the OECD adjusted values
b) 1987
c) 1986

Source: Archibugi and Pianta, 1992.

Table 5.3 Expenditure on R&D as a % of GDP

	Total R&D expenditure				Civil R&D
Countries	1975	1981	1987	1989	1987
United States	2.32	2.45	2.90	2.80	2.1
Japan[a]	1.81	2.14	2.67	–	2.6
EC 12	1.59	1.71	1.95	1.95	1.7[i]
W. Germany	2.24	2.42	2.83	2.85	2.7[h]
France	1.79	1.97	2.29	2.33	1.9
United Kingdom	2.18	2.42	2.27	–	1.8[g]
Italy	0.84	0.87	1.19	1.25	1.1[h]
Netherlands	2.02	1.88	2.33	2.30[f]	2.3
Belgium	1.30	1.31[c]	1.65	1.61[f]	1.6
Denmark	1.01	1.10	1.43	–	1.4
Spain	0.35	0.40	0.62	0.72	0.6
Ireland	0.85	0.73	0.94	0.94[f]	0.9
Portugal	0.27[b]	0.35[d]	0.45[e]	–	–
Greece	–	0.21	0.33[e]	0.37[f]	0.3[h]
Switzerland	2.40	2.29	2.88[e]	–	–
Sweden	1.80	2.30	2.99	–	–
Austria	0.92	1.17	1.32	1.32	1.3
Canada	1.10	1.21	1.36	1.29	1.3
Australia	1.00[b]	1.00	1.19	–	1.1[e]
Finland	0.91	1.19	1.73	1.80	1.7
Norway	1.34	1.29	1.81	1.87	1.7

Notes:) Data for Japan are the OECD adjusted values; b) 1976; c) 1979; d) 1982; e) 1986; f) 1988; g) 1985; h) Estimate (share of GDP on GERD less government defence R&D); i) Estimate
–: not available

Source: Archibugi and Pianta, 1992.

Table 5.4 Annual % rate of growth of R&D expenditure in real terms for OECD countries
(using OECD implicit GDP price indexes).

Countries	1975–78	1979–82	1983–85	1986–89	1975–89
United States	3.71	4.46	9.55	2.34	4.58
Japan	4.62	9.28	9.81	7.41[k]	7.42[o]
EC 12[a]	2.89	4.38	5.86	4.23	4.05
W. Germany	2.06[b]	2.07[d]	6.20	4.38[n]	4.25
France	2.48	6.92	4.92	4.31	4.43
United Kingdom	3.14	3.04[e]	3.59	1.23[l]	2.61
Italy	-0.06	8.82	11.74	6.60	6.10
Netherlands	0.63	1.28	4.66	3.70[k]	2.87
Belgium	4.24[b]	5.99[g]	3.49	2.20[k]	3.72
Denmark	1.91	6.53	6.97	7.37[l]	5.39
Spain	2.38	8.19	10.46	12.05	7.76
Ireland	0.50[b]	4.51	12.41	6.48[k]	4.34
Portugal	12.81[c]	4.98[g]	5.54[j]	–	7.27
Greece	–	5.79	17.05	7.30[k]	–
Switzerland	0.75	0.46[d]	11.15[h]	–	3.35[q]
Sweden	2.22[b]	12.32[d]	9.39	4.48[m]	6.20[p]
Austria	–	–	3.52	3.42	5.21
Canada	3.93	8.66	8.88	0.23	4.66
Australia	1.88[c]	3.32[e]	8.61[i]	0.74[l]	4.79[r]
Finland	4.77[b]	10.09[d]	11.34	7.19	8.32
Norway	6.43	4.02	13.00	3.31[n]	5.41

Notes: a) Where possible missing values were estimated by regression; b) 1975–77; c) 1976–77; d) 1979–81; e) 1978–81; f) 1979–83; g) 1978–83; h) 1983–86; i) 1984–86; j) 1981–84; k) 1986–88; l) 1986–87; m) 1985–87; n) 1985–89; o) 1975–88; p) 1975–87; q) 1975–86; r) 1976–87.

Source: Archibugi and Pianta, 1992.

Table 5.5 Source of funds and sector where R&D performed (1987)

Countries	Sector where R&D performed (%)				Total	Source of funds (%)			
	Business enterprise	Govern-ment	Higher Education	Private non-profit		Business enterprise	Govern-ment	Other national	From abroad
United States	72.6	10.6	14.1	2.7	100	49.5	48.7	1.8	0.0
Japan[a]	70.9	10.3	14.0	4.8	100	73.5	19.6	6.8	0.1
W. Germany	72.2	12.7	14.6	0.5	100	63.6	34.7	0.4	1.3
France	58.9	25.2	15.0	0.9	100	41.8	51.7	0.6	5.9
United Kingdom	67.0	15.1	14.2	3.7	100	49.7	38.7	2.5	9.2
Italy	57.2	22.6	20.2	–	100	41.7	54.0	–	4.3
Netherlands	59.2	17.3	21.4	2.1	100	51.8	44.3	2.0	2.0
Belgium	72.9	4.4	18.9	3.8	100	70.7	27.6	0.7	1.1
Denmark	55.6	19.4	23.9	1.1	100	48.7	45.9	2.8	2.7
Spain	57.3	26.3	15.5	0.9	100	48.8	48.5	1.1	1.5
Ireland[b]	53.6	24.3	20.8	1.3	100	48.0	43.8	1.5	6.6
Portugal	26.3	36.0	30.1	7.6	100	26.8	63.5	6.7	2.9
Greece[b]	28.6	49.8	21.6	–	100	23.2	74.4	–	2.4
Switzerland	77.7	6.3	12.8	3.2	100	78.9	21.1	–	–
Sweden	66.8	4.2	28.9	0.1	100	60.0	36.9	1.5	1.6
Austria	–	–	–	–	100	48.8	48.5	0.3	2.4
Canada	55.0	20.4	23.3	1.3	100	41.7	41.7	3.9	9.2
Australia[b]	36.5	34.9	27.1	1.5	100	35.9	60.7	2.5	0.9
Finland	58.9	20.1	20.6	0.3	100	58.8	38.9	1.2	1.0
Norway	62.0	15.8	21.2	1.0	100	50.3	46.8	1.1	1.7

Notes: a) Data for Japan are the OECD adjusted values; b) 1986.
Source: Archibugi and Pianta, 1992.

Table 5.6 Technology Balance of Payments (TBP) for OECD countries, 1988

	Receipts (x) ($ millions)	Payments (m) ($ millions)	Balance (x – m)	Export/ Import ($ millions)
United States[a]	10 735	2 048	+8 687	2.61
Japan	1 922	2 436	–514	0.79
Germany	3 794	4 532	–738	0.84
France	1 479	1 860	–381	0.80
Italy	638	1 178	–540	0.54
United Kingdom[b]	1 534	1 672	–138	0.92
Canada[b]	561	591	–30	0.95
Spain	182	1 380	–1 198	0.13
Australia	72	186	–114	0.38
Netherlands	524	962	–438	0.54
Belgium	1 265	1 811	–546	0.70
Sweden[b]	149	51	+98	2.90
Austria	59	238	–179	0.25
Denmark[b]	184	161	+23	1.14
Greece	–	13	–	–
Norway[b]	28	77	–49	0.37
Finland[b]	52	81	–29	0.64
Portugal[b]	4	33	–29	0.11
Yugoslavia[b]	6	22	–16	0.27
OECD	23 188	19 332	+3 856	1.20
Europe	9 898	14 071	–4 160	0.70
EC	9 604	13 602	–3 985	0.71

Notes: Data at current prices and exchange rates

a) Royalties and licence fees only. We have used these different types of data because they are much closer to the amounts declared by Japan, the United Kingdom and Australia, for which a cross-check was possible. Total data for the United States (royalties and licence fees plus other private services) diverge too greatly;

b) Data for the United Kingdom, Canada, Turkey and Yugoslavia are 1987 instead of 1988; for Australia, 1986; and for Finland, 1982.

Source: OECD, *Main Science and Technology Indicators* (various issues).

Table 5.7 ***Patents registered in the main patenting institutions***
(% distribution of patents registered at the EPO, in Japan, FR Germany, France and the US, by country of origin)

Countries	EP0 1980-89 applications	Japan 1979-87 applications	Japan 1979-87 granted	W. Germany 1982-87 applications	W. Germany 1982-87 granted	France 1981-87 applications	France 1981-87 granted	United States 1979-88 granted	United States 1979-88 citations
United States	25.82%	4.47%	7.86%	6.48%	13.71%	10.79%	15.54%	56.31%	59.86%
Japan	15.57%	89.42%	83.67%	9.48%	13.85%	7.36%	9.40%	16.26%	17.46%
EC 12	47.64%	4.50%	6.09%	75.75%	63.03%	74.24%	62.50%	19.47%	16.72%
W Germany	23.26%	2.28%	2.98%	71.00%	52.74%	10.58%	15.54%	9.41%	7.92%
France	8.98%	0.71%	0.99%	1.30%	3.61%	55.88%	36.03%	3.36%	2.81%
United Kingdom	7.26%	0.68%	0.90%	1.14%	2.16%	1.91%	3.49%	3.55%	3.41%
Italy	3.27%	0.27%	0.30%	1.25%	1.33%	3.10%	3.31%	1.31%	0.96%
Netherlands	3.22%	0.40%	0.70%	0.59%	1.98%	1.01%	2.58%	1.07%	1.01%
Belgium	0.90%	0.06%	0.10%	0.15%	0.29%	0.59%	0.66%	0.37%	0.34%
Denmark	0.33%	0.05%	0.09%	0.19%	0.60%	0.36%	0.31%	0.23%	0.17%
Spain	0.27%	0.03%	0.03%	0.11%	0.28%	0.76%	0.55%	0.12%	0.06%
Ireland	0.09%	a	a	0.01%	0.01%	0.03%	0.02%	0.04%	0.02%
Portugal	0.01%	a	a	a	a	0.01%	0.01%	0.01%	0.01%
Greece	0.03%	a	a	0.01%	0.03%	0.01%	0.01%	0.01%	0.01%
Switzerland	4.46%	0.52%	0.82%	2.19%	3.61%	2.05%	3.32%	1.81%	1.50%
Sweden	1.63%	0.23%	0.32%	0.67%	1.28%	0.76%	1.58%	1.16%	0.92%
Austria	1.07%	0.08%	0.12%	0.57%	1.83%	0.60%	0.49%	0.44%	–
Canada	0.91%	0.11%	0.17%	0.15%	0.33%	0.29%	0.42%	1.83%	1.50%
Australia	0.57%	0.10%	0.08%	0.07%	0.34%	0.25%	0.23%	0.47%	–
EPO countries	54.66%		-	-	-	-	-	-	-
Others	2.35%	0.59%	0.87%	5.06%	2.21%	3.66%	6.51%	2.24%	2.04%
WORLD	100%	100%	100%	100%	100%	100%	100%	100%	100%

Notes: a) Less than 0.00%. - Not available; *Source*: Archibugi and Pianta, 1992.

Table 5.8 Rates of change in domestic, foreign and external patents

Countries	Domestic Patents 1979–88	Rates of change in Foreign Patents 1979–88	External Patents 1979–88	Ratio of external to domestic patents 1979	1988
United States	2.44%	6.30%	7.50%	1.73	2.67
Japan	8.30%	3.85%	11.53%	0.25	0.33
EC 12	1.10%	9.38%	7.49%	2.06	3.90
W. Germany	0.54%	4.87%	6.79%	2.28	3.93
France	1.16%	5.95%	7.64%	2.41	4.22
United Kingdom	0.64%	5.49%	8.34%	1.37	2.65
Italy	-11.59%[a]	10.01%[a]	8.50%	1.97[b]	–
Netherlands	2.00%	10.17%	6.91%	5.18	7.90
Belgium	-1.05%	10.15%	6.38%	3.65	7.00
Denmark	3.28%	7.24%	13.47%	2.74	6.38
Spain	-0.31%	11.77%	5.06%	0.92	1.48
Ireland	8.39%	4.26%	14.12%	0.81	1.29
Portugal	-6.19%	5.33%	29.86%	0.10	1.94
Greece	-0.18%	27.88%	8.96%	0.07	0.15
Switzerland	-2.21%	9.87%	3.38%	4.60	7.58
Sweden	-2.39%	10.12%	8.56%	2.51	6.52
Austria	-0.75%	13.51%	7.44%	1.66	3.39
Canada	6.28%	2.88%	8.31%	2.83	3.35
Australia	3.26%	5.31%	17.36%	0.70	2.22

Notes: Column one refers to patents by residents of the country, column two to patents by foreigners of the country, and column three to patents by residents extended in other countries. Columns four and five refer to the average number of patent applications extended abroad for each domestic patent application.

a) 1980–88

b) 1980

– Not available.

Table 5.9 World breakdown for patents in 1980 and 1988

	Domestic Applications		Foreign Applications		Total National Applications	
	1980	**1988**	**1980**	**1988**	**1980**	**1988**
OECD countries	327222 61.5%	483723 67.7%	360310 87.7%	632873 89.2%	687532 73.0%	1116596 78.1%
Africa	3367 0.6%	5257 0.7%	7505 1.8%	11813 1.7%	10872 1.1%	17070 1.2%
Asia except Japan	3645 0.7%	18386* 2.6%	12921 3.1%	34442* 4.8%	16566 1.8%	52828 3.7%
Latin America	4936 0.9%	3713 0.5%	17742 4.3%	13435 1.9%	22678 2.4%	17148 1.2%
Eastern Europe	192205 36.2%	209595 29.1%	12370 3.0%	16563 2.3%	204875 21.7%	226158 15.7%
TOTAL	531677	720674	410859	709128	942536	1429802

* Including China, Democratic People's Republic of Korea and Republic of Korea.

Source: OECD, *Main Science and Technology Indicators* (various issues).

Table 5.10 Countries' shares of patents in fast growing sectors
(patents granted in the US for 30 out of the 118 3-digit IPC classes).

	1975–78		1985–88	
Countries	**% of total patents specialisation**	**Index of specialisation**	**% of total patents**	**Index of**
United States	25.52%	1.04	33.69%	1.01
Japan	24.19%	0.98	37.10%	1.11
EC 12	22.87%	0.93	28.50%	0.85
Germany	20.01%	0.81	27.19%	0.82
France	26.63%	1.08	34.68%	1.04
United Kingdom	25.87%	1.05	34.73%	1.04
Italy	21.63%	0.88	28.37%	0.85
Netherlands	25.51%	1.04	33.44%	1.00
Belgium	18.30%	0.74	27.68%	0.83
Denmark	27.90%	1.13	32.94%	0.99
Spain	19.15%	0.78	23.82%	0.71
Ireland	20.25%	0.82	40.60%	1.22
Portugal	5.56%	0.23	0.00%	0.00
Greece	19.84%	0.81	25.95%	0.78
Canada	21.88%	0.89	28.78%	0.86
Switzerland	18.06%	0.73	26.75%	0.80
Sweden	26.18%	1.06	32.29%	0.97
Australia	21.88%	0.89	25.99%	0.78
WORLD	24.60%	1.00	33.34%	1.00

Source: Archibugi and Pianta, 1992.

Table 5.11 OECD area export patterns (%)

	1963–64	**1975–79**	**1985–87**
Technological intensity			
High	14.06	16.80	22.57
Medium	39.17	43.83	44.06
Low	46.77	39.37	33.37
Total	100	100	100
Aerospace	2.57	2.28	2.86
Computers	1.30	1.91	4.30
Electronics	3.31	4.34	6.10
Pharmaceuticals	1.25	1.14	1.34
Scientific instruments	2.92	3.22	3.97
Electrical machinery	2.71	3.91	4.01
Total	14.06	16.80	22.57

Source: OECD STAN database.

Table 5.12 Exports of highly R&D intensive products: countries' rank and share

Country	1969 Rank	1969 %	1979 Rank	1979 %	1987 Rank	1987 %
Japan	3	10.05	3	12.07	1	18.16
United States	1	29.26	1	20.95	2	17.34
Germany	2	15.95	2	15.04	3	12.59
United Kingdom	4	8.70	5	7.02	4	6.52
France	5	5.77	4	7.24	5	6.41
Taiwan	15	0.55	12	2.03	6	3.82
Italy	8	4.35	7	3.99	7	3.55
Netherlands	6	5.15	6	4.09	8	3.14
Switzerland	7	4.91	8	3.93	9	3.10
South Korea	20	0.13	14	1.44	10	2.83
Canada	9	3.03	10	2.09	11	2.36
Singapore	23	0.06	15	1.38	12	2.23
Belgium	10	2.15	9	2.84	13	2.04
Hong-Kong	13	0.91	13	1.82	14	1.93
Mexico	16	0.48	16	1.31	15	1.84
Sweden	11	2.15	11	2.05	16	1.75
Austria	14	0.89	17	1.26	17	1.10
Denmark	12	1.19	18	1.25	18	1.10
Finland	19	0.15	19	0.34	19	0.44
Brazil	21	0.08	21	0.30	20	0.37
Norway	17	0.34	20	0.34	21	0.30
Australia	18	0.16	22	0.15	22	0.18
Argentina	22	0.07	23	0.06	23	0.03

Source: OECD STAN database, Paris.

Table 5.13 Market shares of high-technology exports (EC Trade, 1987)

	Automated machine tools	Data-processing machines	Telecommunications	Electronic consumer goods	Electronic components	Aerospace & electronic instruments and apparatus	Electrical	Chemicals	TOTAL
Germany	64.5	26.1	38.8	32.5	29.8	25.7	40.6	26.3	30.3
UK	7.5	17.7	13.8	13.5	16.1	33.6	23.4	11.3	19.1
France	3.5	14.2	15.9	12.9	21.7	28.2	12.5	20.0	18.6
Netherlands	2.0	10.0	5.9	8.9	10.7	2.8	7.3	20.2	9.8
Italy	12.2	9.2	7.3	9.4	12.6	5.4	7.6	8.0	8.4
Belgium	6.8	4.3	8.8	16.2	2.6	1.3	1.8	8.7	5.4
Ireland	–	13.9	3.3	0.3	2.0	0.5	1.1	0.9	4.0
Denmark	1.0	1.1	4.4	2.6	1.3	1.1	4.8	2.3	2.0
Spain	2.6	3.4	1.5	1.3	1.9	1.3	0.8	2.0	2.0
Portugal	–	–	0.1	2.4	1.3	0.1	–	0.2	0.4
Greece	–	–	0.2	–	0.1	0.1	–	–	0.04

Source: Amendola and Perrucci, 1991.

Table 5.14 ***Papers and citations***

(% distribution across countries of the number of papers and paper citations 1973–78, 1979–84, 1981–86).

	1973-78		1979-84		1981-86	
	Papers	Citations	Papers	Citations	Papers	Citations
United States	37.17%	52.62%	37.05%	51.60%	35.85%	50.59%
Japan	5.60%	4.21%	7.14%	5.70%	7.26%	5.85%
EC 12	26.54%	24.72%	26.00%	24.76%	26.32%	25.57%
W. Germany	6.42%	5.22%	6.18%	5.85%	6.07%	8.40%
France	5.49%	3.92%	5.14%	4.27%	4.84%	4.31%
UK	9.10%	10.67%	8.26%	8.90%	8.30%	8.24%
Italy	1.82%	1.27%	2.08%	1.57%	2.31%	1.75%
Netherlands	1.35%	1.57%	1.55%	1.75%	1.72%	1.92%
Belgium	0.82%	0.73%	0.81%	0.78%	0.87%	0.85%
Denmark	0.80%	0.99%	0.86%	0.97%	0.84%	0.92%
Spain	0.38%	0.18%	0.68%	0.36%	0.89%	0.47%
Ireland	0.19%	0.09%	0.18%	0.10%	0.17%	0.11%
Portugal	0.04%	0.02%	0.05%	0.30%	0.06%	0.03%
Greece	0.14%	0.06%	0.21%	0.90%	0.18%	0.80%
Switzerland	1.38%	1.57%	1.34%	1.76%	1.29%	1.78%
Sweden	1.58%	2.17%	1.65%	1.93%	1.68%	1.99%
Austria	0.58%	0.29%	0.55%	0.34%	0.55%	0.35%
Canada	4.30%	4.31%	4.20%	4.05%	4.14%	4.00%
Australia	1.76%	0.63%	2.01%	1.87%	2.14%	2.02%
Others	21.10%	9.50%	20.07%	7.98%	20.81%	7.87%
WORLD	100%	100%	100%	100%	100%	100%

Source: Archibugi and Pianta, 1992.

6. State Expenditure and Economic Performance

David Coates and Mette Wiggen

Political institutions play a critical role in economic performance in each major industrial nation, such that it is impossible to capture a full statistical picture of economic activity both within and beyond the EC without looking at the scale and character of state activity in each European economy in turn. It is not that the comparative statistical indicators that we have can tap the full detail and determinants of such state activity. They cannot; but what they can and do give us is a broad sense of the *trends* visible in state economic activity at this stage of capitalist development, and some indication of the *range* of state involvement in economic performance across the advanced industrial nations as a whole.

1. Problems of methodology and approach

As we approach the statistical material associated with this section of the book, we need to be aware of the procedures by which the statistics have been acquired, and of the degree to which characteristics of those procedures set limits on what we can say about the role of the state as an economic actor.

Even when taking the statistics simply as broad aggregates, the numbers that emerge depend critically on the collating institution from which they are drawn. The broad choice we face here is between data on public expenditure drawn from the International Monetary Fund and data drawn from the National Account statistics of the OECD. As Pedone and others have noted, the two sources generate figures which differ markedly, with the resulting danger that if the sources are used interchangeably, our sense of variations in government expenditure becomes seriously distorted through the artefact of different accounting systems. Pedone's calculations on the variations in the statistics from the two collating agencies are given in Table 6.1; in this instance for the year 1973 (Pedone, 1982, p. 407). They are stark enough to require that all our data come from one source or the other; and here we will rely entirely on OECD data, since the OECD national accounts give a fuller and more detailed set of aggregates than do the IMF, and since they are the product of what Pedone called a serious effort 'to assemble information on public expenditure by function' (Pedone, 1982, pp. 392–3).

But even then, if we rely on OECD figures alone, two sets of indeterminacies remain. One is a variation of figures which derives from different national practices in the gathering and classifying of statistical data.

The second indeterminacy in the figures derives from the limited range of state economic activities which are open to statistical compilation of any kind. Statistical series on government economic activity cannot do more, in the end, than chart broad changes in outlays and receipts, and those outlays and receipts are only part of the full range of government initiatives that help/hinder local economic performance. As economic actors, states do more than tax and spend. They establish legal systems, negotiate complex sets of trade relationships, establish and police codes of social interaction around production and distribution, and develop detailed policy initiatives of various sorts that touch individual industries, regions, firms, classes and consumers. The legal and trade agreements they initiate and supervise fix the broad context within which all economic activity in their areas of sovereignty goes on. The specific industrial policies on which they settle, and the broad monetary and fiscal decisions they take, put an equally potent – if more transient – general context behind all economic activity. The decisions they take about systems of ownership, the legitimacy of private rewards, the education and training of labour forces, and the rights of workers and consumers – and the balance they strike between expenditure on industry and on welfare or defence – all profoundly affect the way industries perform and economies compete. Elements of these varying policy initiatives and decisions do then surface in the figures we will examine here; but those that do are only the tip of the iceberg of state interventions that now play so central a part in European economic performance.

2. Dominant trends in State outlays and receipts

Nonetheless the figures gathered here do provide important information about trends in state economic activity.

The first is that there has been a significant and general *increase* in the scale of public expenditure in virtually all western European industrial nations since the 1960s. In every EC and EFTA economy, total government outlays as a percentage of GDP were higher in the 1980s than they had been thirty years before; and considerably so in certain cases. As Table 6.2 indicates, the average Belgian figure for total government outlays as a percentage of GDP rose by 29 percentage points over those three decades, the Danish figure rose by 30%, the Swedish by nearly 28%. The table also shows a degree of *convergence* in the totals of outlays by different European states. The range of variation in the percentage points cited here reduces slightly over the period; as the unweighted average moves from 31.09% for the EC twelve in the 1960s to 51.5% by the end of the 1980s, and as, Spain and Portugal apart, the remaining ten all cluster around the new average. The need to place exceptions into the record, however, also points to the persistence of *variations* in the size of state activity between different national economies, even within the EC twelve. Across Western Europe as a whole, the small states, relative to their GDPs, are Spain, Portugal, Switzerland, even Greece; while the big ones are Austria, Germany, the Benelux countries and the

Scandinavians. We can also see differential timings in the main periods of state expansion: with the majority of European states experiencing their greatest expansion in the 1970s, but with a significant minority (Greece, Spain and Portugal) continuing that expansion well into the 1980s, thereby narrowing the gap between the big states and the small. The full set of figures on this growth pattern in the 1970s and 1980s is given in Table 6.3.

Not all outlays by the state reflect a real call on resources by state institutions. Much of what passes in and out of state hands are transfers between sections of the population; which is why – if we are to determine the scale of the state's own presence as an economic actor – we also need to look at figures on the amount of final consumption undertaken by public bodies, to see what percentage of GDPs are actually absorbed by state institutions themselves. Figures for final consumption, for average years in three decades, are provided here in Table 6.4.

The general trends in Table 6.4 confirm what Table 6.3 also implied; an increase in the role of the state as a consumer in every EC and EFTA economy between 1960 and 1990. Over the thirty years as a whole, the big state spenders stand out clearly in that table: Sweden, Denmark, the United Kingdom and West Germany. So too do the small ones: Spain, Switzerland and Portugal. What is slightly more difficult to extract are those economies whose governmental spending expanded significantly in the 1980s and those whose general period of growth occurred in the decade before. That information is clearer in Table 6.5, where the figures on governmental final consumption are reset as index numbers, with 1978 as 100. Then the growth states of the 1980s are clearly Spain, Portugal, Finland, Norway, Greece and Italy. What Table 6.5 suggests is that there has been a convergence here too. Governments which consumed small percentages of their GDP in the 1960s (Spain, Portugal and Greece in particular) have now caught up: to put normally between 15–20% of GDP into state consumption, with the Scandinavian countries still averaging higher percentages (in the range 21–27%). The full figures for the 1970s and 1980s are given in Table 6.6.

When we turn to look at what governments chose to spend their money on, a different pattern begins to emerge. It is not easy to put a full set of reliable statistics together on all EC and EFTA countries, to give a detailed breakdown of government expenditure over time; but it can be done for seven of the major EC economies (Belgium, Denmark, France, Germany, Italy, the Netherlands and the United Kingdom). Data on military expenditure is more readily available on a wider range of states; and when these statistics are combined, the following patterns emerge.

Firstly, the priority accorded to defence expenditure differs across nation states. This difference is already clear (at least by implication) in the statistics gathered in Table 6.7 on military expenditure as a percentage of GNP in the 1980s. The weight of military expenditure in both the Greek and the US economy is starkly demonstrated there. Greece devoted 5.9% of its GNP to military expenditure in 1990, down slightly from the 7% of a decade before; and the United States devoted 5.6%, also down on the 1984 peak of 6.4%. The American figure reflects world obligations and ambitions by the leading superpower; the Greek figure reflects more local internal and external political concerns. But the legacies of earlier phases of world domination and colonial expansion are there in the data on the United Kingdom and on France. The UK recorded 5.1% and 3.9% of its GNP going to military concerns in 1982 and 1990, France recorded 4.1% and 3.6%: all to be set against German figures of 3.4% and 2.8%, and a consistent Japanese figure of 1%. These patterns are discussed more fully in a later chapter.

These patterns are even more evident when we look at the distribution of spending priorities *within* state outlays themselves. In 1980 the United Kingdom directed 11.1% of all government expenditure to the defence budget. In 1990 that figure was still 10%; against figures for Belgium of 4.5% (1985), West Germany 5.5% (1989) and even France of only 6.4% (1985). What swallowed the lion's share of government expenditure in all seven EC countries, however, was not military expenditure but spending on social security and welfare. Between 30% and 40% of the budgets of each of the seven states shown in Table 6.8 went to this heading in 1990, drowning the weight (inside the public accounts) of education spending (between 9% and 12%), health expenditure (anything from 8%–18%) and services to industry and the economy (of again, anything between 9% and 12%). The West European states differed to a degree on their military pretensions, but each of them carried a substantial social security budget, and a fairly consistent pattern of total expenditures on education and services to the economy.

Finally we need to look at the total flows of revenues that finance state expenditures of this level. We have two ways of indicating key features of those flows, as between national economies. One is to look at the total receipts that flow to governments as a percentage of GDP. As is to be expected, these mirror clearly the total outlays given in Table 6.3; but they are reproduced here for completeness – in summary form as Table 6.9, and with greater detail for the 1980s as Table 6.10. The 1980s story can also be charted in terms of government borrowing: as the size of the PSBR in Gross Domestic Product. Not all the figures on this are easily available; but those that are, are gathered in Table 6.11. They show very significant differences in net lending as between different governments, with the consistently high borrowers being the Italian State, the Irish and the Belgian.

To a UK audience that might be surprising, given the fuss made about the PSBR in the early years of the Thatcher government. More often than not, the policy debate in the UK goes on – at least in its public face – in ignorance of where the UK stands in European terms on levels of public expenditure, consumption, spending priorities and debt; with public figures prone to stress the UK's uniqueness in state spending (either as something to defend, or something to blame). But in fact, there is very little about the total flows associated with UK state expenditure which set them apart from the western

European norm. That is why Table 6.12 is particularly illuminating, demonstrating as it does that the UK is in the middle of the European pack for the scale of government outlays, a leading consumer among European states (though slowing in that role in the 1980s) and less and less out of line from the rest of Europe in terms of its borrowing requirements. Indeed, there is very little in these figures – with the possible exception of military expenditures – to lend any credence to the arguments of those blaming the volume of state expenditures in the UK for anything unique and deficient in local economic performance.

Bibliography

Pedone A, (1982), 'Public expenditure', in A Botho (ed) *The European Economy: growth and crisis*, Oxford University Press, pp. 390-408

Table 6.1 Public expenditure on various definitions, 1973 (in per cent of GDP at current prices)

	Total expenditure			Current expenditure	
	OECD-UN[a]	IMF[b]	IMF[c]	OECD-UN[d]	IMF[e]
France	43.3	37.4	23.6	39.5	35.3
Germany	45.5	30.1	15.9	41.7	27.8
Italy	45.6	42.5	32.8	41.9	36.6
United Kingdom	46.3	40.2	38.5	41.4	37.7
Spain	25.4	21.2	12.2	22.5	18.5
Sweden	51.2	29.6	–	46.9	27.4

a. General government current disbursements plus gross capital formation
b. Total expenditure
c. Government expenditure
d. General government current disbursements
e. Current expenditure

Sources: OECD, National Accounts of OECD Countries, 1976, and UN, Yearbook of National Accounts Statistics, 1978 (for first and fourth columns); IMF, Government Finance Statistics Yearbook, 1978 (for second and fifth columns); IMF, International Financial Statistics, December 1979 (for third column)

Table 6.2 Total outlays of Government as a percentage of GDP (average years)

	1960–67	1968–73	1974–79	1980–90	1960–90
Belgium	31.6	37.5	52.1	60.7	47.0
Denmark	29.1	40.1	49.1	59.0	45.7
France	37.4	38.9	43.3	50.2	43.4
Germany (West)	35.9	39.8	47.5	47.7	43.0
Greece	19.7	22.4	28.0	41.4	29.5
Ireland	31.4	38.3	45.1	–	42.5
Italy	31.9	36.0	42.9	49.1	40.9
Luxembourg	32.9	35.8	48.2	–	42.4
Netherlands	37.8	44.8	52.8	59.3	49.7
Portugal	19.6	21.5	33.0	–	30.2
Spain	–	22.5	26.8	–	29.0
United Kingdom	34.7	39.5	44.4	44.8	41.1
Austria	37.6	40.2	46.7	50.9	44.6
Finland	29.3	31.7	36.3	39.9	34.9
Norway	32.8	41.8	48.5	–	43.3
Sweden	34.8	44.3	54.4	62.7	50.3
Switzerland	19.0	22.0	29.2	30.3	25.6
USA	28.3	31.1	32.6	–	32.3
Japan	18.7	20.5	28.4	32.7	25.9

Source: OECD Economic outlook, *Historical Statistics 1960-1990*, p. 68 Table 6.5.

Table 6.3 Total outlays of Government as a percentage of GDP

	1974	1980	1981	1982	1983	1984	1985	1986	1987	1988	1989	1990
Belgium	39.4	59.0	64.2	64.2	64.1	62.8	62.5	61.8	60.1	57.7	55.7	55.2
Denmark	45.9	56.2	59.8	61.2	61.6	60.3	59.3	55.7	57.3	59.4	59.4	58.4
France	39.3	46.1	48.7	50.4	51.4	52.0	52.2	51.4	50.9	50.2	49.4	49.9
Germany (West)	44.6	48.5	49.4	49.6	48.5	48.1	47.6	47.0	47.3	46.9	45.5	46.0
Greece	25.0	30.5	35.9	37.0	38.2	40.2	43.7	42.9	44.8	45.2	46.4	50.9
Ireland	43.0	50.8	52.5	55.8	55.8	54.0	54.8	54.6	52.8	49.6	43.1	-
Italy	37.9	41.7	45.8	47.4	48.6	49.4	50.9	50.7	50.2	50.4	51.5	53.0
Luxembourg	35.6	54.8	58.5	55.8	55.1	51.8	51.7	51.0	–	–	–	–
Netherlands	47.9	57.5	59.7	61.6	62.2	61.0	59.7	59.6	60.8	58.3	55.9	55.6
Portugal	24.7	25.9	43.9	43.0	47.9	44.4	43.4	43.9	43.5	43.5	41.7	–
Spain	23.1	32.9	35.6	37.5	38.8	39.3	42.2	41.7	40.5	40.5	–	–
United Kingdom	44.8	44.8	47.5	47.0	46.7	47.3	46.2	45.2	43.1	41.3	41.2	42.1
Austria	41.9	48.9	50.3	50.9	51.2	50.8	51.7	52.4	52.7	51.1	50.0	49.6
Finland	32.0	36.6	37.5	39.1	40.3	39.8	41.6	42.2	42.2	40.0	38.2	41.2
Norway	44.6	48.3	47.9	48.3	48.4	46.3	45.6	49.9	51.1	53.7	54.6	–
Sweden	48.1	61.6	64.2	66.3	66.0	63.5	64.7	63.0	59.2	59.5	59.9	61.4
Switzerland	25.5	29.3	28.9	30.1	30.9	31.4	31.0	30.5	30.1	30.5	30.2	30.7
USA	32.2	33.7	34.1	36.5	36.9	35.8	36.7	37.1	36.8	36.1	36.1	–
Japan	24.5	32.6	33.4	33.6	33.9	32.9	32.3	32.6	32.8	32.2	31.5	32.3

Source: OECD Economic outlook, *Historical statistics 1960-1990*, p. 68 Table 6.5.

Table 6.4 Government final consumption as a percentage of GDP: average for years

	1960–67	1968–73	1974–79	1980–90	1960–90
Belgium	12.7	14.0	16.6	16.6	15.1
Denmark	15.6	20.2	24.2	26.1	21.9
France	14.4	14.8	16.9	18.8	16.5
Germany (West)	14.9	16.5	19.8	19.9	17.9
Greece	11.8	12.4	15.4	19.3	15.3
Ireland	13.0	14.6	17.7	18.2	16.1
Italy	13.1	14.0	13.9	16.3	14.6
Luxembourg	11.0	11.4	14.8	16.2	13.7
Netherlands	14.1	15.5	17.3	16.5	15.9
Portugal	12.2	13.3	14.1	15.4	13.9
Spain	8.5	9.5	11.4	14.5	11.4
United Kingdom	16.9	17.7	20.5	20.8	19.2
Austria	13.3	14.8	17.4	18.6	16.3
Finland	13.2	14.9	17.5	19.8	16.7
Norway	14.4	17.4	19.6	19.8	17.9
Sweden	17.5	22.0	26.2	27.7	23.7
Switzerland	10.1	10.7	12.7	13.1	11.8
United States	17.5	18.3	17.7	18.2	17.9
Japan	8.0	7.8	9.7	9.6	8.8

Source: OECD Economic Outlook; *Historical Statistics 1960-1990*, p. 66 Table 6.2.

Table 6.5 The growth of government final consumption expenditure (at constant prices) 1978-1990 (1978 = 100).

	1978	1980	1985	1990
Belgium	100	104.0	105.6	106.9
Denmark	100	110.4	119.2	122.3
France	100	105.6	119.4	133.1
Germany (West)	100	106.1	112.2	119.8
Greece	100	106.1	126.6	139.0
Italy	100	105.2	120.7	134.2
Netherlands	100	103.4	108.3	113.8
Portugal	100	114.9	130.1	160.5
Spain	100	108.5	129.7	175.3
United Kingdom	100	103.7	107.8	115.9
Austria	100	105.7	115.4	120.9
Finland	100	108.2	131.0	154.6
Norway	100	109.2	133.3	149.0
Sweden	100	107.1	116.8	125.3

Source: OECD National Accounts 1978–1990, Paris 1992.

Table 6.6 Government final consumption as a percentage of GDP

	1974	1980	1981	1982	1983	1984	1985	1986	1987	1988	1989	1990
Belgium	14.7	17.8	18.6	18.0	17.5	17.0	17.1	16.8	16.2	15.2	14.5	14.3
Denmark	23.4	26.7	27.8	28.2	27.4	25.9	25.3	23.9	25.2	25.7	25.5	25.2
France	15.4	18.1	18.8	19.3	19.5	19.6	19.4	18.9	18.8	18.5	18.0	18.0
Germany (West)	19.3	20.2	20.7	20.6	20.2	20.0	20.1	19.9	20.0	19.7	18.9	18.4
Greece	13.8	16.4	18.0	18.3	18.8	19.5	20.4	19.4	19.6	20.0	20.5	21.2
Ireland	17.2	19.9	19.9	19.8	19.3	18.7	18.6	18.8	17.7	16.4	15.3	15.7
Italy	13.8	14.7	16.0	16.0	16.4	16.3	16.4	16.2	16.7	16.9	16.7	17.3
Luxembourg	11.5	16.7	17.4	16.4	15.8	15.4	15.7	15.7	16.9	16.3	15.9	16.3
Netherlands	16.2	17.9	17.8	17.7	17.5	16.6	16.2	16.0	16.4	15.8	15.3	14.8
Portugal	14.1	14.5	15.0	14.9	15.1	15.0	15.5	15.4	15.2	16.0	16.1	16.7
Spain	10.0	13.3	13.9	14.1	14.6	14.4	14.7	14.7	15.1	14.8	15.2	15.2
United Kingdom	20.0	21.2	21.8	21.7	21.7	21.5	20.8	20.8	20.3	19.7	19.4	19.9
Austria	15.8	18.0	18.5	18.9	18.9	18.6	18.9	19.0	18.9	18.5	18.2	18.0
Finland	15.2	18.1	18.7	19.0	19.4	19.4	20.4	20.7	20.8	20.1	19.7	21.1
Norway	18.3	18.8	19.1	19.4	19.4	18.6	18.5	19.8	20.7	21.0	21.0	21.0
Sweden	23.4	29.1	29.4	29.3	28.7	27.8	27.6	27.2	26.5	25.8	25.9	27.1
Switzerland	11.6	12.7	12.7	13.0	13.4	13.4	13.3	13.1	12.8	13.0	13.1	13.3
United States	18.1	17.6	17.5	18.4	18.4	18.0	18.4	18.7	18.6	18.3	17.9	18.3
Japan	9.1	9.8	9.9	9.9	9.9	9.8	9.6	9.7	9.5	9.2	9.2	9.1

Source: OECD Economic Outlook; *Historical Statistics 1960–1990*, p. 66 Table 6.2.

Table 6.7 Military Expenditure as a percentage of GNP

	1981	1982	1983	1984	1985	1986	1987	1988	1989	1990
Belgium	3.4	3.3	3.2	3.1	3.0	3.0	2.9	2.7	2.5	2.4
Denmark	2.5	2.5	2.5	2.3	2.2	2.0	2.1	2.2	2.1	2.0
France	4.1	4.1	4.1	4.0	4.0	3.9	4.0	3.8	3.7	3.6
Germany (West)	3.4	3.4	3.4	3.3	3.2	3.1	3.1	2.9	2.8	2.8
Greece	7.0	6.8	6.3	7.1	7.0	6.2	6.3	6.4	5.7	5.9
Ireland	1.8	1.7	1.5	1.5	1.5	1.6	1.4	1.4	1.3	1.3
Italy	2.1	2.1	2.1	2.2	2.2	2.1	2.3	2.3	2.3	2.1
Luxembourg	1.1	1.0	1.1	1.0	0.9	0.9	1.1	1.1	1.1	1.1
Netherlands	3.2	3.2	3.2	3.2	3.1	3.1	3.1	3.0	2.9	2.7
Portugal	3.5	3.5	3.3	3.3	3.1	3.2	3.1	3.2	3.2	3.1
Spain	2.4	2.4	2.4	2.4	2.4	2.2	2.4	2.1	2.0	1.8
United Kingdom	4.7	5.1	5.1	5.3	5.1	4.9	4.6	4.3	4.1	3.9
Austria	1.2	1.2	1.3	1.2	1.2	1.3	1.2	1.1	1.1	1.0
Finland	1.9	2.1	2.1	2.0	1.9	2.0	1.9	1.9	1.9	1.8
Norway	2.9	3.0	3.1	2.8	3.1	3.1	3.3	3.2	3.3	3.2
Sweden	3.0	2.9	2.8	2.7	2.6	2.6	2.5	2.4	2.4	2.4
Switzerland	1.8	1.9	1.9	1.9	2.0	1.8	1.7	1.7	1.6	1.6
USA	5.7	6.3	6.5	6.4	6.6	6.7	6.4	6.1	5.9	5.6
Japan	0.9	0.9	1.0	1.0	1.0	1.0	1.0	1.0	1.0	1.0

Source: 1981-90: S.I.P.R.I Yearbook 1992, Table 7.A.3.

Table 6.8 Percentage of government expenditure directed to particular areas (1980-1990)

	Defence		Education		Health		Social Security & Welfare		Economic Service	
	1980–1990		1980–1990		1980–1990		1980–1990		1980–1990	
Belgium	4.7	4.5[a]	13.6	12.7	10.2	10.0[a]	34.9	34.5[a]	12.3	12.2
Denmark	4.5	3.5[b]	13.8	11.6[b]	10.3	8.7[b]	37.9	38.9[b]	10.9	9.7[b]
France	6.6[c]	6.4[a]	10.9	10.5[a]	17.0	18.6[a]	35.6	34.0[a]	7.0	6.9[a]
Germany	5/8	5/5[b]	10.6	9.2[b]	12.9	13.1[b]	38.9	40.5[b]	10.8	9.9[b]
Italy	3.9	3.8	11.4	10.1	13.3	11.0	31.4	31.2	15.2	12.0
Netherlands	5.6	5.0	13.7	9.9[a]	–	–	37.9	35.0[a]	–	–
UK	11.1	10.0	12.4	11.7	11.3	12.1	27.9	31.5	8.9	9.4

a = 1985 Figure
b = 1989 Figure
c = 1983 Figure

Source: OECD Historical Outlook, *Historical statistics 1960-1990*, passim

Table 6.9 ***Current receipts of governments as a percentage of GDP: average in years.***

	1960–67	1968–73	1974–79	1980–90	1960–90
Belgium	30.1	35.2	46.2	51.3	41.7
Denmark	30.1	42.5	48.3	55.6	45.0
France	37.2	38.4	40.8	46.5	41.4
Germany (West)	36.1	39.5	44.0	44.9	41.4
Greece	23.6	26.7	29.1	33.6	28.8
Ireland	27.2	33.9	35.9	–	35.3
Italy	29.7	30.8	33.5	37.9	33.5
Luxembourg	34.2	36.7	50.1	–	43.5
Netherlands	36.4	43.5	49.8	52.9	46.2
Portugal	19.5	23.0	27.6	–	27.4
Spain	18.6	22.5	25.7	–	25.5
United Kingdom	32.5	37.9	39.0	41.3	37.9
Austria	37.4	40.3	43.9	47.2	42.7
Finland	30.8	35.0	38.2	39.1	36.0
Norway	36.2	45.4	49.8	n.a	46.6
Sweden	37.3	47.6	54.4	60.2	50.7
Switzerland	23.6	26.6	32.7	34.1	29.7
USA	26.5	29.1	29.8	–	29.3
Japan	19.3	20.9	24.6	31.0	24.8

Source: OECD Historical Outlook, *Historical statistics 1960-1990*, p. 68 Table 6.6.

Table 6.10 Current receipts of government as a percentage of GDP

	1974	1980	1981	1982	1983	1984	1985	1986	1987	1988	1989	1990
Belgium	37.7	49.3	50.3	52.4	52.0	53.0	53.2	52.2	52.4	50.7	48.9	49.5
Denmark	48.4	52.2	52.1	51.1	53.6	55.5	56.5	58.3	58.8	59.1	57.9	56.1
France	38.4	44.5	45.1	45.9	46.6	47.5	47.6	46.9	47.3	46.7	46.4	46.5
Germany (West)	42.8	44.9	45.0	45.6	45.2	45.5	45.8	45.0	44.7	44.1	45.0	43.4
Greece	27.0	30.5	29.1	32.3	33.6	34.8	34.6	35.5	37.0	35.1	32.5	34.7
Ireland	35.2	38.8	39.6	41.9	43.6	43.8	43.2	43.2	43.4	44.1	40.1	–
Italy	30.6	33.0	34.1	35.9	37.7	37.5	38.1	38.8	39.0	39.3	41.1	42.2
Luxembourg	40.2	53.3	53.8	53.8	56.2	54.2	55.9	52.9	–	–	–	–
Netherlands	47.0	52.8	53.5	53.8	55.3	54.1	54.3	53.0	53.6	52.4	49.9	49.5
Portugal	23.0	31.4	33.3	35.4	37.8	37.3	35.9	37.6	36.2	38.1	38.7	–
Spain	22.8	29.7	31.2	31.4	35.3	33.2	34.2	34.7	36.4	36.2	–	–
United Kingdom	39.6	39.9	42.1	42.8	42.1	42.1	42.2	41.3	40.7	40.5	40.2	40.0
Austria	42.5	46.4	47.8	46.7	46.4	47.5	48.5	47.9	47.6	47.3	46.4	46.7
Finland	35.7	35.8	37.5	37.3	37.4	39.0	40.5	41.8	39.4	40.0	39.8	41.2
Norway	48.5	53.2	51.8	51.9	51.8	53.0	55.1	54.7	55.2	55.1	54.9	–
Sweden	48.8	56.3	57.6	58.0	59.6	59.2	59.5	60.4	62.3	61.7	64.2	63.9
Switzerland	29.7	32.8	32.8	33.3	33.9	34.7	34.4	35.0	34.5	35.0	34.1	34.2
USA	30.4	30.8	31.6	31.1	30.7	30.7	31.3	31.4	32.0	31.5	31.8	-
Japan	24.5	27.6	29.0	29.4	29.6	30.2	30.8	31.0	32.6	33.1	33.4	34.6

Source: OECD Historical Outlook, *Historical statistics 1960-1990*, p. 68 Table 6.6.

Table 6.11 Net lending of government as a percentage of GDP

	1974	1980	1981	1982	1983	1984	1985	1986	1987	1988	1989	1990
Belgium	–	−9.3	−13.5	−11.5	−11.8	−9.4	−8.9	−9.3	−7.4	−6.7	−6.5	−5.4
Denmark	+3.1	−3.3	−6.9	−9.1	−7.2	−4.1	−2.0	+3.4	+2.4	+0.6	−0.5	−1.4
France	+0.3	–	−1.9	−2.8	−3.2	−2.8	−2.9	−2.7	−1.9	−1.8	−1.2	−1.7
Germany (West)	−1.3	−2.9	−3.7	−3.3	−2.6	−1.9	−1.2	−1.3	−1.9	−2.2	+0.2	−1.9
Greece	–	–	–	–	–	–	–	–	–	–	–	–
Ireland	−7.0	−11.1	−12.2	−13.2	−11.5	−9.5	−10.7	−10.7	−8.7	−4.7	−2.3	–
Italy	−7.0	−8.5	−11.4	−11.3	−10.6	−11.6	−12.6	−11.6	−11.0	−10.8	−10.0	−10.6
Luxembourg	+5.3	−0.4	−3.5	−1.0	+2.0	+3.4	+5.3	+3.1	–	–	–	–
Netherlands	−0.2	−4.0	−5.5	−7.1	−6.4	−6.3	−4.8	−6.0	−6.6	−5.2	−5.2	−5.3
Portugal	−1.6	+5.5	−10.6	−7.6	−10.1	−7.0	−7.4	−6.4	−7.3	−5.4	−3.1	–
Spain	+0.2	−2.6	−3.9	−5.6	−4.8	−5.5	−6.9	−6.0	−3.1	−3.3	–	–
United Kingdom	−3.8	−3.5	−4.0	−2.9	−3.4	−4.0	−2.8	−2.8	−1.3	+0.3	+0.2	−1.0
Austria	+1.3	−1.7	−1.8	−3.4	−4.0	−2.6	−2.5	−3.7	−4.3	−3.1	−2.8	−2.2
Finland	+4.6	−0.3	+1.2	−0.6	−1.7	+0.4	+0.1	+0.8	−1.5	+1.3	+2.9	+1.4
Norway	+4.7	+5.7	+4.7	+4.4	+4.2	+7.4	+10.2	+5.6	+4.6	+2.3	+1.3	–
Sweden	+2.0	−4.0	−5.3	−7.0	−5.0	−2.9	−3.8	-1.3	+4.3	+3.5	+5.6	+3.8
Switzerland	–	–	–	–	–	–	–	–	–	–	–	–
USA	−0.3	−1.5	−1.1	−4.0	−4.9	−3.8	−4.2	−4.4	−3.6	−3.5	−3.1	–
Japan	+0.4	−4.4	−3.8	−3.6	−3.6	−2.1	−0.8	−0.9	+0.5	+1.5	+2.5	+3.0

Source: OECD Economic Outlook, *Historical Statistics 1960-1990*, p. 69 Table 6.7.

Table 6.12 The UK's position in European League Tables on State Expenditure (1990)

		Out of EC(12)	Out of OECD (19)
total government outlay 1960–7		4th highest	6th
total government outlay 1980–9		7th	9th
total government outlay 1960–90		8th	11th
government final consumption 1960–7		1st	3rd
government final consumption 1980–9		2nd	3rd
government final consumption 1960–90		2nd	3rd
government final consumption growth rate 1978–1990		8th	12th
Expenditure priorities:	defence	1st (out of 7)	
	education	3rd (out of 7)	
	health	3rd (out of 7)	
	social security	6th (out of 7)	
	econ. services	5th (out of 7)	
PSBR (as % of GDP):	1974	3rd	3rd
	1980	5th	6th
	1985	8th	10th
	1990	6th (out of 7)	7th (of 11)

7. The Military Economy in Europe

Paul Dunne

The second half of the 1980s and the early 1990s was a period of considerable change in the military economy in Europe and globally. The end of the Cold War removed the justification for huge expenditure on arms by the superpowers and their allies. Despite the rush by vested interests in these countries to replace the Cold War with new threats, there have been clear changes in policy. The biting economic constraints and the increasing need to use resources for other purposes suggests we should look forward to continued reductions in defence budgets. This means that the size, structure, and form of the military economy in Europe is likely to continue to experience considerable change. For many countries, the importance of the defence industrial base to their economies suggests that these changes will have important implications for their future economic and industrial performance.

This chapter looks at the changes that have been taking place in the military economy in Europe. It first discusses the changing strategic environment and the implications of these changes to provide a context for the analysis. Section 2 then discusses the sources of information accessible to those researching the subject and the problems involved in using the available measures and especially in making comparisons using such data. Section 3 considers the world trends in military spending and arms production and trade, with section 4 focusing in more detail on the developments in Western Europe. Section 5 considers the employment effects of military expenditure, followed by a discussion of arms production (section 6), research and development (section 7) and the arms trade (section 8). Section 9 then presents some discussion of conversion and the 'peace dividend'. Finally, section 10 presents some conclusions and considers the likely future of the military economy in Europe.

1. Changing strategic environment

The strategic environment in Europe has seen profound changes in recent years. The dissipation of the East–West conflict, the success of arms control negotiations, the demise of the CIS and the breakup of the Warsaw Treaty Organisation, have broken the Cold War posturing. Most countries have cut arms spending and are reviewing their force and procurement plans, as the experience of the European Fighter Aircraft (EFA) project illustrates, but they are also finding themselves in a situation characterised by greater uncertainties. Globally, the collapse of the USSR has shifted the balance of power towards US hegemony in military terms, but the burden of being the world's policeman rests heavily on an economy in relative decline. At the same time, the growing economic power of Japan and the integration of Western Europe suggests a changing international order.

It is generally agreed that the new potential threats will not require the same level of resources as were devoted to the military during the Cold War. But there remain many who argue the contrary, that it is important to maintain or develop advanced weapon production capabilities and to continue research and development projects without producing the final output, the weapon (Taylor, 1993). In addition, the vested interests within the 'military industrial complex' are continually defining new threats which, not surprisingly, require the maintenance of the present force and procurement levels and the same expensive hi-tech weaponry. This is not to say there are no real threats. The world has become an uncertain and more dangerous place for many countries. But such threats require different types of force structure and weaponry, while powerful industrial and employment lobbies are supporting elements of the old structure. At the same time, there are still weapon systems such as Trident in the UK whose role is unclear in the changing world order but whose necessity remains relatively unquestioned.[1]

Nowhere are these conflicts and contradictions more apparent than in NATO. The organisation has not folded but is in the process of creating a more global role for itself, with the development of heavily armed rapid deployment forces. The defence industries in the constituent countries are likely to argue that the weapons they have under development, especially their expensive hi-tech ones, are just what is required for these forces. Even with successful lobbying by the defence companies, however, such forces will require far less resources than those devoted to the Cold War.

All of these developments have increased the uncertainties facing the defence industrial base, and have engendered considerable changes in the military economy in Europe. In principle these changes should be beneficial, as most of the research on the economic effects of military expenditure suggest that high military spending is an economic burden. It has been found to have influenced the pattern of economic development adversely, and to have reduced the industrial competitiveness of economies in high-tech sectors. This does not mean, however, that cutting defence spending will immediately lead to improved economic performance, particularly in the short run. There are problems of structural adjustment which need to be dealt with, using the resources made available to achieve any improved economic performance (Dunne, 1990). Such problems are clearly illustrated by the experience of Russia and the other ex-Warsaw Pact countries, (Renner, 1992).

[1]See PRODEM (1993a) for a more detailed discussion.

2. Finding and Interpreting Data

There are a number of sources of information on military spending in the world. The Stockholm International Peace Research Institute's (SIPRI) *Yearbook* provides the most consistent and, given their impartiality, in some ways most reliable data. In the 1992 Yearbook (SIPRI, 1992) they do warn that though there seems to be an increase in the quantity of information provided relative to the past, with an increasing number of sources, there has been a qualitative decline and the reliability of the data has gone down. The problems caused by the changes in East and Central Europe and the uncertainties of the allocations of the costs of the Gulf War require a specific warning about the interpretation of recent figures.

SIPRI use the NATO definition as a guideline:

> 'Where possible, the following items are included: all current and capital expenditure on the armed forces, in the running of defence departments and other government agencies engaged in defence projects as well as space projects; the cost of paramilitary forces and police when judged to be trained and equipped for military operations; military R&D, tests and evaluation costs; and costs of retirement pensions of service personnel, including pensions of civilian employees. Military aid is included in the expenditure of the donor countries. Excluded are items on civil defence, interest on war debt and veterans' payments. Calendar year figures are calculated from fiscal year data where necessary, on the assumption that expenditure takes place evenly throughout the year.' (SIPRI Yearbook, SIPRI, 1992)

Other sources of data include *The Military Balance* from the International Institute for Strategic Studies, Brasseys; *Janes Yearbooks* (various), from Janes Publishing Company, London; and *World Military Expenditure and Arms Transfers,* US Arms Control and Disarmament Agency, US Government Printing Office, Washington DC. This last publication is comprehensive but care must be taken as some data suggest that they reflect government views rather than verifiable information (see for example figure for arms exports to Iraq). Relevant data are also available from NATO, the OECD, the IMF, and the United Nations.[2] Other organisations which provide information and analysis include Saferworld; Campaign Against the Arms Trade (CAAT); Oxford Research Group; Project on Demilitarisation (ProDem); BASIC; and DFax.

It is also possible to go back to the source figures in government publications to overcome the various deficiencies in the secondary sources. For an example of this approach see Scheetz (1990) on Argentina, Chile and Peru.

Despite attempts by the international organisations to provide accurate and

---

[2]Useful summaries are provided by Sivard (1989).

comprehensive data on a consistent basis, there are still considerable problems with the data that need to be borne in mind when using it. SIPRI, although impartial and careful collectors of information, cannot report other than what they can find out. Their definition of military expenditure reproduced above hints at the sort of problems involved in interpreting the data. Comparisons are particularly difficult because the authorities can lie or mislead. Items of defence spending can be put under other headings, either hidden as the UK government did with the costs of Chevaline in the 1960s, or conventions used to allocate items may simply differ across countries. It is likely that countries will differ in the way they treat such items as expenditure on military hospitals, forces' housing, pensions and education and in the way they treat conscripts and paramilitary groups, if they have them. Countries may also differ in their treatment of military infrastructure expenditures; and defence firms may benefit from general government initiatives.

To overcome some of these problems, comparisons of military spending are often based upon the military burden, which is usually measured as the share of GDP devoted to military spending. This ratio has the advantage that it does not require adjusting for differing inflation rates or population levels.

Attempts to measure and compare the employment generated by military expenditure create similar problems. It is fairly straightforward to get the direct employment effects (apart from the different conventions in the treatment of conscripts and paramilitary groups); the number of troops plus civil servants in the ministry of defence, and, in some cases, directly employed industrial labour. But to get total employment requires some estimate of indirect employment within companies and their subcontractors, together with the multiplier effects of the expenditures. Given the diversified nature of many firms any simple direct method, such as surveys of the companies, is of little use and some indirect method using macroeconomic models is needed. Where these are available the problems of making comparisons are acute.[3]

As for resources devoted to research and development (R&D), military R&D is difficult to distinguish from civil R&D, and may take place in the same companies. In the public sector, for instance in the universities, the problems are similar. It is therefore likely that the share of resources devoted to military R&D is in general underestimated. A fundamental problem in interpreting all of these indicators is that they are all measures of inputs, not output, and so there is no obvious means of judging whether any changes in effectiveness of the use of military resources have taken place. Just cutting military expenditure does not necessarily mean that there is a cut in capability.

It is clear from this discussion that there are real problems in undertaking research on the military economy in any country and that these are exacerbated when international comparisons are attempted. However, the

[3]See Dunne (1991) for a discussion of these issues and the problems involved.

problems should not be overplayed. All empirical research has similar, though maybe not such severe, problems and with care it is possible to undertake research. At the same time the importance of understanding what is happening to the military cannot be overemphasised. The next section looks at trends in world military indicators.

3. World Military Spending Trends

In 1966 world military expenditure was around $568 billion dollars in 1990 prices; by 1990 it had increased to $950 billion, an increase of 70 per cent over 25 years. Most of this was accounted for by the arms race between NATO and the Warsaw Treaty Organisation (WTO). The changes in the strategic environment with the collapse of the WTO has seen the rate of growth in world military expenditure slow down and in 1990 actually start to decline (SIPRI, 1991).

Table 7.1 shows the trends in military spending and other indicators from 1960 to 1987 for developed and developing countries. The growth in real military expenditure from 1960 to 1987 was much more marked in the developing world, although still dwarfed by the developed world in terms of absolute expenditure. This was reflected in an increasing average burden, as measured by the share of GNP devoted to military spending, for the developing countries, from 3.9 per cent in 1960 to 5.2 per cent by 1987, whereas there was a decline from 6.9 per cent to 5.5 per cent for the developed countries. Military expenditure per capita more than doubled in the developing countries over the period, while the size of the armed forces remained relatively constant and military expenditure per soldier almost trebled. The developed world saw a smaller increase in military expenditure per capita, a decline in the size of the armed forces and a doubling of military expenditure per soldier. These trends are reflected in the massive growth of arms imports to the developing world, a 36-fold increase between 1960 and 1987, and the growth in arms exports from the developed countries.

Both superpowers have since cut defence spending. US spending, which had increased rapidly in the early 1980s in line with the NATO commitment to 3 per cent growth in real terms, declined by over 5 per cent between 1986 and 1989. The USSR saw a rapid growth in defence spending in the 1980s despite growing economic problems. By 1991 the USSR no longer existed and the loose confederation of states which replaced it has been forced to reduce defence expenditures. Table 7.2 shows how between 1978 and 1988 military spending rose in real terms for both NATO and the Warsaw Pact, though more for NATO. At the same time the share of GDP devoted to military expenditure remained stable for both NATO and the WTO, though the actual share in the WTO was more than twice that of NATO, which is also reflected in the higher military expenditure per capita. Real military expenditure per capita remained relatively stable for the WTO, but increased from $557 to $763, in 1988 prices, for NATO. All of these trends were dominated by the US and the USSR.

More recently, SIPRI report that the former USSR states halved defence spending in 1992, with their military burden falling from around 10% in the former USSR to around 6% in what is now Russia. In contrast, total NATO military expenditure actually rose in 1992 in real terms, with the figure for NATO (Europe) falling but only by 2.9% from the previous year. This suggests that Western military expenditure still remains high relative to the former USSR despite the cuts that have taken place. This certainly suggests potential for further cuts.

As regards the arms trade, the period saw an increase in NATO imports and a slight reduction in exports, while the WTO reduced its imports and increased its exports. The US saw a large increase in imports and exports, though the absolute level of imports remained relatively low. These trends do not show the underlying dynamics, with increasing competition from intermediate producers, such as Brazil and Israel, and the desperate push for arms exports by the eastern European and ex-CIS economies, making the international arms market increasingly competitive (Anthony *et al,* 1990).

4. Military Spending Trends in Western Europe

Western Europe has a combined GDP close to the US and a larger population. As Table 7.3 shows, European NATO countries, including France, spend just under 60 per cent as much on the military as the US, though Europe's expenditure, relative to the US, has increased over the last twenty years. In the early 1980s NATO did have a commitment to an annual 3 per cent growth for member countries' military expenditure in real terms. However, as the figures show, only the US and the UK really met that commitment. The average annual growth over the period 1980–87 was in fact just under 2 per cent, with spending levels then stabilising and then in 1990 starting to decline.

Military Expenditure in Europe is dominated by France, Germany and the UK, who spend almost 70 per cent of the total for all European NATO countries. In 1973 it was Germany that had the highest spending of the three, but by 1983 their expenditures had converged, with the UK slightly ahead of the others. The reduction in UK military spending in the mid-1980s left France, with a continued increase in spending, as Europe's highest military spender. Overall, although there were increases in expenditure between 1983 and 1991, the pattern for most countries was one of growth to the mid-1980s and then a general decline in constant price military spending in the late 1980s.

There are numerous problems in making such absolute comparisons (as discussed above) and the picture is rather different if we look at the share of military spending in GDP. If we ignore the special cases of Greece and Turkey, whose military gov ernments maintained high military spending, then Table 7.4 shows the US and the UK to have the highest military burdens. The pattern for the European NATO countries shows the average military burden increasing in the early 1980s followed by a relatively sharp decline in the late 1980s. There is some variation in the speed of reduction across countries but the pattern is generally consistent, with the most marked changes being seen in the UK and US.

Table 7.5 shows that the US spends more than twice as much on procurement of major weapons systems as all European NATO countries put together, including France. It also indicates that while the real military expenditure in France and Germany was of similar magnitudes to the UK, the UK had much the highest procurement expenditure. Again the pattern over time shows a general increase in the early 1980s and a general decline in expenditure in the late 1980s. Indeed, the pattern is more pronounced for procurement expenditure than for general military expenditure, which made the effect of the declining expenditure on the defence industrial base more marked.

5. Employment Effects of Military Spending

Table 7.6 gives the figures for direct employment as a share of the working population. Although there are problems with the treatment of conscripts in these figures, they show a wide variation across countries, with a general decline over the period. In 1980 the highest were France and Norway with just under 1.5 per cent and the lowest Japan with 0.3 per cent. This military-related employment tends to be more highly skilled than the average. By 1988 all countries had reduced the share of the working population directly employed by military expenditure. Japan was still by far the lowest, with the US and Belgium now the highest, as a result of smaller falls than the other countries.

These estimates only give the direct employment effects and, as discussed above, finding the total effects requires considerable further work. The measurement of the indirect employment effects will require individual country studies usually involving some form of modelling. Not surprisingly this makes comparisons very difficult

Table 7.7 gives some idea of the relative magnitudes of military-related employment.[4] The findings reported in the Table were based upon various forms of static input-output models, except for Sweden which used survey techniques. To provide a basis for comparison, the figures for military expenditure in each study were translated into US dollars and then deflated by the US GDP deflator for 1980. The fairly large differences for some countries between the IISS figures for military expenditure and those of the studies, largely reflected definitional differences. The figures showed a wide dispersion in the number of jobs supported by military expenditure; the number of jobs per one billion US dollars being highest in France and lowest in Sweden.

These results suggested that military expenditures supported around 4 per cent of the labour force. While this is not a particularly high proportion the

---

[4]From Dunne (1991), which is one of the few attempts to provide a consistent comparative analysis.

studies also showed that the effects were concentrated around particular industries and regions. As expected, the higher the burden of military expenditure, the higher was the share of the labour force dependent on it. In addition, the countries with the highest burdens also have employment shares higher than their expenditure shares, possibly reflecting changes in the nature of military expenditure as it increases. Care is needed in interpretation, however, as these differences might reflect variations in the success of the studies in measuring indirect employment, rather than any fundamental differences across countries.

6. Arms Production

The changing international environment has led to considerable changes in the structure of arms production in Europe. The drive of technology towards more complex and expensive systems has challenged the ability of national economies to support major players. While the changing relation between military and civilian technology (see below) has led to new competition from civil producers, there is limited regulation of the arms producers internationally and the trend is towards a reduced role for the state in many countries. Although arms production is not covered by the Treaty of Rome, these developments are underpinned in the EC by the Independent European Policy Group (IEPG) Action Plan announced in 1986, which is intended to remove the protectionist policies in national arms markets. It is not intended to create a free market, but to allow 'balanced' access to markets. This has spurred the restructuring of the industry in Europe (Brzoska and Lock, 1992). More recent developments have seen the IEPG being absorbed into the Western European Union (WEU) as the institutional architecture of Europe continues to develop and it attempts to develop an alternative security agenda.

As Table 7.8 shows, the major arms producing companies in Europe are highly concentrated within the UK, France and Germany and the developments above have led to increasing concentration and a marked restructuring. As Table 7.9 shows, there has been a growth of cross border mergers, and international takeovers. This is a relatively new phenomenon and is a response to the increasing uncertainties of the market, with cuts in procurement and the anticipation of further cuts, and partly a response to the Single European Market. The international arms market has become increasingly competitive with an increase in intermediate producers and some switch in patterns of demand away from hi-tech equipment. In addition, as former WTO countries have tried to sell weapons for hard currency, often at bargain prices, they have squeezed out less sophisticated weapons. This 'cascadence' has increased pressures in the arms market in particular for marginal and intermediate producers. These developments, as well as having security implications, have influenced the pattern of development of the arms companies. A further development has been the growth of cross share ownership and the creation of new companies by the defence giants to integrate production and research and development. This is shown in Table

7.10, which also illustrates the formation of transnational defence companies, as East Asian companies become involved (Walker and Willett, 1993).

These changes mean that the introduction of competitive procurement policies in countries such as the UK, have actually led to the creation of monopolies for certain military equipment. Companies failing to secure contracts have collapsed, restructured, merged or been taken over, and potential competition has been removed. Monopoly has been the dialectical result of the introduction of competition.

As regards future prospects, the differing economic situations and the differing forms of defence industrial base within the main producers mean that the effects of the cuts and restructuring are likely to differ across countries. Germany is likely to suffer least, given its strong industrial and technological capacity, while France is likely to retain a high level of government involvement to maintain its industry (Walker and Willett, 1993). The UK is the most vulnerable, with a weak technological and industrial base and government policies biased towards introducing competition (Dunne and Smith, 1992). Also, British companies tend to be poorly placed for change relative to their main competitors. For example DASA is very strong in civil markets compared to BAe and Thomson CSF is stronger than GEC in civil electronics.[5]

7. Research and Development

There is considerable debate over the effects of defence R&D on innovation, technological development and hence on economic growth. On the one hand military R&D can provide a stimulus to innovation, with important spin-offs to the civilian sector. On the other it can take resources away from civilian R&D without providing benefits to the civil economy. It is most likely that the role of R&D is historically specific. During wars it is likely to provide innovations, and certainly after the second world war there were a number of important civilian innovations that came from defence, such as transistors, semiconductors and computing (though one can never say what the opportunity cost was). In general, however, it has been the countries with limited military R&D that have advanced faster, economically and technologically. Indeed, it would appear that civilian technology is actually leading military technology, with 'spin-in' becoming increasingly important. Many advanced weapons systems are relying on civil production for advanced components. There are some exceptions, such as stealth technology, but the dominant trend is towards a dependence on civil innovation, or at least a limiting of freedom to pursue technologies where there is no civil connection (Markusen and Yudken, 1992).

Table 7.11 shows an irregular distribution of government funded defence R&D among the six largest R&D spenders in the OECD. In 1990 the US was by far the largest spender on military R&D. It allocates some 13 per

---

[5]Renner (1992) and the collection in Brzoska and Lock (1992) provide detailed country studies.

cent of its defence budget to R&D, a figure which reflects a growth of 80 per cent between 1980 and 1990, mainly due to the Strategic Defence Initiative (SDI). Despite some cuts in the late 1980s the US defence R&D still remains high, four times as high as the total for the other countries in 1990. At the other extreme, Japan has by far the smallest allocation of R&D resources to defence, which is not surprising given its commitment to limiting its military spending to less than 1 per cent of GDP. In 1990 just over 5 per cent of government R&D spending was military related in Japan, only 0.02 per cent of GDP.

The UK, France, and Germany all spent about the same amount on defence in absolute terms, but the expenditure patterns for R&D are very different. The share of GDP devoted to R&D was considerably higher in Germany, but the share of defence R&D was considerably lower than both France and the UK. Only 13.5 per cent of government R&D was defence related in Germany, while the figures for the UK and France were 44 per cent and 40 per cent respectively. In addition, in the UK and France nuclear R&D is an important element of the high military R&D expenditure.

Between 1967 and 1988 there is some evidence of a slight increase in industry-financed R&D as a share of GDP in most countries. In the late 1980s there does seem to have been a decline in defence R&D as a share of GDP allocation to R&D, but rather less than expected given the cuts in spending. There is also some evidence that, while the Cold War arms race may be over, the dynamic of weapons development may be continuing (PRODEM, 1993b).

8. The Arms Trade

In looking at the arms trade it is important to take care in interpreting the figures. Not only may they be misleading if countries wrongly report the destinations, or use 'middlemen' countries, or, as with the Iraqi supergun affair, do not export as weapons, but also because the figures are very lumpy. If we look at year on year changes the pattern will be dominated by a small number of large arms sales. Further problems are created by the use of offset arrangements and barter in arms sale agreements between countries (for example the UK's Al Yamanah agreement with Saudi Arabia).

To overcome this problem of lumpiness Table 7.12 reports the exports of major weapons for the periods 1981–85 and 1986–91. This shows that between these two periods arms exports fell globally by 7 per cent. In fact the averaging hides a marked general decline towards the end of the 1980s. All of the individual European countries saw a reduction in arms exports apart from Sweden, while total European arms exports fell by around 12 per cent. Intra-European trade held up better, falling by about 9 per cent, indicating that the main reduction in demand came from the 'other world' category. It is worth emphasising that these SIPRI data are measures of the volume of weapons transferred, not the amounts paid. The value of transfers is almost impossible to discover because of elements of aid and credit as well as offsets and countertrade.

Arms exports are important to the European defence industrial base as Table 7.13 shows. For many of the largest defence contractors, exports make up a majority of their sales. It is also clear that arms exports to the US are more important than transfers within Europe for many of the contractors, particularly for UK firms, and that exports outside Europe are important. There are, however, some noteworthy exceptions, with a minority of companies heavily dependent on their domestic markets.

This is consistent with the changing international environment and economic situation of potential importers. The World Bank and IMF are pushing for reduced military burdens in debtor countries and many countries have reduced their orders of equipment from the industrialised countries. It is likely that these trends will continue. Indeed, it is also likely that the market will become increasingly competitive, as former WTO countries fall back on arms exports in desperation, and intermediate producers develop their facilities.

It is also important to emphasise that the arms trade is not as profitable to an exporting country as it might appear. Arms production is highly subsidised by national governments, particularly in the development costs, while the market is highly competitive. Once a country has produced a weapons system it will sell at close to marginal cost, writing off most of the fixed costs. Thus most exports carry high hidden subsidies. The reduction of national procurement has led companies to intensify their efforts to export despite declining markets and attempts to support diversification.

9. Conversion and the Peace Dividend

It is clear that the military economy in Europe is changing. At present there seems little economic benefit or 'peace dividend' being attained, and little in the way of coherent policies on conversion to aid the restructuring taking place by reducing its economic and social costs. Despite the restructuring there are no major examples of conversion by the European defence contractors. They have tended to diversify, but this has generally meant rationalisation and acquisition rather than any shift in production resources (Renner, 1992). This is a situation that should not be allowed to continue as, given the developments discussed above, it is likely to have large economic costs.

Most research suggests that with political will large cuts in defence spending can be undertaken. There will be problems of structural adjustment, but these are little different to those presented by any declining industry. The availability of the resources released by the cuts in military spending mean that it is possible to ease the costs of adjustment. Certainly with compensatory policies, reductions in military expenditure can represent an opportunity rather than a cost (Dunne and Smith, 1984; Dunne and Willett, 1992).

It is necessary for national policies to address the effects of reduced military spending on industrial structure, on individual companies, and on the labour force. The regional distribution of defence spending is also important, as in many countries there is an inequitable distribution of defence spending to wealthier regions. A further consideration is the specific impact on local communities which may be dependent upon defence installations, factories or shipyards.

These issues have a European dimension and it will be necessary to develop EC policies and institutions to replace the anarchic restructuring that is taking place at the moment. The Independent European Programme Group (IEPG) has attempted to take the lead in unifying the European armaments market, with suggestions of 'juste retoure' rather than free market liberalisation. Yet this is simply a debate over how to adjust the market rather than how to have a planned adjustment to lower arms production and to achieve a peace dividend. The EEC and WEU will also need to sort out defence production and procurement in the context of broader regulatory issues created by dual use technologies. If the opportunity is not to be lost, some change of attitude and direction is necessary (Lovering, 1993).

10. Conclusions

The changing international environment has led to considerable cuts in military expenditure and has resulted in the restructuring of the military economy in Europe. This chapter has identified some of these changes and has attempted to assess their general policy implications. The first consideration in undertaking any research on military spending is to get to know your data and the reliability of the sources. There are reliable sources of data on the military industrial complex, but care has to be taken in interpreting them, and even more care when making comparisons.

From the data presented in this chapter, it can be seen that world military expenditure, in relation to GDP, is indeed on a downward path, though the gradient should not be overstated, nor should one underestimate the potential for vested interests to level off the path. Nevertheless, there is likely to be a reduced demand for arms while competition within the international arms market is increasing. Such trends mean that the defence industry in Europe needs to restructure, yet within the EC restructuring has taken place in something of a policy vacuum. There has been little attempt to convert to civilian production, while diversification has tended to be by rationalisation or acquisition, rather than by transferring resources. The national governments which have tried to introduce competition have found themselves faced by monopolists in certain areas as contractors have folded and been taken over. The decline in military related employment has caused considerable problems in countries with already high unemployment rates. Certain local regions dependent on defence have been particularly hard hit.

This all seems a far cry from the expectations of a 'peace dividend', but is the result of a failure to recognise the importance of planning the structural adjustments precipitated by the cuts in military expenditure. The evidence suggests that military expenditure is an economic burden and that in the long run there can be benefits to cuts in military expenditure. The problem is that the evidence for improved economic performance always assumes a reallocation of expenditures and implicitly assumes some form of policy to aid structural change. The failure to develop such polices, both at national and international level is likely to be costly.

It is also important to recognise the strength of the military related vested interests within Europe. There have been a number of cases in which the development of unnecessary weapons systems has been maintained, such as the European Fighter Aircraft; and the dynamics of the Cold War arms race is still apparent in R&D. Advanced weapons systems are sold abroad and then it is argued that development needs to be continued to keep ahead. Such arguments are supported by suggesting that cuts are leading to a 'peace penalty' or a negative peace dividend. Yet it is clear that with agreements on arms control and, in particular, controls on the arms trade, the continued development of weapons of mass destruction would be unnecessary and the potential for cuts in military expenditure greater. The recent Konver programme where EC funds are provided to aid conversion shows awareness but fails to recognise the problems of plant conversion. What is needed is a European industrial policy to aid structural adjustment, reallocate resources, retrain skilled workers, and reorientate science and technology away from the military. In this way, rather than allowing a specialised European defence cartel to develop, a broader industrial/technological base capable of satisfying civilian needs and the diminishing defence requirements could be created. Such developments could provide a genuine 'peace dividend', both regenerating European manufacturing industry and making the world a safer place in which to live.

Bibliography

Anthony, I., Allebeck, A.C. and Wulf, H. (1990), *West European Arms Production*, SIPRI.

Brzoska, M. and Lock, P. (eds) (1992), *Restructuring of Arms Production in Western Europe*, SIPRI, Oxford University Press.

Cusack, T.R. (1991), 'The Changing Contours of Government', *FIB Papers*, Wissenschaftszentrum Berlin Für Sozialforschung Veröffentlichungsreihe der Forschungsgruppe Internationale Beziehungen, Berlin, Germany.

Deger, S. and Sen, S. (1990), *Military Expenditure: The Political Economy of International Security*, SIPRI, Oxford University Press.

Dunne, P. (1990), 'The Political Economy of Military Expenditure: An Introduction', *Cambridge Journal of Economics*, Vol. 14, No. 4, Dec, pp. 395–404.

Dunne, P. (1991), 'Quantifying the Relation of Defence Expenditure to Employment', Chapter 2 in Paukert, L. and Richards, P. (eds) (1991) *Defence Expenditure, Industrial Conversion and Local Employment*, International Labour Office, Geneva.

Dunne, P. (1993), 'The Changing Military Industrial Complex in the UK', *Defence Economics*, Vol. 4, No. 2, March.

Dunne, P. and Smith, R. (1992), 'Thatcherism and the UK Defence Industry', Chapter 5 in Michie, J. (1992), *1979–92 The Economic Legacy*, Academic Press.

Dunne, P, and Smith, R. (1984), 'The Economic Consequences of Reduced UK Military Expenditure', *Cambridge Journal of Economics*, Vol. 8, No. 3, September 1984, pp. 297–310.

Dunne, P. and Willett, S. (1992), *Disarming the UK: The Economics of Conversion*, Discussion Paper No. 2, Centre for Industrial Policy and Performance, University of Leeds.

Hartley, K. (1991), *The Economics of Defence Policy*, Brasseys, London.

IISS (1992), *The Military Balance 1992–3*, International Institute for Strategic Studies, Brasseys.

IISS (1992), *Strategic Survey*, International Institute for Strategic Studies, Brasseys.

Lovering, J. (1990), 'Military Expenditure and the Restructuring of Capitalism: The Military Industry in Britain', *Cambridge Journal of Economics*, Vol. 14, No. 4, Dec. pp. 453–468.

Lovering, J. (1993), 'After the Cold War: The Defence Industry and the New Europe', Chapter in P. Brown and R. Crompton (1993, forthcoming), *The New Europe? Economic Integration and Social Exclusion*, University of London Press.

Markusen, A. and Yudken, J. (1992), *Dismantling the Cold War Economy*, Basic Books.

PRODEM (1993a), *The Triumph of Unilateralism: The Failure of Western Militarism*, The New Militarism Briefings, No. 1, Project on Demilitarisation, March 1993.

PRODEM (1993b), *Militarism versus Disarmament – Challenging the New Arms Race*, The New Militarism Briefings, No. 2, Project on Demilitarisation, forthcoming July 1993.

Renner, M. (1992), *Economic Adjustment After the Cold War: Strategies for Conversion*, UNIDIR, Dartmouth Publishing Co.

Scheetz, T. (1990), 'The Evolution of Public Sector Expenditures: Changing Political Priorities in Argentina, Chile, Paraguay and Peru', *Journal of Peace Research*, Vol. 29, No. 2, May, pp. 175–190.

SIPRI (various years), *SIPRI Yearbook*, Stockholm International Peace Research Institute, Blackwell.

Sivard, R.L. (1989), *World Military and Social Expenditures 1989*, World Priorities, Washington DC.

Smith, R.P. (1990), 'Defence Procurement and Industrial Structure in the UK', *International Journal of Industrial Organisation,* No. 8, pp. 185–205.

Southwood, P. (1991), *Disarming Military Industries*, Macmillan.

Taylor, T. (1993), 'West European Defence Industrial Issues for the 1990s', *Defence Economics*, Vol. 4, No. 2, March.

Walker, W. and Gummett, P. (1989), *Britain and the European Armaments Market*, International Affairs.

Walker, W. and Willett, S. (1993), 'Restructuring the European Defence Industrial Base', *Defence Economics*, Vol. 4, No. 2, March.

Willett, S. (1991), *Defence Expenditure Trends and R&D*, Mimeo, Centre for Defence Studies, King's College, London.

Table 7.1 Military Expenditure for Developed and Developing Countries

	1960	1970	1980	1987
Military Spending (1986 US $ billion):				
World	372	559	681	866
Developed	344	497	574	722
Developing	28	62	107	144
Military Spending as a Percentage of GNP:				
World	6.5	5.9	5.1	5.5
Developed	6.9	6.2	5.2	5.5
Developing	3.9	4.7	4.6	5.2
Military Spending per capita (1986 US $):				
World	131	158	157	176
Developed	379	492	524	631
Developing	15	25	33	38
Armed Forces per 10,000 persons:				
World	617	583	566	532
Developed	1117	1031	928	896
Developing	400	414	448	424
Military Expenditure per Soldier (1986 US $ thousand):				
World	20.1	26.0	27.1	32.5
Developed	33.9	47.7	56.5	70.5
Developing	3.3	5.6	7.2	8.8
Arms Imports (1986 US $ billion):				
World	2.4	5.9	34.7	47.2
Developed	1.3	2.0	8.2	11.3
Developing	1.1	3.9	26.5	35.9
Arms Exports (1986 US $ billion):				
World	2.4	5.8	34.6	47.4
Developed	2.3	5.6	33.3	44.6
Developing	0.1	0.2	1.3	2.7

Source: Sivard (1989).

Table 7.2 ACDA Figures for NATO and WTO; US and USSR

	1978	1988
Military Expenditure (1988 US $ million):		
NATO	317100	467300
WTO	316800	358600
US	183500	307700
USSR	268000	299800
Share of GNP		
NATO	4.1	4.8
WTO	11.3	11.0
US	4.9	6.3
USSR	12.5	11.9
Military Expenditure per capita (1988 US $):		
NATO	557	763
WTO	856	898
US	824	1250
USSR	1023	1047
Armed Forces per thousand persons:		
NATO	9.3	9.1
WTO	14.1	13.2
US	9.3	9.1
USSR	14.9	13.6
Imports (1988 US $ million):		
NATO	3459	5695
WTO	4299	3665
US	202	725
USSR	1847	1100
Exports (1988 $m)		
NATO	19570	18540
WTO	21160	24040
US	10750	14300
USSR	17970	21400

Source: US Arms Control and Disarmament Agency (ACDA) (1990).

Table 7.3 Military expenditures in millions of US $ at 1988 prices and exchange rates

	1973	1983	1991
Canada	5932	8534	9699
US	208391	258828	264383
Belgium	3484	4323	4026
Denmark	1798	2342	2256
France	25513	34252	36403
FRG	30714	34054	34268
Greece	2091	3128	3078
Italy	12270	14708	18711
Luxembourg	38	64	89
Netherlands	5403	6497	6368
Norway	1882	2656	3083
Portugal	1733	1099	1416
Spain	4673	6738	6674
Turkey	1337	2393	3870
UK	26729	34981	34008
Eur NATO	117665	147235	154250
%USA	56	57	58
Austria	845	1426	1340
Finland	1116	1726	2107
Sweden	4199	4253	4250
Switzerland	2627	2926	3109
Japan	15899	22400	31083

Source: *SIPRI Yearbook*, various years.

Table 7.4 Military expenditure as a share of GDP

	1973	1983	1990
Canada	1.9	2.1	2.0
US	6.0	6.5	5.6
Belgium	2.8	3.2	2.4
Denmark	2.1	2.5	2.0
France	3.8	4.1	3.6
FRG	3.5	3.4	2.8
Greece	4.1	6.3	5.9
Italy	2.9	2.3	2.1
Luxembourg	0.8	1.1	1.1
Netherlands	3.3	3.2	2.7
Norway	3.1	3.1	3.2
Portugal	6.0	3.3	3.1
Spain	4.1	2.4	1.8
Turkey	4.9	4.8	4.9
UK	4.9	5.1	3.9
Eur Nato	3.6	3.4	3.0
Nato	3.6	3.6	3.1
Austria	1.0	1.3	1.0
Finland	1.4	2.1	1.8
Ireland	1.4	1.5	1.3
Sweden	3.6	2.8	2.4
Switzerland	2.0	1.9	1.6
Japan	0.8	1.0	1.0

Source: *SIPRI Yearbooks*, various years.

Table 7.5 Procurement expenditure 1988 US $ million

	1982	1986	1991
Canada	1405	1887	1579
USA	51493	78219	63415
Belgium	611	548	310
Denmark	390	301	358
France	7878	8850	9101
FRG	6533	7082	5715
Greece	583	498	704
Italy	2540	3122	3272
Luxembourg	1.5	2	4
Netherlands	1344	1346	1038
Norway	499	588	699
Portugal	59	73	115
Spain	1180	1593	999
Turkey	271	496	711
UK	8307	9270	6791
NATO	83095	113875	94811
Eur NATO	30197	33769	29817
%US	59	43	47
EC	29427	32685	28435

Source: *SIPRI Yearbooks*, various years.

Table 7.6 Direct Military Employment as a percentage of the population of working age

	1973	1983	1987
Canada	0.58	0.49	0.48
US	1.59	1.36	1.33
Belgium	1.44	1.37	1.33
Denmark	1.15	0.93	0.85
France	1.53	1.31	1.20
FRG	1.23	1.12	1.11
Italy	1.18	0.96	0.97
Netherlands	1.32	1.00	0.99
Norway	1.40	1.38	1.29
UK	1.01	0.88	0.85
Austria	0.79	0.99	1.07
Finland	1.13	1.10	1.05
Sweden	1.37	1.22	1.23
Switzerland	–	–	–
Japan	0.31	0.30	0.29

Source: Cusack (1991).

Table 7.7 Comparison of the effects of military expenditure in seven industrialised countries

	Canada	France	Fed. Rep. of Germany	Norway	Sweden	United Kingdom	United States
IISS military expenditure figures (US $ billion)	5.2	23.9	15.5	1.3	3.9	23.9	122.3
Years of study	1981	1981	1976	1978	1980	1981	1979
Military expenditure from studies (1980 US $ billion)	4.6	17.5	18.4	1.6	5.9	22.8	133.5
Industrial employment (thousand)							
Direct	105.8[a]	–	837.0[b]	46[e]	18.0	330.0	–
Indirect	120.5	–	121.0	35	18.0	270.0	–
Total employment		451.0		81			1844.2[c]
Total overall	226.3	1105.0[d]	959.0	1442	138.0	1134.0	4810.3
Jobs per US $ billion	48.8	63.1	52.2	50.6	23.3	49.7	36.0
Jobs as per cent of labour force	1.9	4.6	3.5	5.6	3.4	4.3	4.5
Military expenditure as per cent of GDP	1.8	4.0	3.3	2.9	3.3	5.0	5.6

Notes: Billions referred to in this table are thousand millions.
a) Total direct employment. b) Total direct employment composed of 152,000 direct industrial and 685,000 public sector employment. c) Private sector employment. d) Total including conscripts and gendarmerie (896,000 if they are excluded). e) Total direct employment (no. of person years) including officers and conscripts.

Source: Dunne (1991) which also contains comparative information

Table 7.8 Top 40 European defence contractors in 1989 (ECUM, 1989)

Rank/companies	Country	Arms sales	% of total sales
1 British Aerospace	UK	5535	42
2 Thompson CSF*	France	3760	78
3 Daimler-DASA	FRG	3710	48
4 GEC	UK	2691	20
5 Aerospatiale	France	1985	44
6 Dassault	France	1930	78
7 DCN	France	1810	100
8 Rolls Royce	UK	1361	32
9 GIAT	France	970	100
10 STC	UK	930	25
11 Selenia	Italy	922	75
12 Ferranti	UK	908	68
13 Aeritalia	Italy	871	55
14 Matra	France	780	65
15 SNECMA	France	770	40
16 VSEL	UK	671	100
17 Lucas	UK	630	20
18 Philips	Netherlands	625	3
19 Siemens	FRG	590	2
20 Augusta	Italy	585	80
21 Dlehl	Germany	561	45
22 Finbreda	Italy	538	84
23 Smiths Industries	UK	528	52
24 Westlands	UK	498	80
25 Thorne EMI	UK	474	10
26 Rheinmetall AG	FRG	461	36
27 Dassault	France	450	77
28 GKN	UK	396	13
29 Racal	UK	389	17
30 Dowty	UK	379	36
31 HSA	Netherlands	372	95
32 RVI	France	365	7
33 Fiat Aviazone	Italy	356	60
34 Hunting	UK	345	32
35 SNIA-BDP	Italy	324	20
36 Krauss, Maffei	FRG	232	50
37 CASA	Spain	320	50
38 Sextant	France	320	37
39 Fincantieri	Italy	304	25
40 Shorts	UK	283	90

Source: Eurostrategies, 1991.

Table 7.9 International takeovers in the European arms industry 1989–1990

Buyer company companies	**Country of buyer**	**Seller company**	**Country or of seller**
Alcatel	France	ACEC Space, Defence and Telecom.Division	Belgium
Astra	UK	MARC	Switzerland
Astra	UK	Poudriere Reunie	Belgium
Bombardier Inc.	Canada	Short Brothers plc	UK
Diehl	FRG	BGT	USA
Dowty	UK	Palmer Chenard Industries	USA
Elsag	Italy	Bailey Controls	USA
Nobel Industries	Sweden	Philips Elektronik	Netherlands
Plessey	UK	Leigh Instruments	Canada
SNECMA	France	FN Moteurs	Belgium
SABCA	Belgium	Dassault Belgique	France/Bel
Siemens	FRG	Plessey	UK
Thompson CSF	France	HSA	Netherlands
Thompson CSF	France	Ocean Defence Corporation	USA
Thompson-CSF	France	Philips MBLE Def	Netherlands
Thompson-CSF	France	Link Miles	UK
Thompson-CSF	France	Ferranti Sonar Division	UK
Thompson-Brandt	France	Forges de Zeebrugge Armaments	Belgium
GIAT	France	Fabrique Nationale (and part of Baretta)	Belgium
Aerospatiale	France		
Alcatel	France	Parts of Space Systems Loral	USA
Selenia	Italy		
MAN	Germany	Steyr-Daimler-Puch	Austria
Sauer	Germany	Sundstrand-Sauer Co	USA
Fincantieri	France		
Bremer	Germany	Sulzer Diesel AG	Switzerland
Vulcan AG	Italy	Ferranti Italiana	UK
Finmeccanica	Italy	Ferranti Italiana	UK
Finmeccanica	Italy	FIAR (Italy owned by Ericsson, Sweden)	Sweden
FIAT	Italy	Enesa	Spain
Thorn-EMI	UK	MEL (UK military part of Philips)	Netherlands
		(electronics division part of Philips)	UK
Astra Holdings	UK	PRB	Belgium
Dowty Group	UK	Resdel Engineering	USA
BEI Electronics	USA	4 divisions of Systron Donner	UK

Source: *SIPRI Yearbook, 1990.*

Table 7.10 The formation of new transnational companies in the arms production sector 1990

Companies	**Countries of origin**	**Name of merged/new company**
Matra	France	
MBB	Germany	Eurodrone
Aerospatiale	France	
MBB	Germany	Eurocopter
Selenia	Italy	
CSEE	France	CSEE Defence
Aerospatiale	France	
OFEMA	France	
AIROD	Malaysia	
Thompson-CSF	France	Defence Electronics
Allied Ordnance	Singapore	of Singapore
Thompson-CSF	France	
Ferranti International sonar division	UK	Ferranti-Thompson Sonar
MBB	Germany	
Santa Barbara	Spain	DEFTEC
BMW	Germany	
Rolls Royce	UK	BMW-Rolls Royce
CESELSA	Spain	Aeronautical Systems
SD-Scicon	UK	Designers
Ferranti-Tech	UK	
Allied Ordnance	Singapore	Ferranti Tech Asia

Source: *SIPRI Yearbook, 1991*, p. 290.

Table 7.11 Research and Development

(a) Military R&D in 1990

	US	**Jap**	**Fr**	**Ger**	**It**	**UK**
Current Price £m 1990	24294	324	3145	991	255	2183
% GDP	0.74	0.02	0.57	0.14	0.05	0.40
% Total Govt R&D Expend	62.6	5.4	40.0	13.5	6.1	44.0

Source: Cabinet Office, *Annual Review of Government Funded R&D*, London: HMSO, 1992.

(b) Defence R&D as % GDP

	1967	**1975**	**1985**	**1988**
US	1.01	0.63	0.85	0.83
Japan	0.01	0.01	0.02	–
France	0.54	0.35	0.46	0.52
Germany	0.21	0.14	0.14	0.13
Italy	0.02	0.01	0.08	0.08
UK	0.60	0.64	0.67	0.51

Source: OECD Statistics.

(c) Industry financed R&D as % GDP

	1967	1975	1985	1988
US	1.01	1.01	1.35	1.38
Japan	0.83	1.12	1.84	1.95
France	0.61	0.69	0.94	0.96
Germany	0.94	1.12	1.58	1.78
Italy	0.35	0.47	0.58	0.54
UK	1.00	0.80	0.96	1.06

Source: OECD Statistics.

Table 7.12 ***Exports of major weapons from Western Europe, 1981-90***

Figures are values of major conventional weapons systems transferred, in US $m., at constant (1985) prices.

	Exporting Nation												
1981-85 Recipient	France	FRG	Italy	Spain	Sweden	UK	BLN	GPT	Other Europe	Total Europe	USA	Other World[a]	Total
France	-	-	-	-	-	-	-	-	-	-	26	112	138
FRG	81	-	16	-	-	66	-	-	-	163	1502	2	1667
Italy	97	110	-	-	-	-	-	-	28	235	759	-	994
Spain	683	60	13	-	-	15	-	-	-	771	624	14	1409
Sweden	-	3	-	-	-	159	-	-	118	280	176	-	456
UK	1174	-	-	-	-	-	-	-	1	1175	1724	6	2905
BLN	41	1210	-	-	-	44	-	-	3	1298	5317	-	6615
GPT	182	1481	110	-	-	243	908	-	491	3415	2201	40	5656
Other Europe	472	-	26	-	289	1050	44	-	21780	23661	3244	219	27124
Total Europe	**2730**	**2864**	**165**	**-**	**289**	**1577**	**952**	-	**22421**	**30998**	**15573**	**393**	**46964**
USA	37	177	44	-	-	404	12	-	-	674	-	258	932
Other World[a]	16738	4659	5136	1662	243	5831	521	93	44240	79123	49821	11352	131296
Total 1981-85	**19505**	**7700**	**5345**	**1662**	**532**	**7812**	**1485**	**93**	**66661**	**110795**	**56394**	**12003**	**179192**

Exporting Nation

1986-90 **Recipient**	France	FRG	Italy	Spain	Sweden	UK	BLN	GPT	Other Europe	Total Europe	USA	Other World[a]	Total
France	-	-	-	22	-	22	50	-	-	94	487	19	600
FRG	70	-	8	-	-	78	-	-	-	156	2756	57	2969
Italy	32	81	-	-	24	-	-	6647	28	232	634	-	866
Spain	742	53	136	-	-	11	-	-	75	1017	4478	57	5552
Sweden	76	33	-	10	-	48	-	-	-	167	232	-	399
UK	496	-	-	-	-	-	18	-	4	518	795	178	1491
BLN	57	303	-	-	-	-	-	-	11	371	2130	9	2510
GPT	991	1458	92	225	-	133	205	-	191	3295	4565	336	8196
Other Europe	216	828	28	-	915	623	59	-	19775	22444	1006	50	23500
Total Europe	**2680**	**2756**	**264**	**257**	**939**	**915**	**332**	**67**	**20084**	**28294**	**17083**	**706**	**46083**
USA	6	7	3	31	3	316	-	-	112	478	-	558	1036
Other World[a]	11111	1956	1311	802	859	6483	1495	25	45092	69134	37502	12181	118817
Total 1986-90	**13797**	**4719**	**1578**	**1090**	**1801**	**7714**	**1827**	**92**	**65288**	**97906**	**54585**	**13445**	**165936**

Notes: a: All countries except Europe and the USA.
BLN is Belgium, Luxembourg, Netherlands
GPT is Greece, Portugal, Turkey

Source: SIPRI arms trade data base.

Table 7.13 Export performance of European defence contractors 1989

Exporting companies	Value ECUs	Exports as a % of total sales		
		Total	to US	to Europe
British Aerospace	8045	61.5	11.0	21.0
Rolls Royce	3194	74.9	38.3	16.0
Daimler-DASA	3072	39.0	–	–
Thompson-CSF	3024	63.0	10.0	10.0
GCE	1804	18.8	3.8	5.7
Dassault	1556	63.0	12.0	17.0
SNECMA	1459	76.0	54.0	9.0
Racal	1281	56.0	20.0	17.0
Aerospatiale	943	20.9	7.9	55.6
Smiths	735	72.4	42.6	15.2
Matra	648	54.0	–	–
Dowty	608	57.8	26.5	16.3
Vickers	599	60.0	27.55	21.5
Hunting	588	54.6	40.6	7.6
Rheinmetall	522	41.0	11.0	25.0
Ferranti	468	35.0	20.4	14.2
Westland	323	52.0	11.0	9.0
Selenia	290	60.0	–	–
Augusta	268	45.0	–	–
GIAT	97	10.0	0	<5.0
VSEL	21	3.1	0.2	0.04

Source: *Eurostrategies*, 1991.

Table 7.14 Military expenditure as a share of GDP

	US	Bel	Den	Fr	FRG	Gre	It	Lux	Neth	Jap
1973	6.0	2.8	2.1	3.8	3.5	4.1	2.9	0.8	3.3	0.8
1974	6.1	2.8	2.4	3.7	3.6	4.3	2.8	0.8	3.3	0.9
1975	6.0	3.0	2.6	3.9	3.6	6.5	2.7	1.0	3.5	0.9
1976	5.4	3.1	2.3	3.8	3.5	6.9	2.3	0.8	3.2	0.9
1977	5.3	3.2	2.3	3.9	3.4	7.0	2.4	0.8	3.3	0.9
1978	5.1	3.3	2.3	4.0	3.3	6.7	2.4	0.8	3.1	0.9
1979	5.1	3.3	2.3	3.9	3.3	6.3	2.4	0.9	3.2	0.9
1980	5.4	3.3	2.4	4.0	3.3	6.7	2.1	1.0	3.1	0.9
1981	5.7	3.4	2.5	4.1	3.4	7.0	2.1	1.1	3.2	0.9
1982	6.3	3.3	2.5	4.1	3.4	6.8	2.3	1.0	3.2	0.9
1983	6.5	3.2	2.5	4.1	3.4	6.3	2.3	1.1	3.2	1.0
1984	6.4	3.1	2.3	4.0	3.3	7.1	2.3	1.0	3.2	1.0
1985	6.6	3.0	2.2	4.0	3.2	7.0	2.3	0.9	3.1	1.0
1986	6.7	3.0	2.0	3.9	3.1	6.2	2.2	0.9	3.1	1.0
1987	6.4	2.9	2.1	4.0	3.1	6.3	2.4	1.1	3.1	1.0
1988	6.1	2.7	2.2	3.8	2.9	6.4	2.5	1.1	3.0	1.0
1989	5.9	2.5	2.1	3.7	2.8	5.7	2.4	1.1	2.9	1.0
1990	5.6	2.4	2.0	3.6	2.8	5.9	2.1	1.1	2.7	1.0

	Nor	Por	Sp	Tur	UK	Au	Fin	Ir	Sw	Swi
1973	3.1	6.0	1.6	4.9	4.9	1.0	1.4	1.4	3.6	2.0
1974	3.1	7.4	1.7	5.1	5.1	1.1	1.3	1.7	3.5	2.0
1975	3.2	5.3	1.7	5.0	5.0	1.2	1.4	1.6	3.4	2.0
1976	3.1	4.0	1.8	6.2	4.8	1.2	1.4	1.6	3.3	2.3
1977	3.1	3.5	1.7	5.8	4.7	1.2	1.4	1.6	3.4	2.1
1978	3.2	3.5	1.7	5.2	4.5	1.3	1.4	1.5	3.4	2.1
1979	3.1	3.5	1.7	4.3	4.6	1.3	1.4	1.6	3.3	2.2
1980	2.9	3.5	2.3	4.3	4.7	1.2	1.9	-	3.0	1.9
1981	2.9	3.5	2.4	4.9	4.7	1.2	1.9	1.8	3.0	1.8
1982	3.0	3.5	2.4	5.2	5.1	1.2	2.1	1.7	2.9	1.9
1983	3.1	3.3	2.4	4.8	5.1	1.3	2.1	1.5	2.8	1.9
1984	2.8	3.3	2.4	4.4	5.3	1.2	2.0	1.5	2.7	1.9
1985	3.1	3.1	2.4	4.5	5.1	1.2	1.9	1.5	2.6	2.0
1986	3.1	3.2	2.2	4.8	4.9	1.3	2.0	1.6	2.6	1.8
1987	3.3	3.1	2.4	4.2	4.6	1.2	1.9	1.4	2.5	1.7
1988	3.2	3.2	2.1	3.8	4.3	1.1	1.9	1.4	2.4	1.7
1989	3.3	3.2	2.0	4.3	4.1	1.1	1.9	1.3	2.4	1.6
1990	3.2	3.1	1.8	4.9	3.9	1.0	1.8	1.3	2.4	1.6

Source: *SIPRI*.

Table 7.15 Direct military employment as a percentage of work age population

	US	Bel	Den	Fr	FRG	It	Neth
1972	1.68	1.45	1.23	1.55	1.20	1.20	1.32
1973	1.59	1.44	1.15	1.53	1.23	1.18	1.32
1974	1.53	1.39	1.06	1.52	1.25	1.17	1.29
1975	1.48	1.40	1.07	1.54	1.25	0.97	1.27
1976	1.45	1.34	1.07	1.50	1.23	0.91	1.23
1977	1.42	1.36	1.04	1.46	1.20	0.98	1.22
1978	1.36	1.34	1.05	1.47	1.19	0.99	1.20
1979	1.36	1.36	1.06	1.44	1.17	0.99	1.18
1980	1.34	1.38	0.98	1.42	1.15	0.98	1.08
1981	1.37	1.43	0.93	1.37	1.14	0.98	1.07
1982	1.37	1.44	0.91	1.34	1.13	0.97	1.05
1983	1.36	1.37	0.93	1.31	1.12	0.96	1.00
1984	1.35	1.38	0.87	1.28	1.12	0.98	1.01
1985	1.34	1.37	0.86	1.26	1.14	0.98	1.01
1986	1.34	1.36	0.85	1.21	1.11	0.99	1.02
1987	1.33	1.33	0.85	1.20	1.11	0.97	0.99

	Au	Fin	Sw	Jap	Nor	UK
1972	1.11	1.26	1.42	0.36	1.43	1.03
1973	0.79	1.13	1.37	0.31	1.40	1.01
1974	0.81	1.14	1.33	0.31	1.40	0.98
1975	0.79	1.12	1.30	0.31	1.55	0.97
1976	0.79	1.25	1.30	0.31	1.54	0.95
1977	0.78	1.24	1.24	0.31	1.53	0.88
1978	0.79	1.24	1.24	0.31	1.52	0.90
1979	1.04	1.23	1.24	0.31	1.44	0.91
1980	1.02	1.23	1.20	0.31	1.43	0.95
1981	0.99	1.12	1.20	0.31	0.90	1.61
1982	1.00	1.22	1.26	0.30	1.63	0.87
1983	0.99	1.10	1.22	0.30	1.38	0.88
1984	1.07	1.09	1.22	0.30	1.39	0.88
1985	1.07	1.04	1.20	0.29	1.38	0.87
1986	1.07	1.03	1.24	0.29	1.38	0.87
1987	1.07	1.05	1.23	0.29	1.29	0.85

No data available for 1988–90

Source: Cusack (1991).

Table 7.16 Constant price military expenditure in US $m 1988 prices

	US	Bel	Den	Fr	Jap	FRG	Gr	It	Lux	Neth
1973	208391	3484	1798	25513	15899	30714	2091	12270	38	5403
1974	206017	3532	1970	25402	16135	32058	2002	12284	41	5653
1975	199787	3847	2136	26531	16776	31913	3206	11432	44	5928
1976	188970	4048	2109	27684	16944	31683	3131	11377	47	5864
1977	196738	4151	2119	29242	17426	31566	3318	12219	46	6532
1978	197903	4426	2202	30953	18496	32904	3389	12740	50	6309
1979	199134	4524	2216	31656	19702	33346	3283	13547	52	6689
1980	206573	4614	2235	32222	20099	33807	2841	14174	60	6510
1981	220955	4657	2260	32995	20628	34216	3360	14269	62	6575
1982	240616	4502	2323	33668	21291	33786	3428	14248	63	6555
1983	258828	4323	2342	34252	22400	34054	3128	14708	64	6497
1984	270923	4139	2287	34104	23504	33712	3717	15262	64	6608
1985	290026	4092	2234	34103	24672	33796	3688	15902	63	6533
1986	305076	4261	2153	35118	25924	34719	3152	16293	66	6633
1987	300890	4287	2275	36137	27289	35320	3144	18463	75	6753
1988	295841	4097	2320	36105	28521	35097	3326	19625	86	6729
1989	290593	4035	2263	36494	29491	35008	3116	19771	79	6791
1990	277037	3959	2265	36463	30340	36890	3151	19024	82	6599
1991	264383	4026	2256	36403	31083	34268	3078	18711	89	6368

	Nor	Por	Sp	Tur	UK	Aus	Fin	Sw	Swi
1973	1882	1733	4673	1337	26729	845	1116	4199	2627
1974	1932	2076	5073	1402	27294	951	1149	4232	2618
1975	2094	1429	5282	2206	27281	1061	1237	4353	2469
1976	2146	1116	5657	2531	27800	1086	1260	4344	2798
1977	2187	1030	5671	2438	26669	1122	1166	4391	2652
1978	2339	1041	5652	2232	27548	1227	1222	4521	2657
1979	2396	1057	5929	1980	28769	1300	1364	4677	2781
1980	2422	1145	6423	1876	31100	1272	1467	4596	2765
1981	2447	1142	6413	2316	30549	1238	1496	4539	2761
1982	2545	1142	6518	2528	33283	1278	1714	4380	2907
1983	2656	1099	6738	2393	34981	1426	1726	4253	2926
1984	2558	1021	6669	2325	36511	1366	1733	4263	2949
1985	2946	1036	6952	2467	36548	1429	1765	4268	3255
1986	2853	1166	6772	2772	36173	1501	1895	4357	3022
1987	3037	1212	7672	2647	35713	1401	1919	4431	2926
1988	2895	1348	7171	2664	34629	1344	2013	4442	3047
1989	2971	1415	7396	3082	34290	1409	2070	4508	3100
1990	2994	1455	6949	3725	32672	1341	2044	4492	3233
1991	3083	1416	6674	3870	34008	1340	2107	4250	3109

Source: *SIPRI*.

Table 7.17 Constant Price Military Expenditure: Annual Percentage Growth

	US	Bel	Den	Fr	FRG	Gr	It	Lux	Neth
1973	-5.19	4.50	-5.17	3.60	3.85	-0.18	-0.15	9.14	1.56
1974	-1.15	1.35	9.16	-0.44	4.28	-4.32	0.12	7.57	4.52
1975	-3.07	8.55	8.08	4.35	-0.45	47.06	-7.19	6.28	4.75
1976	-5.57	5.09	-1.26	4.26	-0.72	-2.37	-0.48	6.98	-1.09
1977	4.03	2.53	0.46	5.48	-0.37	5.81	7.14	-1.97	10.79
1978	0.59	6.42	3.84	5.69	4.15	2.12	4.17	8.33	-3.48
1979	0.62	2.19	0.63	2.25	1.33	-3.18	6.14	2.92	5.86
1980	3.67	1.96	0.87	1.77	1.37	-14.46	4.53	15.19	-2.71
1981	6.73	0.93	1.11	2.37	1.20	16.78	0.67	3.28	0.99
1982	8.52	-3.38	2.75	2.02	-1.26	2.00	-0.15	1.60	-0.30
1983	7.30	-4.06	0.81	1.72	0.79	-9.16	3.18	1.57	-0.89
1984	4.57	-4.35	-2.38	-0.43	-1.01	17.25	3.70	0.00	1.69
1985	6.81	-1.14	-2.34	0.00	0.25	-0.78	4.11	-1.57	-1.14
1986	5.06	4.05	-3.69	2.93	2.69	-15.70	2.43	4.65	1.52
1987	-1.38	0.61	5.51	2.86	1.72	-0.25	12.50	12.78	1.79
1988	-1.69	-4.53	1.96	-0.09	-0.63	5.63	6.10	13.69	-0.36
1989	-1.79	-1.52	-2.49	1.07	-0.25	-6.52	0.74	-8.49	0.92
1990	-4.78	-1.90	0.09	-0.08	5.24	1.12	-3.85	3.73	-2.87
1991	-4.68	1.68	-0.40	-0.16	-7.37	-2.34	-1.66	8.19	-3.56

	Nor	Por	Sp	Tur	UK	Aus	Fin	Swe	Swi	Jap
1973	0.86	-7.87	8.91	7.05	-1.22	0.98	1.60	0.39	-3.16	5.39
1974	2.63	18.08	8.22	4.76	2.09	11.80	2.90	0.78	-0.34	1.47
1975	8.09	-37.39	4.02	45.32	-0.05	11.02	7.41	2.81	-5.87	3.90
1976	2.45	-24.71	6.86	13.77	1.89	2.31	1.82	-0.21	12.49	1.00
1977	1.88	-7.99	0.25	-3.77	-4.16	3.27	-7.69	1.08	-5.34	2.80
1978	6.74	1.02	-0.34	-8.79	3.24	8.88	4.62	2.93	0.20	5.96
1979	2.39	1.51	4.79	-11.98	4.34	5.82	11.05	3.39	4.54	6.32
1980	1.08	8.03	8.00	-5.42	7.79	-2.18	7.26	-1.76	-0.57	2.00
1981	1.03	-0.26	-0.16	21.07	-1.79	-2.71	1.96	-1.25	-0.14	2.60
1982	3.93	0.00	1.62	8.76	8.57	3.18	13.60	-3.57	5.15	3.16
1983	4.27	-3.84	3.32	-5.49	4.98	10.96	0.70	-2.94	0.65	5.08
1984	-3.76	-7.36	-1.03	-2.88	4.28	-4.30	0.40	0.23	0.78	4.81
1985	14.12	1.46	4.16	5.93	0.10	4.51	1.83	0.12	9.87	4.85
1986	-3.21	11.82	-2.62	11.66	-1.03	4.92	7.11	2.06	-7.43	4.95
1987	6.25	3.87	12.48	-4.61	-1.28	-6.89	1.26	1.68	-3.23	5.13
1988	-4.79	10.64	-6.75	0.64	-3.08	-4.15	4.78	0.25	4.05	4.42
1989	2.59	4.85	3.09	14.57	-0.98	4.72	2.79	1.47	1.72	3.34
1990	0.77	2.79	-6.23	18.95	-4.83	-4.95	-1.26	-0.36	4.20	2.84
1991	2.93	-2.72	-4.04	3.82	4.01	-0.07	3.04	-5.54	-3.91	2.42

8. The Social Consequences of Industrialism

Mark Rudd

In order to interpret fully the economic performance of the major Western Industrial Nations, it is important that a study is made of the social conditions within each of those economies. Before drawing conclusions about how well each nation is performing, questions must be addressed regarding non-economic areas such as standards of health, housing, education and the environment which directly affect the welfare of the population.

The social consequences of industrialism are as important to a nation's citizens as the economic consequences. Along with a successful economy may come a broad and comprehensive system of education; a social benefit system for the poor, sick and elderly; and levels of health provision allowing higher life expectancies and a generally fitter population. On the other hand industrialism may be accompanied by high levels of crime, higher rates of divorce and homelessness, a bigger divide between the 'haves' and the 'have-nots', and an environment which becomes more polluted and dangerous every day. Whether your political judgement sways you to the advantages or disadvantages of capitalist industrialism, social factors are a vital ingredient in understanding the performance of each nation and the welfare of its people.

Population 1. Size and density

According to the office for Official Publications of the European Communities, the population of Europe on January 1st 1993 stood at almost 347 million, a figure greater than that of the United States and former Soviet Union. (Individual country data is given in Table 8.1.) The total population of the Community in 1993 was divided between the member states in the following proportions: Belgium 2.9%, Denmark 1.49%, France 16.59%, Germany 23.25%, Greece 2.98%, Ireland 1.03%, Italy 16.42%, Luxembourg 0.11%, Netherlands 4.39%, Portugal 2.84%, Spain 11.28%, UK 16.71%. When we take into consideration the population density of the community (Table 8.2), the figure rises to five times that of the USA. Furthermore the density of the individual countries' population is generally concentrated in industrial, financial and administrative centres. Only in a limited number of regions, such as in Southern Spain, has the population found itself concentrated in particular areas for other reasons. The most densely populated nation in Europe in 1988 was the Netherlands, with 358 people per square kilometre. The second most densely populated country was Belgium, with 325 per km^2, contrasting sharply with Ireland, at only 51 per

km^2 and Greece at 76. The population density of all the European countries increased between 1985 and 1989, except for Ireland where the density of population remained constant. The sharpest rises in total population since 1975 have occurred in France (a rise of just under five million) and Spain (just under four million), whilst the population of most other countries have risen by around the million mark. The clear exception is Germany, the population of which rose by nineteen million with unification. Portugal is the only country to show a decline in the total population since 1989, dropping by 455,000 in four years. Figures on population change in 1992 are given in Table 8.3.

2. Structure

In 1990 a quarter of the population in the European Community was below twenty years of age and approximately one fifth was over the age of sixty. Ireland has the highest proportion of its population under twenty within the EC (37%) and also has the lowest percentage of those over sixty (15.1%). No other country has such a starkly contrasting population structure, as the rest stand very close to the Community average. The United Kingdom has the highest percentage of over sixtys (20.7%) which is not far above the average of 19.6%. Country by country data on age structure is given in Table 8.4.

3. The foreign population

The majority of the foreign population in Europe comes from non-member countries, and more than 80% of these are resident in only three countries – Germany, France and the United Kingdom. In 1989 they accounted for 5.7%, 3.8% and 1.8% of the respective populations. Luxembourg has the highest percentage of foreign population at 28.2%, yet the majority of these are from other member states. Taking Community and non-Community foreigners together, the European average is around 4%. Belgium has the highest percentage of foreign residents at 8.7%, followed by Germany at 7.8% and France at 6.6%. Only Spain, Portugal and Italy stand at 1% or less. (Table 8.5)

4. Births, deaths, marriages and divorces

During the 1980s birthrates in Southern Europe fell considerably, leading to a reduction in natural population growth rates between 1982 and 1992. Meanwhile birthrates in the countries of Northern Europe went in the opposite direction; but overall fertility has fallen for three consecutive years to date.. Despite the fall in the number of births, the proportion of extra-marital births is rising steadily. In Scandinavia this figure amounts to almost half of all births, down to about one in three in the UK and France, and one in four in Austria. At the same time the divorce rate across Europe is still rising whilst the marriage rate has declined. Life expectancy at birth continues to rise across Europe, where in 1992 the figure stood at 72.8 years for males and 79.4 years for females.

Male life expectancy is highest in Greece at 74.6 years and amongst women Italians can expect to live the longest, averaging 80.4 years. The average life expectancy for men and women across Europe in 1992 was 76.1 years. The highest life expectancy in this respect is in the Netherlands, with an average of 77.3 years, closely followed by Greece, France and Italy at 77.2 years. The lowest life expectancy rate is in Portugal, 73.55, and Ireland 73.85. Portugal also has the highest infant mortality rate (9.3 per 1000 live births) and the Netherlands has the lowest (6.3). Ireland however has the highest fertility rate, with 2.11 children per woman, whilst Spain has marginally the lowest (1.23). The systematic data under this heading is given in Table 8.6.

5. Standards of living, poverty and health

Depending upon individual national criteria, about 49 million people in the European Community were considered to be 'poor' in 1980, rising to around 50 million in 1985. This amounts to around 15% of the total population of the EC. Member states with the highest poverty rates were Portugal (33%), Ireland (20%), Spain (19%), and Greece and the UK (18%). On a standardised measure of poverty, with the poverty threshold set at 50% of mean national adult expenditure (Table 8.7), Belgium had the least poverty in 1985 (5.9%) and Portugal the most (32.7%). Households in which the head was unemployed or non-active, female-headed households and households headed by persons with low qualifications figure significantly among the EC poor. In terms of the geographical distribution of poverty in relation to the resident population, the figures read quite differently: for example, Denmark has 1.6% of the Community's population, but only 0.8% of its poor. The United Kingdom on the other hand has 17.6% of the Community's population, and 20.7% of its poor.

Incidences of poverty among the elderly and among children rate higher than among any other groups in Europe (Table 8.8). In 1985 the poverty rate of children was worst in the Netherlands, followed by Germany and the UK, although European nations fare much better in comparison with other regions of the world. However, poverty in Europe amongst these two highly dependent groups has shown a steady rise since 1980.

One indication of the commitment to eradicating child poverty and promoting welfare can be found in the Unicef league tables of measles immunisation for children (Table 8.9). Most European nations achieve a figure above 80% (of children immunised), and the Community average lies at 82.5% (excluding Luxembourg). However, these figures compare unfavourably with selected 'poorer' nations across the world, as the table shows.

6. Social Protection

What sort of protection can the sick, elderly or unemployed expect from the state? When given as a percentage of Gross Domestic Product, the amount spent by each member state on social protection (benefits) becomes more revealing than when given in sheer total of money spent in this area. Since 1970 all European community states have increased their welfare spending as a percentage of GDP (Table 8.10). Social protection spending in these terms appeared to peak in 1983 with an EC average of 26.2% in that year. This figure has declined steadily since then, but in 1989 the Netherlands stood out on its own as the only nation committed to spending over 30% on its welfare system. Greece, Spain and Portugal were the only countries to spend less than 20% of GDP, and the Community average dropped from 25.7% to 24.7% in only two years from 1987 to 1989. The per capita totals devoted to social protection show that six countries (Luxembourg, Netherlands, Germany, France, Denmark and Belgium) spend above the Community average. In 1987 Luxembourg, Netherlands and Germany remained way ahead of the pack in this respect with 130%, 129% and 128% respectively of the Community average. Only Portugal finds itself under neighbours Spain, with 30% and 53% respectively (Table 8.11).

What are the individual priorities of governments within Europe on welfare spending? In 1987 the largest share of social benefits now devoted to 'Old Age Survivors' (45%) and 'Health' (36%) which alone accounted for over 80% of community benefit expenditure. Areas of family benefits, maternity, unemployment (and promotion of employment) and housing were far lower, varying between 8% and 3.5% (Table 8.12). Expenditure on the elderly followed a rather close pattern across the EC, ranging from 59.4% in Italy to 31.1% in Ireland. The diversity of expenditure on unemployment, however, was far greater, ranging from Luxembourg on just over 1% to Spain on nearly 17%: the Community average in 1987 stood at 7% (Table 8.13).

7. Homelessness

The figures on homelessness in Europe (Table 8.14) show clearly that Germany, France and the UK have a disproportionate number of homeless in relation to the rest of Europe. Portugal, Denmark and Spain remain the only countries in the table to show a homeless figure of less than 1 in 1000, whereas the European average is 7.5. Taking the figures from the European Statistical Office (Table 8.15), we can calculate that the percentage of residences which are unoccupied amounts to 22.9% in Spain, and, at the other end of the scale, 2.9% in the Netherlands. Furthermore, a breakdown of Europe's homeless reveals the same trends as with poverty – the young, females and ethnic minorities are disproportionately affected. In Europe over 70% of the homeless are under 40 years old; in Denmark, where immigration accounts for a very low percentage, 17% of homeless women were immigrants. In London, households headed by a black person are said to be three times more likely to become officially homeless than households headed by a white person.

Germany, France and the UK together contain over two million homeless people. The problem of interpretation in such figures is not just with estimating discrepancies as mentioned, but that those countries with the most extensive provisions for the homeless will emerge with the highest figures. As a result of this, the relatively low numbers of homeless people as expressed in the figures from Italy, Portugal and Spain, may result from a lack of service provision rather than an actual lack of homelessness. The hidden homeless are those who do not come into contact with welfare services, those who exist where welfare services may be inadequate, or those who receive help from elsewhere. The potential homeless are those who have only a precarious hold on their housing tenure or for other reasons are at risk from losing their accommodation. On this basis Shelter insists that up to 1.2 million people may be defined as homeless in Britain, and across the EC as many as 10% of the community population may be affected.

Table 8.1 Total population on 1 January 1975–1993 (000s)

	1975	1980	1985	1989	1993
Belgium	9,783.0	9,843.3	9,857.7	9,927.6	10,068.3
Denmark	5,054.4	5,122.1	5,111.1	5,129.8	5,180.6
France	52,600.0	53,731.4	55,062.5	56,017.0	57,526.6
Germany	61,991.5	61,439.3	61,049.3	61,715.0	80,614.1
Greece	8,986.2	9,587.5	9,919.5	10,019.0	10,320.0
Ireland	3,164.0	3,392.8	3,537.3	3,515.0	3,556.5
Italy	55,293.0	56,388.5	57,080.5	57,504.7	56,932.7
Luxembourg	357.4	363.5	366.2	374.9	395.2
Netherlands	13,599.1	14,091.0	14,453.8	14,805.2	15,238.9
Portugal	8,879.1	9,713.6	10,128.9	10,305.3	9,850.3
Spain	35,338.0	37,242.0	38,423.0	38,794.6	39,114.2
UK	56,230.7	56,285.9	56,538.8	57,135.2	57,959.0
Europe: total	311,276.3	317,200.8	321,528.5	325,243.3	346,756.3

Source: 1975–1989 are taken from Eurostat (1990), *Demographic Statistics* p. 101.
1993 data comes from Eurostat (1993), *Rapid Reports: Population and Social Conditions*, No. 7 p. 2.

Table 8.2 Total population, area, population density (1985)

Country	Population (thousands)	Area (1000 km²)	Persons (per km²)
B	9,858	31	323
DK	5,114	43	245
D	61,024	249	245
GR	9,935	132	75
E	38,602	505	76
F	55,170	544	101
IRL	3,540	69	51
I	57,141	301	190
L	367	3	141
NL	14,492	42	352
P	10,157	92	110
UK	56,618	244	232
EUR 12	322,000	2,253	143
USA	239,300	9,372	26
USSR	278,600	22,402	12
JAPAN	120,700	372	324
WORLD	4,837,000	135,837	37

Source: Eurostat (1989) *Rapid Reports: Population and Social Change*, No. 7 p. 4.

Table 8.3 Population change in 1992 – EUR 12 (in 000s)

Country	Population	Births	Deaths	Natural Increase	Net Migration	Total Increase
B	10068.3	125.1	105.7	19.4	25.4	44.7
DK	5180.6	67.8	60.8	7.0	11.5	18.4
D	80614.1	805.8	881.2	–75.5	345.0	269.5
GR	10320.0	104.0	98.0	6.0	35.0	41.0
E	39114.2	381.3	341.1	40.2	18.1	58.3
F	57526.6	742.8	523.0	219.8	90.0	309.8
IRL	3556.5	51.6	30.8	20.8	–6.0	14.8
I	56932.7	561.3	547.1	14.2	89.2	103.4
L	395.2	5.1	4.0	1.1	4.3	5.4
NL	15238.9	196.7	129.9	66.8	57.9	124.7
P	9850.3	115.0	101.2	13.9	-10.0	3.9
UK	57959.0	781.0	634.2	146.8	59.0	205.8
EUR 12	346756.3	3937.5	3457.0	480.5	719.3	1199.7

Source: Eurostat (1993) *Rapid Reports: Population and Social Conditions*, No. 7 p. 2.

Table 8.4 Population by age group on 1 January 1990 (%)

	0-19	20-39	40-59	>60 of which	>80
B	24.8	30.7	24.0	20.4	3.5
DK	24.3	30.0	25.3	20.4	3.7
D	21.8	31.6	26.3	20.3	3.7
GR[a]	26.8	28.3	25.6	19.4	3.0
E	28.5	30.3	22.7	18.5	2.8
F	27.7	30.1	23.0	19.1	3.7
IRL	37.0	28.0	19.9	15.1	6.0
I	24.4	30.1	25.3	20.2	4.0
L	23.2	32.4	25.5	18.9	3.0
NL	25.7	33.0	24.1	17.3	2.9
P	29.3	30.2	22.3	18.2	2.5
UK	25.9	29.9	23.5	20.7	3.6
EUR 12	25.5	30.5	24.3	19.6	3.3

Notes:
a 1989 figures

Source: Eurostat (1992), *Europe in figures*, Third Edition, p. 82.

Table 8.5 Breakdown of resident population

	Non-Community foreigners		Community foreigners		Total foreign population
	000s	%	000s	%	%
B	332	3.3	536	5.4	8.7
DK	115	2.3	26	0.5	2.8
D	3520	5.7	1325	2.1	7.8
GR	123	1.2	102	1.0	2.2
E	165	0.4	231	0.6	1.0
F	2102	3.8	1578	2.8	6.6
IRL	17	0.5	62	1.8	2.3
I	236	0.4	100	0.2	0.6
L	–	–	–	–	–
NL	464	3.1	160	1.1	4.2
P	74	0.7	27	0.3	1.0
UK	1025	1.8	828	1.4	3.2
EUR 12	8175	2.5	4976	1.5	4.0

Source: Eurostat (1992), *Europe in figures*, Third Edition, p. 90.

Table 8.6 Main demographic indicators 1992 - EUR 12

Country	Average population 1992 (000s)	Total fertility[d]	Marriages (000s)	Divorces (000s)	Mortality		
					Deaths under one year	Life expectancy at birth[e] males	females
B	10045.2	1.56	58.3	22.3	1027	72.8*	79.5*
DK	5171.4	1.77*	32.3	13.0	471[c]	72.5*	78.0*
D	80569.7	1.30*	452.1	136.3[c]	5711[c]	72.1*	78.7*
GR	10300.0	1.41	50.0	6.5	850	74.6*	79.8*
E	39085.1	1.23	215.1	23.1[a]	3005	73.3*	80.3*
F	57372.1	1.73	269.9	108.1[c]	5400	73.1	81.3
IRL	3547.6	2.11	16.1	–	343	71.0	76.7
I	56845.0	1.26	306.9	24.0	4675	74.0*	80.4*
L	392.5	1.65	2.5	0.8[c]	44	72.0*	79.1*
NL	15184.0	1.59	93.6	30.1	1233	74.3	80.3
P	9898.1	1.48	69.9	12.4	1068	69.8*	77.3*
UK	57854.0	1.80*	375.4[b]	165.7[b]	5445	73.2*	78.6*
EUR 12	372356.0	1.48*	2053.3*	602.1[c]*	31400	72.9*	79.5*

Notes: * Estimation EUROSTAT (a) 1989; (b) 1990; (c) 1991; d) children per woman; (e) The data refer to the year 1991, with the exception of France, Ireland and the Netherlands, for which data refer to the year 1990.

Source: Eurostat (1993) *Rapid Reports: Population and Social Conditions*, No. 7 p. 4.

Table 8.7 Rates of poverty in the European Community (households and total population)

Country	1980				1985			
	households		persons		households		persons	
	%	1000s	%	1000s	%	1000s	%	1000s
B	6.3	226.	7.1	701	5.2	189	5.9	583
DK	8.0	166	7.9	407	8.0	166	8.0	409
D	10.3	2592	10.5	6448	9.2	2306	9.9	6074
GR	20.5	604	21.5	2073	17.4	527	18.4	1817
E	20.3	2129	20.9	7829	17.8	1924	15.7	7257
F	18.0	3503	19.1	10313	14.8	2947	15.7	8681
IRL	18.5	167	18.4	625	17.4	162	19.5	684
I	12.0	2237	14.1	7941	14.7	2760	15.5	8880
L	–	–	–	–	–	–	–	–
NL	6.9	345	9.6	1363	7.9	403	11.4	1661
P	31.4	906	32.4	3167	31.7	948	32.7	3310
UK	14.1	2808	14.6	8226	18.9	3790	18.2	10324

Source: Eurostat (1990), *Rapid Reports: Population and Social Conditions*, No. 7 p. 2.

Table 8.8 Poverty among children and the elderly

	Children			Elderly		
	Poverty index*		variation in the absolute no of poor	Poverty index*		variation in the absolute no of poor
	1980	**1985**	%	**1980**	**1985**	%
Belgium	113	114	–20.3	175	181	–17.7
Denmark	110	114	–5.4	238	255	12.1
F.R. of Germany	110	138	3.5	136	141	–8.1
Greece	96	103	–16.5	145	153	–2.9
Spain	106	107	–14.5	157	125	–21.7
France	108	124	–6.6	159	136	–31.2
Ireland	122	143	23.8	163	73	–50.5
Italy	114	97	–14.4	132	129	1.5
Netherlands	136	155	25.6	44	46	31.9
Portugal	112	112	–2.3	139	139	8.1
United Kingdom	138	132	12.2	163	119	–7.1

* National poverty rate = 100

Source: Eurostat 1990, *Rapid Reports: Population and Social Conditions*, No7 p3

Table 8.9 Comparisons of Child Immunisation Performance

Measles Immunisation	%		%
Ireland	99	Hungary	100
Portugal	96	North Korea	99
Netherlands	94	Cuba	99
Germany	90	China	95
UK	89	Chile	93
Denmark	86	Mauritius	88
Spain	84	Syria	87
Greece	76	India	86
Belgium	75	Israel	86
France	69	Zimbabwe	83
Italy	50		
EC Average (excl. Lux)	82.5		

Source: UNICEF, *The Progress of Nations*, 1993.

Table 8.10 Current expenditure on social protection (as % of GDP)

	1970	1980	1983	1985	1987	1989
B	18.7	28.0	30.8	29.3	29.0	26.7
DK	19.6	28.7	30.1	27.8	27.5	29.6
D	21.5	28.7	28.8	28.2	28.3	27.3
GR	7.6	9.1	13.6	15.4	16.0	16.3
E	10.0	15.6	17.4	17.8	17.2	17.3
F	18.9	25.4	28.3	28.8	28.2	28.0
IRL	13.7	21.6	24.1	24.0	23.6	20.6
I	14.4	19.4	22.9	22.5	23.0	23.2
L	15.6	26.5	27.2	25.5	26.1	25.6
NL	19.6	30.4	33.8	31.1	31.4	30.2
P	9.1	14.6	16.1	16.1	16.1	18.1
UK	14.3	21.5	23.9	24.4	23.6	20.6
EUR12	17.3	24.2	26.2	25.9	25.7	24.7

Source: Eurostat (1991), *Rapid Reports: Population and Social Conditions*, No. 4 p. 6.

Table 8.11 Per capita social protection benefits, in purchasing power standards,as % of the Community average, 1987

	% of Community average
EUR 12	100
B	111
DK	117
D	128
GR	–
E	53
F	119
IRL	58
I	92
L	130
NL	129
P	30
UK	96

Table 8.12 Breakdown of social protection benefits by group of functions EUR12[a] - 1987

	%
Old age	45.0
Health[b]	36.0
Family	8.0
- maternity	
Unemployment	7.5
- promotion of employment	
Housing etc	3.5

Notes: a) Excluding Greece
b) Health: sickness, invalidity, disability and occupational accidents and diseases.

Source: Eurostat (1990), *Rapid Reports: Population and Social Conditions*, No. 3 p. 2.

Table 8.13 Breakdown of social protection benefits by function as % of overall benefits – 1987

Country	Old age (survivors)	Health	Family (maternity)	Unemployment (promotion of employment)	Housing (miscellaneous)
	%	%	%	%	%
Belgium	43.5	34.1	8.6	12.6	1.2
Denmark	37.6	31.3	12.1	12.8	6.2
Germany	41.7	40.8	7.1	6.8	3.6
Greece	-	-	-	-	-
Spain	45.9	34.9	1.8	16.9	0.5
France	45.0	34.2	10.7	6.6	3.4
Ireland	31.1	34.4	12.7	16.2	5.6
Italy	59.4	33.0	5.0	2.4	0.2
Luxembourg	44.2	44.3	9.4	1.3	0.8
Netherlands	31.9	45.7	8.0	11.1	3.3
Portugal	41.5	45.8	7.2	3.0	2.5
UK	42.7	30.8	10.9	8.1	7.4

Source: Eurostat (1990), *Rapid Reports: Population and Social Conditions*, No. 3 p. 3.

Table 8.14 The extent of estimated homelessness in the European Communities, 1992

Member State	Total Population	No of Homeless	Homeless per 1000
Belgium	9,987,000	26,000	2.6
Denmark*	5,135,000	2,800	0.5
Germany	80,440,000	1,030,000	12.8
Spain	39,322,000	30,000	0.8
France	56,614,000	627,000	11.1
Greece	10,269,000	?	?
Ireland	3,536,000	5,000	1.4
Italy	57,739,000	90,000	1.6
Luxembourg	378,000	500	1.3
Netherlands	14,891,000	30,000	2.0
Portugal	10,497,000	2,500	0.2
UK	56,490,000	688,000	12.2
Total	335,029,000	2,531,800	7.5

* Denmark = 1989, based on a one-day census of users of accommodation centres.

Source: The Second Report of the European Observatory on Homelessness, 1993, Mary Daly.

Table 8.15 Unoccupied residences in the EC

Country	No of main residences	Unoccupied dwellings	% of unoccupied residences
Belgium	3,660	152	4.1
Denmark	2,029	120	5.9
France	19,438	1854	9.5
Germany	23,797	–	–
Greece	2,896	–	–
Ireland	876	–	–
Italy	17,542	2,032	11.6
Luxembourg	2,124	–	–
Netherlands	4,941	113	2.9
Portugal	2,769	430	15.5
Spain	10,470	2,396	22.9
UK	19,635	1583	8.1

Source: Eurostat (1992), *Rapid Reports: Population and Social Conditions*, No. 4 p. 3.